Based on the Common Core State Standards (CCSS)

PARCC

SUCCESS STRATEGIES

High School
Algebra I

**Comprehensive Skill Building
Practice for the Partnership
for Assessment of
Readiness for College and
Careers Assessments**

Dear Future Exam Success Story:

Congratulations on your purchase of our study guide. Our goal in writing our study guide was to cover the content on the test, as well as provide insight into typical test taking mistakes and how to overcome them.

Standardized tests are a key component of being successful, which only increases the importance of doing well in the high-pressure high-stakes environment of test day. How well you do on this test will have a significant impact on your future, and we have the research and practical advice to help you execute on test day.

The product you're reading now is designed to exploit weaknesses in the test itself, and help you avoid the most common errors test takers frequently make.

How to use this study guide

We don't want to waste your time. Our study guide is fast-paced and fluff-free. We suggest going through it a number of times, as repetition is an important part of learning new information and concepts.

First, read through the study guide completely to get a feel for the content and organization. Read the general success strategies first, and then proceed to the content sections. Each tip has been carefully selected for its effectiveness.

Second, read through the study guide again, and take notes in the margins and highlight those sections where you may have a particular weakness.

Finally, bring the manual with you on test day and study it before the exam begins.

Your success is our success

We would be delighted to hear about your success. Send us an email and tell us your story. Thanks for your business and we wish you continued success.

Sincerely,

Mometrix Test Preparation Team

Need more help? Check out our flashcards at:
http://MometrixFlashcards.com/PARCC

TABLE OF CONTENTS

Top 15 Test Taking Tips

1. Know the test directions, duration, topics, question types, how many questions
2. Setup a flexible study schedule at least 3-4 weeks before test day
3. Study during the time of day you are most alert, relaxed, and stress free
4. Maximize your learning style; visual learner use visual study aids, auditory learner use auditory study aids
5. Focus on your weakest knowledge base
6. Find a study partner to review with and help clarify questions
7. Practice, practice, practice
8. Get a good night's sleep; don't try to cram the night before the test
9. Eat a well balanced meal
10. Wear comfortable, loose fitting, layered clothing; prepare for it to be either cold or hot during the test
11. Eliminate the obviously wrong answer choices, then guess the first remaining choice
12. Pace yourself; don't rush, but keep working and move on if you get stuck
13. Maintain a positive attitude even if the test is going poorly
14. Keep your first answer unless you are positive it is wrong
15. Check your work, don't make a careless mistake

Algebra I

Seeing Structure in Expressions

The expression $6s^2$ gives the surface area of a cube with edge length s. What is the coefficient of this expression?

A term is a product and/or quotient of a real number and one or more variables, each of which may be raised to a nonnegative integer exponent. The real number is the coefficient of the term. A polynomial expression is a term or sum of several terms. The expression $6s^2$ is therefore a single term, and the coefficient is the real number 6. Note that if a term is written, for example, as simply s^2, then the coefficient is 1, because $s^2 = 1s^2$. A coefficient may also be negative, such as in the term $-0.5ab$.

The expression $2W + 2L$ gives the perimeter of a rectangular frame with side lengths W and L. How many terms does this expression have?

A polynomial expression is the sum and/or difference of one or more terms. Each term is a product and/or quotient of one or more variables, each of which may be raised to a nonnegative integer exponent, and a real number. The expression $2W + 2L$ has 2 terms, one of which is $2W$ and the other of which is $2L$. It is important to realize that terms are separated by addition or subtraction. Therefore an expression such as $4xy$ has only 1 term. Also, since an expression such as $2x - 3y$ can be written as $2x + (-3y)$ the second term could be referred to as positive or negative.

What are the factors of the expression $x(5x + 2)(x - 4)$?

The factors of the expression $x(5x + 2)(x - 4)$ are the expressions x, $5x + 2$, and $x - 4$. To identify the factors of an expression, the expression must be written as a product of terms and/or expressions (with any expressions delineated by parentheses). The factors themselves may involve addition or subtraction of multiple terms, but if the expression is not written only as the product of terms or expressions, the expression is not in factored form. For example, the polynomial $x^2 + 2x + 8$ cannot be factored with real numbers, so it is considered to be one factor. The polynomial $x^2 + 6x + 8$ can be factored as $(x + 2)(x + 4)$, and therefore has two factors, $(x + 2)$ and $(x + 4)$.

Interpret the exponent in the expression $5000(1 + \frac{r}{12})^{12t}$. The expression gives the value of an account that earns annual interest rate r, after t years.

The exponent in the expression is $12t$. Since the variable t represents the number of years, the exponent represents the number of months in t years. For example, if $t = \frac{1}{2}$ or half a year, then $12t = 12 \cdot \frac{1}{2} = 6$ months. Similarly, if $t = 2$, then $12t = 12 \cdot 2 = 24$ months. This means that the exponent $12t$ converts the time since the initial deposit from years to months. Note that this relates to the expression $\frac{r}{12}$, in which 12 represents the number of times annually the interest is compounded (monthly, in this case). For t = 1, the initial amount 5000 is multiplied by the expression $(1 + \frac{r}{12})$ 12 times, corresponding the number of times the interest is compounded by one-twelfth the annual interest rate. [If the interest were compounded quarterly, the expression would read $5000 \left(1 + \frac{r}{4}\right)^{4t}$].

In the expression $18,000(1 + r)^{20}$, what is the base of the exponent 20? Evaluate the expression for r = 0.1, 0.4, and 0.7 and round to the nearest integer.

In the expression $18,000(1 + r)^{20}$, the base of the exponent 20 is $(1 + r)$, not 1 or r. This is because by the order of operations, the sum in parentheses is calculated first, and then this sum is raised to the power of 20. The last step is to then multiply this result by the coefficient 18,000. For r = 0.1, 0.4, and 0.7, the expression is equal to the following values (to the nearest integer):

$$8,000(1 + r)^{20} = 18,000(1.1)^{20} \approx 121,095$$

$$18,000(1 + r)^{20} = 18,000(1.4)^{20} \approx 15,060,286$$

$$18,000(1 + r)^{20} = 18,000(1.7)^{20} \approx 731,561,653$$

Simplify the expression $\frac{2-x}{x-2}$.

To simplify a rational expression, factor both the numerator and denominator, and then simplify by noting that the ratio of identical factors equals 1. In this particular expression, the numerator is the opposite of the denominator. That is, $2 - x = -(-2 + x) = -(x - 2)$. Rewrite the numerator and then simplify:

$$\frac{2 - x}{x - 2} = \frac{-(x - 2)}{x - 2} = -1$$

The expression simplifies to –1. Note that the original expression is equal to –1 for all values of x except x = 2. This is because the original expression is not defined for x = 2: the denominator would be equal to zero in this case, and division by zero is undefined.

What is the role of the number 2 in the expression $\log_2 \frac{1}{8}$**?**

The given expression is a logarithm. A logarithm asks the question: "to what exponent does the base need to be raised to equal the argument?" The $\frac{1}{8}$ is the argument, and the 2 is the base of the logarithm. This means that the expression yields the value of the exponent to which 2 must be raised to equal $\frac{1}{8}$. Such an expression can be simplified using the identity $b^{(\log_b x)} = x$ as follows:

$$a = \log_2 \frac{1}{8}$$
$$2^a = 2^{\left(\log_2 \frac{1}{8}\right)}$$
$$2^a = \frac{1}{8} = \frac{1}{2^3} = 2^{-3}$$
$$a = -3$$
$$\log_2 \frac{1}{8} = -3$$

Write the leading term of the expanded form of $(3x - 1)^5$**.**

In order to expand a binomial that is raised to a power apply the binomial theorem. The number of terms will be equal to the exponent, which in this case is 5. The leading term contains the greatest occurring power of x, which will be x^5 in this case. Thus, to obtain the leading term, raise the x-term of the binomial to the 5th power: $(3x)^5 = 243x^5$. Then multiply the result by the first entry (corresponding to the leading term of the expansion) of the 5th row (corresponding to the exponent) of Pascal's triangle. In any row, though, the first entry is 1. Therefore the leading term of the expanded form of $(3x - 1)^5$ is $243x^5$.

How can $9 - (m + 1)^2$ **can be rewritten in factored form?**

The expression $9 - (m + 1)^2$ can be rewritten by first noting that the expression is a difference of squares. Since $9 = 3^2$, the expression can be written as $(3)^2 - (m + 1)^2$. In general, a difference of squares is factored as $a^2 - b^2 = (a + b)(a - b)$. In this case, $a = 3$ and $b = m + 1$:

$$9 - (m + 1)^2 =$$
$$3^2 - (m + 1)^2 =$$
$$(3 + m + 1)(3 - (m + 1)) =$$
$$(4 + m)(2 - m)$$

How $x^6 - y^6$ **is both a difference of squares and a difference of cubes.**

A difference of squares can be written as $a^2 - b^2$, and a difference of cubes can be written as $a^3 - b^3$. Both of these are factorable binomials. By using the property of exponents that states
$(a^m)^n = a^{mn}$, the term x^6 can be written as either $(x^2)^3$ or $(x^3)^2$. The term y^6 can be rewritten in a similar way. Therefore $x^6 - y^6 = (x^3)^2 - (y^3)^2$ and, equivalently, $x^6 - y^6 = = (x^2)^3 - (y^2)^3$. Regardless of which method is used, there is only one *completely* factored expression that is equivalent to $x^6 - y^6$. (Since one of the factors of the difference of squares method is $x^3 - y^3$,

- 4 -

which is itself a difference of cubes, the resulting expressions from either method are essentially equivalent).

Rewrite $2x^2 - 6xy - 2x + 6y$ in factored form.

The expression $2x^2 - 6xy - 2x + 6y$ has 4 terms, and therefore may be factorable by grouping. Group terms of like degree: group terms containing the square of a single variable or the product of two variables, for example. The GCF of the first two terms $2x^2$ and $6xy$ is $2x$. The GCF of the last two terms $2x$ and $6y$ is 2. Rewrite the expression as follows:
$$2x^2 - 6xy - 2x + 6y =$$
$$2x(x - 3y) - 2(x - 3y)$$

The factored parts of the expression have a common binomial factor, $(x - 3y)$. Complete the factoring by factoring out $(x - 3y)$:

$$2x(x - 3y) - 2(x - 3y) =$$
$$(x - 3y)(2x - 2)$$

Solve $4^{3x} = 2^{x+10}$.

Two exponential expressions are equal if they have the same base and exponent. To solve for x, rewrite the expressions so they have the same base, and then set the resulting exponents equal to each other. Because $4 = 2^2$, rewrite 4^{3x} with a base of 2:

$$4^{3x} = 2^{x+10}$$
$$(2^2)^{3x} = 2^{x+10}$$
$$2^{6x} = 2^{x+10}$$
$$6x = x + 10$$
$$5x = 10$$
$$x = 2$$

What is the relationship between the linear factors $(x - a)$ and $(x - b)$ of a quadratic expression and the zeros of the related function?

If the linear factors of a quadratic expression are $(x - a)$ and $(x - b)$, then the quadratic function can be written as $y = k(x - a)(x - b)$, where k is a nonzero constant. The zeros of this function are the values of x for which $y = 0$. Direct substitution of a or b for x makes the value of y equal to 0, so $x = a$ and $x = b$ are zeros of the quadratic function. Note that the value of k may affect the shape or direction of the graph of the function, but not the x-intercepts (the zeros of the function).

What are the zeros of the function
$y = 4x^2 - 10x$**?**

The zeros of the function $y = 4x^2 - 10x$ are the values of x for which $y = 0$. To find the zeros, factor the right side of the equation, and set $y = 0$:

$$y = 4x^2 - 10x$$
$$y = 2x(2x - 5)$$
$$0 = 2x(2x - 5)$$

Next, since a product is only equal to zero if at least one of the terms is zero, set the linear factors of the function $2x$ and $(2x - 5)$ equal to 0:

$$2x = 0 \qquad 2x - 5 = 0$$
$$x = 0 \qquad 2x = 5$$
$$x = \frac{5}{2}$$

The zeros of the function $y = 4x^2 - 10x$ are $x = 0$ and $x = \frac{5}{2}$.

Give an example of a quadratic function with zeros $x = 1$ and $x = -3$

If a is a zero of a quadratic function, then $(x - a)$ is a factor of the quadratic expression that defines the function. Therefore $(x - 1)$ and $(x + 3)$ are both factors of the quadratic function. Quadratic functions with these zeros therefore have the form $y = k(x - 1)(x + 3)$. The reason that this is just a form, and not a unique function, is because multiplying the two binomial factors by any nonzero constant results in another quadratic function with the same zeros. For example, the functions $y = -5(x - 1)(x + 3)$ and $y = 7(x - 1)$ $(x + 3)$ have zeros $x = 1$ and $x = -3$.

Find the x-intercepts of $y = 9x^2 - 6x + 1$.

The x-intercepts of $y = 9x^2 - 6x + 1$ are the zeros of the function. These can be determined by first factoring the quadratic expression $9x^2 - 6x + 1$:

$$9x^2 - 6x + 1 = (3x - 1)(3x - 1) = (3x - 1)^2$$

The expression is a perfect square trinomial. Because the two factors are the same, there is only one x-intercept of the function. Set the factor equal to 0:

$$3x - 1 = 0$$
$$3x = 1$$
$$x = \frac{1}{3}$$

The x-intercept of $y = 9x^2 - 6x + 1$ is therefore $x = \frac{1}{3}$.

What is the technique of completing the square?

The quadratic expression $ax^2 + bx + c$ can always be written as the square of a linear binomial, plus some constant. This is useful to solve or graph quadratic equations or functions. The technique is as follows:

$a\left(x^2 + \frac{b}{a}x\right) + c =$ Factor a from the quadratic and linear terms.

$a\left(x^2 + \frac{b}{a}x + \frac{b^2}{4a^2}\right) + c - \frac{b^2}{4a} =$ Add the square of half the coefficient of x within the parentheses; subtract the product of that term and a outside the parentheses.

$$a\left(x + \frac{b}{2a}\right)^2 + c - \frac{b^2}{4a} =$$

Rewrite the trinomial as a perfect square.

$a\left(x + \frac{b}{2a}\right)^2 + \frac{4ac - b^2}{4a}$ Simplify.

Complete the square to find the minimum value of $y = x^2 - 4x$.

To complete the square, first factor out the leading coefficient, the coefficient of x^2. This is 1, so no factoring is required. Next, add and subtract the square of half the coefficient of x. This value is $(\frac{-4}{2})^2 = 4$. Finally, rewrite the first three terms as a square of a linear binomial.

$$y = x^2 - 4x$$
$$y = x^2 - 4x + 4 - 4$$
$$y = (x - 2)^2 - 4$$

The term $(x - 2)^2$ will never be negative; its minimum value is 0 (when $x = 2$). The minimum value of the function $y = (x - 2)^2 - 4$ can be found by substituting the minimum value of the squared binomial: $y_{min} = 0 - 4 = -4$.

Complete the square to find the maximum value of $y = -2x^2 + 6x$.

In order to determine the maximum value of the function, write the function in standard form by completing the square:

$$y = -2x^2 + 6x$$
$$y = -2(x^2 - 3x)$$
$$y = -2(x^2 - 3x + \frac{9}{4}) + 2 \cdot \frac{9}{4}$$
$$y = -2\left(x - \frac{3}{2}\right)^2 + \frac{9}{2}$$

Since the first term will always be negative unless it is zero (which happens at $x = 3/2$), the vertex of the graph of the function is $(\frac{3}{2}, \frac{9}{2})$. The coefficient of x^2 is negative, so the parabola opens downward. Therefore the maximum value of the function is $\frac{9}{2}$.

The minimum value of $y = x^2 + 4bx$ is –1. Find two possible values of b.

In order to determine the vertex of the function, write the function in standard form by completing the square:

$$y = x^2 + 4bx$$
$$y = x^2 + 4bx + 4b^2 - 4b^2$$
$$y = (x + 2b)^2 - 4b^2$$

The vertex of the graph of the function is therefore $(2b, -4b^2)$. The coefficient of x^2 is positive, so the parabola opens upward. The minimum value is $-4b^2$, which must be equal to –1 in this case. Solving for b gives $b = \pm\frac{1}{2}$. The equation of the function is either $y = x^2 + 2x$ or $y = x^2 - 2x$.

The number of bacteria in a sample doubles approximately every hour. To the nearest million, by what factor does the number of bacteria increase in one day?

The situation is modeled by an exponential function. The bacteria count doubles every hour, so let t represent the number of hours. The equation $b = 2^t$ will give the number of bacteria b present after t hours. For now assume the actual number of bacteria is not important, so at $t = 0$ there is 1 bacterium. There are 24 hours in a day, so if d represents days, $t = 24d$, and the equation becomes
$b = 2^t = 2^{24d}$. This equation can be rewritten as $b = (2^{24})^d = 16{,}777{,}216^t$, which means that there are about 17 million times more bacteria each day.

Rewrite the expression 1.3^{2x} so that the only exponent present is $3x$.

In order to write the expression with an exponent of $3x$, use the properties of exponents. First, use the property $a^{mn} = (a^m)^n$ to write $1.3^{2x} = (1.3^2)^x$. The exponent can be changed to $3x$ if the expression is cubed, or raised to the power of 3. To do this without changing the value of the expression, also take the cube root, or raise to the power of $\frac{1}{3}$. This can be written as shown:

$$(1.3^2)^x = [(1.3^2)^{\frac{1}{3}}]^{3x}$$

Using a calculator, $(1.3^2)^{\frac{1}{3}} \approx 1.191$. So, $1.3^{2x} \approx 1.191^{3x}$. To check this, each expression can be evaluated for values of x to see that they are approximately equal.

The table shows the number of decibels for certain power ratios. By what factor does the power ratio increase for an increase of 1 decibel?

Decibels	Power Ratio
10	10
20	100
30	1,000

For each increase of 10 in the number of decibels, the power ratio increases by a factor of 10. Equivalently, the power ratio is equal to 10 raised to a power equal to the number of decibels divided by 10. If P represents the power ratio and d the number of decibels, then

$P = 10^{\frac{d}{10}}$. To determine the factor for an increase of 1 decibel, rewrite the equation as $P = 10^{\frac{d}{10}} = (10^{\frac{1}{10}})^d$. Using a calculator, $10^{\frac{1}{10}} \approx 1.259$, so the power ratio increases by a factor of about 1.259 for an increase of 1 decibel.

A cable company has 12,000 current customers. They begin to lose 3% of their current customers each year. On average, about what percent of their customers do they lose each month?

The situation is modeled by an exponential decay function. The number of customers decreases by 3%, or equivalently is multiplied by 0.97 each year. The equation $c = 12,000(0.97)^t$ will give the number of customers c present after t years. There are 12 months in a year, so if m represents months, the equation becomes $c = 12,000(0.97)^{\frac{m}{12}}$. This equation can be rewritten as $= 12,000(0.97^{\frac{1}{12}})^m$ or $c \approx 12,000(0.997)^m$, which means that the cable company loses a factor of $(1 - 0.997)$, or about 0.3%, of its current customers each month.

What is the common ratio of a geometric series?

A series is a sum (finite or infinite) of terms of a (finite or infinite) sequence. The series is called *geometric* if the ratio of any term to the preceding term is the same value. This value is called the *common ratio* of the geometric series. For example, in the finite sum 3 + 6 + 12 + 24 + 48, the ratio of any term to the previous term is 2. Therefore, the series is a finite geometric series with a common ratio of 2.

Derive the formula for the sum S of the first (n +1) terms of a finite geometric series given by the equation $S = a + ar + ar^2 + ... + ar^n$, where $r \neq 1$.

Write the equation for the sum, and then multiply each side by r:

$S = a + ar + ar^2 + ... + ar^n$
$rS = (a + ar + ar^2 + ... + ar^n)r$
$rS = ar + ar^2 + ar^3 + ... + ar^n + ar^{n+1}$

If the first equation above is subtracted from the third equation, many of the terms will cancel. In fact, the only unique terms are the term a in the first equation and the term ar^{n+1} in the other. Subtract the equations and solve for S to obtain the formula for the sum of the first (n + 1) terms of a finite geometric series:

$rS - S = ar^{n+1} - a$
$S(r - 1) = a(r^{n+1} - 1)$

$$S = \frac{a(r^{n+1} - 1)}{r - 1}$$

Is $8 - 8\left(\frac{1}{2}\right) + 8\left(\frac{1}{2}\right)^2 - 8\left(\frac{1}{2}\right)^3 + \cdots - 8\left(\frac{1}{2}\right)^7$ a finite geometric series?

Yes, the series $8 - 8\left(\frac{1}{2}\right) + 8\left(\frac{1}{2}\right)^2 - 8\left(\frac{1}{2}\right)^3 + \cdots - 8\left(\frac{1}{2}\right)^7$ is a finite geometric series with a common ratio of $-\frac{1}{2}$. When the common ratio of a geometric series is negative, the signs of the terms alternate. This is because even powers of a negative number result in a positive

- 9 -

value, and odd powers of a negative number result in a negative value. Also, as required by a geometric series, the ratio of any term and the preceding term will always be $-\frac{1}{2}$, since the ratio has one positive and one negative term. (Any series that has consecutive negative terms must therefore have only negative terms. This occurs when the coefficient of each term is negative, not when the common ration is negative.)

In the formula below, x represents the monthly interest rate and L the loan amount for a 30-year mortgage with a monthly payment P.

$$L = P\left(\frac{1}{1+x} + \frac{1}{(1+x)^2} + \cdots + \frac{1}{(1+x)^{360}}\right)$$

Find the monthly payment for a \$250,000 loan with an annual interest rate of 6%.

The part of the equation in parentheses is a geometric series with common ratio $\frac{1}{1+x}$. Use the general formula for the sum of the first n terms of a finite geometric series, $S_n = \frac{a(1-r^n)}{1-r}$, to rewrite the equation, where a is the first term and r is the common ratio. Then solve for P:

$$L = P\left(\frac{1}{1+x} + \frac{1}{(1+x)^2} + \cdots + \frac{1}{(1+x)^{360}}\right)$$

$$= P\left(\frac{\frac{1}{1+x}\left(1 - \left(\frac{1}{1+x}\right)^{360}\right)}{1 - \frac{1}{1+x}}\right) = P\left(\frac{\frac{1}{1+x} - \left(\frac{1}{1+x}\right)^{361}}{1 - \frac{1}{1+x}}\right)$$

$$P = L\left(\frac{1 - \frac{1}{1+x}}{\frac{1}{1+x} - \left(\frac{1}{1+x}\right)^{361}}\right)$$

Since x represents the monthly interest rate, $x = \frac{0.06}{12} = 0.005$. Substituting this for x and 250,000 for L gives $P = \$1498.88$, rounded to the nearest cent.

What are the coefficients of the x^2 term, x term, and constant term of the quadratic expression $(2x - 3)(x + 4)$?

To find the coefficients of the x^2 term, x term, and constant term, the quadratic expression must be written in the form $ax^2 + bx + c$. The real numbers a, b, and c are the coefficients. Multiplying the binomials of the factor form gives $2x^2 - 3x + 8x - 12$, and combining like terms $-3x$ and $8x$ yields $2x^2 + 5x - 12$. The coefficient of the x^2 term is 2, the coefficient of the x term is 5, and constant term is -12.

When does the expression $\frac{-b\pm\sqrt{b^2-4ac}}{2a}$ represent a unique number?

The expression $\frac{-b\pm\sqrt{b^2-4ac}}{2a}$ gives the solutions to the quadratic equation $ax^2 + bx + c = 0$. The plus or minus symbol, $\pm$, means that one solution is attained by adding the radical term $\sqrt{b^2 - 4ac}$ in the numerator and the other solution is attained by subtracting it. For this reason, if the radical term is equal to zero, the entire expression is equal to the (unique) value $\frac{-b}{2a}$. (The radical term is equal to zero if the radicand is equal to zero, that is if $b^2 = 4ac$.)

Factor the expression $x^2 + 2x + 1 - y^2$ by first recognizing a perfect square trinomial.

The first three terms of the expression, $x^2 + 2x + 1$, represent a perfect square trinomial. This means it factors into two identical binomials. The factorization is $x^2 + 2x + 1 = (x + 1)^2$. Therefore the original expression can be rewritten as $(x + 1)^2 - y^2$, which is a difference of squares. Using the fact $a^2 - b^2 = (a + b)(a - b)$, and setting $a = x + 1$ and $b = y$, the expression $(x + 1)^2 - y^2$ factors as $(x + 1 - y)(x + 1 + y)$.

Find the vertex of the parabola with equation $y = 2x^2 - 4x - 3$.

To find the vertex of the parabola, rewrite the quadratic equation in the form $y = a(x - p)^2 + q$ by completing the square. The point (p, q) is the vertex of the parabola:
$$y = 2x^2 - 4x - 3$$
$$y = 2(x^2 - 2x) - 3$$
$$y = 2(x^2 - 2x + 1) - 3 - 2$$
$$y = 2(x - 1)^2 - 5$$

The vertex of the parabola is $(1, -5)$.

Alternatively, recall the x-coordinate of the vertex is given by $-b/2a$, which in this case is $-(-4)/(2 \cdot 2) = 1$. Substitute this in for x to obtain $y = 2 \cdot 1^2 - 4 \cdot 1 - 3 = -5$. As before, the vertex is at point
$(1, -5)$.

What are the x-intercepts of $y = x^2 - 4x$?

The x-intercepts, or zeros, of the function occur at the values of x that make $y = 0$, that is, when $x^2 - 4x = 0$. A quadratic function can have 0, 1, or 2 x-intercepts. Factor the given expression to get $x(x - 4) = 0$. Since the product of the two factors is equal to zero, either $x = 0$ or $x - 4 = 0$. Therefore the quadratic has two x-intercepts, $x = 0$ and $x = 4$.

Solve for b: $6(4)^b = 3(2)^b$.

The variable b appears in the equation as an exponent. Rewrite the equation so that each side has the same base, then equate the exponent expressions:
$6(4)^b = 3(2)^b$
$3 \cdot 2(4)^b = 3(2)^b$
$2(4)^b = 2^b$
$2^1(2^2)^b = 2^b$
$2^{1 + 2b} = 2^b$
$1 + 2b = b$
$b = -1$

The value of b is -1.

Find the sum $4 + 4(2) + 4(2)^2 + 4(2)^3 + \dots + 4(2)^8$.

The sum represents a finite geometric series. The common ratio r of the series is 2, and the first term a_1 of the series is 4. Note that the first two terms can be written with exponents as $4(2)^0$ and $4(2)^1$. Use the formula for the sum of the first n terms of a finite geometric series $S_n = \frac{a_1(1-r^n)}{1-r}$, where n is equal to 1 more than the greatest power of r in the series:

$$S_9 = \frac{a_1(1-r^9)}{1-r} = \frac{4(1-(2)^9)}{1-2} = \frac{-2044}{-1} = 2044$$

The sum of the series is 2044.

Give an example of a system of two linear inequalities in two variables that has no solution.

A linear inequality in two variables will have a solution described by a half-plane; that is, by the entire region of the plane that is either above or below the line described by the corresponding linear equation. A system of two inequalities will have a solution region that is the intersection of the two half-planes. Therefore, a system that has no solution can be created by choosing lines that are parallel, and choosing the half-planes on opposite sides of the two lines, so there is no intersection. An example is the system

$$\begin{cases} y < 2x + 1 \\ y > 2x + 4 \end{cases}$$

Arithmetic with Polynomials & Rational Expressions

Polynomials are closed under multiplication.

For a set to have closure under a particular operation, applying the operation to two elements of the set must result in a member of the set. This means that the product of any two polynomials results in another polynomial. This is correct, because every term of a polynomial in x is of the form ax^n, where a is a real number and n is a nonnegative integer. The product of any two such terms would be $ax^m \cdot bx^n = abx^{m+n}$, where ab is a real number and $m + n$ is a nonnegative integer. The last statement relies on the fact that real numbers are closed under multiplication, and nonnegative integers are closed under addition.

Subtract the polynomial $3x^2 - 4x + 1$ from the polynomial $-2x^2 - x + 5$.

To subtract polynomials, subtract like terms. Like terms have the same variable part, such as $3x^2$ and $-2x^2$, which are both are x^2 terms. To find the difference of like terms, find the difference of the coefficients, and retain the same variable part. You can use the distributive property to first distribute the subtraction to each term of the polynomial that is being subtracted.

$$(-2x^2 - x + 5) - (3x^2 - 4x + 1) =$$
$$(-2x^2 - x + 5) - 3x^2 + 4x - 1 =$$
$$(-2x^2 - 3x^2) + (-x + 4x) + (5 - 1) =$$
$$-5x^2 + 3x + 4$$

- 12 -

Is the sum of two cubic polynomials also a cubic polynomial?

The sum of two cubic polynomials is not necessarily a cubic polynomial. However, it is either a cubic polynomial or a polynomial of lesser degree. The sum of two cubic polynomials of the form $ax^3 + bx^2 + cx + d$, where $a \neq 0$, will have the same form, however it is possible that individual like terms are opposites and have a sum of 0. For example, the sum of $-3x^3 + 2x - 3$ and $3x^3 + 5x^2$ is $5x^2 + 2x - 3$, which is a quadratic polynomial. (Notice that coefficients b, c, and d in the cubic polynomial form are each allowed to equal zero; that is, cubic polynomials can be missing any of the terms with degree less than 3.)

Multiply a binomial and a trinomial

To multiply a binomial and a trinomial, use the distributive property. Because a binomial has 2 terms and a trinomial has 3 terms, there will be $2 \cdot 3 = 6$ multiplications when multiplying the polynomials. In the example below, each term of the binomial is multiplied by the entire trinomial. Then, that multiplication is distributed to each term of the trinomial. In the final steps, like terms are combined and the answer is expressed in standard form, with terms written in order of descending degree.

$(x + 2)(x^2 - 3x + 9) = x(x^2 - 3x + 9) + 2(x^2 - 3x + 9) =$
$x^3 - 3x^2 + 9x + 2x^2 - 6x + 18 =$
$x^3 - x^2 + 3x + 18$

What is the Remainder Theorem for polynomials?

The Remainder Theorem for polynomials states that for a polynomial $P(x)$ and a real number a, the remainder when $P(x)$ is divided by $(x - a)$ is $P(a)$, the value of the polynomial evaluated at $x = a$. If there is no remainder, that is if the remainder equals 0, then $P(a) = 0$ and $(x - a)$ is a factor of the polynomial $P(x)$. For example, if $P(x) = (2x - 3)(3x + 1)$, this can be written as $P(x) = 6\left(x - \frac{3}{2}\right)\left(x + \frac{1}{3}\right)$. Here $P\left(\frac{3}{2}\right) = 0$ and $P\left(\frac{1}{3}\right) = 0$, so that the remainder is zero when $P(x)$ is divided by $\left(x - \frac{3}{2}\right)$ and $\left(x + \frac{1}{3}\right)$; $\left(x - \frac{3}{2}\right)$ and $\left(x + \frac{1}{3}\right)$ are therefore factors of $P(x)$.

On the other hand, the Remainder Theorem also can be used to obtain the remainder when the above $P(x)$ is divided by any binomial, such as $(x - 4)$:

$$Rem\left[\frac{P(x)}{x - 4}\right] = P(4) = (2(4) - 3)(3(4) + 1)$$
$$= (8 - 3)(12 + 1) = 5 \cdot 13 = 65$$

When a polynomial $P(x)$ is divided by $(x + 2)$, the remainder is –4. What is the value of $P(-2)$?

To solve this question, apply the Remainder Theorem for polynomials. The Remainder Theorem states that for a polynomial $P(x)$ and a real number a, the remainder when $P(x)$ is divided by
$(x - a)$ is $P(a)$. Since $P(x)$ was divided by the factor $(x + 2)$, let $a = -2$ in the theorem. This means that $P(a) = P(-2)$, and this is equal to the remainder. Since the remainder is –4, it must be that

$P(-2) = -4$. Note that it is not required to explicitly know the polynomial $P(x)$ or even its degree to apply the remainder theorem.

Divide the polynomial $x^2 + 2x - 4$ by $(x - 3)$. Verify the Remainder Theorem by evaluating the polynomial at $x = 3$.

Divide the polynomial $x^2 + 2x - 4$ by $(x - 3)$ using synthetic or long division:

$$
\begin{array}{r|rrr}
3 & 1 & 2 & -4 \\
  &   & 3 & 15 \\
\hline
  & 1 & 5 & 11
\end{array}
\qquad
\begin{array}{r}
x\ -\ 5 \\
\hline
x - 3\ |\ x^2 + 2x - 4 \\
-\underline{x^2 + 3x} \\
5x - 4 \\
\underline{5x + 15} \\
R\ 11
\end{array}
$$

In either case, the remainder is 11. By the Remainder Theorem, for a polynomial $P(x)$ and a real number a, the remainder when $P(x)$ is divided by $(x - a)$ is $P(a)$. In this case, this means the remainder when $x^2 + 2x - 4$ is divided by $(x - 3)$ must be $P(3)$. Verify that $P(3) = 11$ by substituting $x = 3$ into the polynomial:
$(3)^2 + 2(3) - 4 = 9 + 6 - 4 = 11$

Let $P(x)$ be a cubic polynomial function such that $P(2) = P(-1) = P(4) = 0$. If the y-intercept of $P(x)$ is 2, what is the equation for $P(x)$?

By the Remainder Theorem, for a polynomial $P(x)$ and a real number a, the remainder when $P(x)$ is divided by $(x - a)$ is $P(a)$. This means that, since their remainders when divided into $P(x)$ are all zero, $(x - 2)$, $(x + 1)$, and $(x - 4)$ are factors of $P(x)$. Because $P(x)$ is a cubic polynomial function, it must then be of the form $P(x) = a(x - 2)(x + 1)(x - 4)$, where a is some real number. To determine a, use the fact that the y-intercept is 2, which means that $P(0) = 2$:

$$P(x) = a(x - 2)(x + 1)(x - 4)$$
$$P(0) = 2 = a(0 - 2)(0 + 1)(0 - 4) = 8a$$
$$2 = 8a$$
$$a = \tfrac{1}{4}$$

The equation for $P(x)$, then, is $P(x) = \frac{1}{4}(x - 2)(x + 1)(x - 4)$.

Find the zeros of $y = 2x^2 + 3x - 5$ by factoring.

The zeros of $y = 2x^2 + 3x - 5$ are the values of x for which $y = 0$. These are also the x-intercepts of the graph of the function. Factor $2x^2 + 3x - 5$ and rewrite the equation as $y = (2x + 5)(x - 1)$. In factored form, the zeros are found by setting each linear factor equal to zero:

$2x + 5 = 0$ $\qquad\qquad$ $x - 1 = 0$
$\quad 2x = -5$ $\qquad\qquad$ $\quad x = 1$
$\quad\ x = -\dfrac{5}{2}$

The zeros of $y = 2x^2 + 3x - 5$ are $x = 1$ and $x = \dfrac{5}{2}$.

Construct a rough graph of $y = x^3 - x^2 - 12x$.

To construct a rough graph of the function, factor the polynomial $x^3 - x^2 - 12x$ to find the zeros of $y = x^3 - x^2 - 12x$. Because $x^3 - x^2 - 12x = x(x^2 - x - 12) = x(x - 4)(x + 3)$, the function has zeros at $x = 0$, $x = 4$, and $x = -3$. The zeroes are x-intercepts of the graph of the function. The coefficient of the leading term x^3 is positive, and x^3 has an odd degree. Therefore the value of y will approach negative infinity as x goes to negative infinity, and approach positive infinity as x goes to positive infinity. Therefore, the value of y increases from $-\infty$ in the range $x = -\infty$ to $x = -3$ where $y = 0$, continues increasing to a local maximum before decreasing through $y = 0$ at $x = 0$ to some local minimum, and finally increases through $y = 0$ at $x = 4$ to $+\infty$ as x goes to $+\infty$. A rough sketch is shown.

Sketch a cubic function with zeros at $x = -1$ and $x = 3$ that does not pass through the 4th quadrant. Explain your reasoning.

The cubic function has zeros at $x = -1$ and $x = 3$, so these will be x-intercepts of the function. The function does not pass through the 4th quadrant, which must mean that the curve is tangent to the x-axis at $(3, 0)$, and does not pass through the x-axis at this point. For this same reason, the value of y will approach negative infinity as x goes to negative infinity, and approach positive infinity as x goes to positive infinity. A possible sketch is shown.

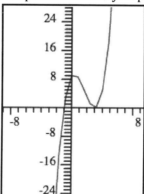

- 15 -

Write the equation for the parabola shown.

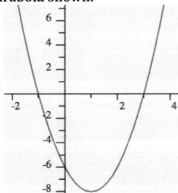

To determine the equation for the parabola, identify the zeros from the graph. The zeros are $x = -1$ and $x = 3$, which means that $(x + 1)$ and $(x - 3)$ are factors of the polynomial that represents the function. Since the parabola is the graph of a quadratic equation, write $y = a(x + 1)(x - 3)$. To determine the value of a, use the fact that the graph passes through the point $(0, -6)$:

$y = a(x + 1)(x - 3)$
$-6 = a(0 + 1)(0 - 3)$
$-6 = -3a$
$a = 2$

Therefore, the equation for the parabola is $y = 2(x + 1)(x - 3)$.

Tony has 4 sections of fence that are *m* feet long, and 4 sections of fence that are *n* feet long. He encloses two square areas with the fencing, one of side *m* and one of side *n*. How much more area can he enclose by making one large square area instead?

Sketch a diagram of what Tony did:

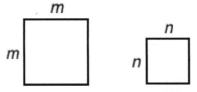

The total area of the enclosures is $m^2 + n^2$. Now sketch a diagram of how Tony could make one large enclosure:

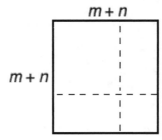

The total area of this enclosure is $(m + n)^2 = m^2 + 2mn + n^2$. Therefore one large fenced area encloses $2mn$ more square feet.

Determine how the expressions m, $\frac{m^2-1}{2}$, and $\frac{m^2+1}{2}$ can be used to generate Pythagorean triples for certain values of m.

A Pythagorean triple is a set of three positive integers that satisfy the Pythagorean Theorem, $a^2 + b^2 = c^2$. For example, the set of numbers {3, 4, 5} is a Pythagorean triple since $3^2 + 4^2 = 5^2$. To show how the given expressions can be used, show that the sum of the squares of two of the expressions equals the square of the remaining term:

$$m^2 + \left(\frac{m^2-1}{2}\right)^2 = m^2 + \left(\frac{m^2-1}{2}\right)\left(\frac{m^2-1}{2}\right)$$
$$= m^2 + \frac{1}{4}(m^4 - 2m^2 + 1)$$
$$= \frac{1}{4}(4m^2 + m^4 - 2m^2 + 1) = \frac{1}{4}(m^4 + 2m^2 + 1)$$
$$= \frac{1}{4}(m^2 + 1)^2 = \left(\frac{m^2+1}{2}\right)^2$$

Clearly, the divisions by 2 require the numerators of those expressions to be even (in order to produce integer results). This occurs for odd m. For $m = 1$, though, one of the terms becomes 0, which is, of course, not allowable. Since negative m produce identical values, for odd m such that $|m| \geq 3$, the expressions generate Pythagorean triples

Meaning of a polynomial identity.

A polynomial identity refers to two polynomials that can be shown equivalent by factoring, multiplying, or simplifying. For any value or values of the variables in the two polynomials, the values of the expressions will be identical. For example, the difference of squares formula $a^2 - b^2 = (a + b)(a - b)$ is a polynomial identity. The left side can be factored to obtain the right side, and/or the right side can be multiplied to obtain the left side. For any real numbers a and b, $a^2 - b^2$ yields the same result as $(a + b)(a - b)$.

Show that the sum of the squares of three consecutive integers a, b, and c, is given by the expression $3b^2 + 2$, where b is the middle integer.

Examples of three consecutive integers are 4, 5, and 6, or 21, 22, and 23. If x represents the middle of 3 consecutive integers, then the other two integers are given by the expressions $x + 1$ and $x - 1$. The squares of these expressions are x^2, $(x + 1)^2$, and $(x - 1)^2$. Now show that $x^2 + (x + 1)^2 + (x - 1)^2 = 3x^2 + 2$:

$$x^2 + (x + 1)^2 + (x - 1)^2 =$$
$$x^2 + x^2 + 2x + 1 + x^2 - 2x + 1 =$$
$$3x^2 + 2$$

What is the Binomial Theorem for expanding the power of a binomial?

The Binomial Theorem gives the expansion of the expression $(x + y)^n$, where x and y are real numbers and n is a positive integer. In other words, it gives a way to write each of the terms of the polynomial that results when $(x + y)$ is written as a multiplicative factor n times. The theorem can be written as follows:

$(x + y)^n = a_0x^ny^0 + a_1x^{n-1}y^1 + a_2x^{n-2}y^2 + \cdots + a_{n-1}x^1y^{n-1} + a_nx^0y^n$ where the coefficients $a_0, a_1,...,$ a_n, are given by the $(n + 1)$th row of Pascal's Triangle. Pascal's Triangle is shown below up to $n = 4$, and the pattern continues such that each entry is the sum of the two entries diagonally above it.

$$1$$
$$1 \quad 1$$
$$1 \quad 2 \quad 1$$
$$1 \quad 3 \quad 3 \quad 1$$

Expand the expression $(b – 2)^4$ using the Binomial Theorem.

The Binomial Theorem is shown below.
$$(x + y)^n = a_0x^ny^0 + a_1x^{n-1}y^1 + a_2x^{n-2}y^2 + \cdots + a_{n-1}x^1y^{n-1} + a_nx^0y^n$$
where the coefficients $a_0, a_1,..., a_n$ are given by the $(n + 1)$th row of Pascal's Triangle. Applying the formula with $x = b$ and $y = -2$ gives:
$$(b - 2)^4 = a_0b^4(-2)^0 + a_1b^3(-2)^1 + a_2b^2(-2)^2 + a_3b^1(-2)^3 + a_4b^0(-2)^4$$
$$= a_0b^4 - 2a_1b^3 + 4a_2b^2 - 8a_3b + 16a_4$$
The coefficients $a_0, a_1,..., a_n$ are given by the 5th row of Pascal's Triangle, which is 1, 4, 6, 4, 1. So the expansion becomes
$b^4 - 8b^3 + 24b^2 - 32b + 16$.

Write the 6th row of. Show what you did.

Pascal's Triangle is a pattern of numbers that give the coefficients of the terms in a binomial expansion. The numbers in row $(n + 1)$ of the triangle represent the coefficients for the terms of the expansion $(x + y)^n$. The first 4 rows of the triangle are shown below:

$$1$$
$$1 \quad 1$$
$$1 \quad 2 \quad 1$$
$$1 \quad 3 \quad 3 \quad 1$$

The pattern continues indefinitely, where each entry is the sum of the two entries diagonally above it.. The first and last entries of every row are 1. Therefore, the next row of the triangle will be 1, 4, 6, 4, 1. The 6th row of Pascal's Triangle is 1, (1 + 4), (4 + 6), (6 + 4), (4 + 1), 1 = 1, 5, 10, 10, 5, 1.

What is the coefficient of the x^5 term in the expansion of $(2x – 1)^5$?

The Binomial Theorem gives the expansion of the expression $(x + y)^n$, where x and y are real numbers and n is a positive integer. The theorem can be written as follows:
$$(x+y)^n = a_0x^ny^0 + a_1x^{n-1}y^1 + a_2x^{n-2}y^2 + ... + a_{n-1}x^1y^{n-1} + a_nx^0y^n$$
where the coefficients $a_0, a_1,..., a_n$ are given by the $(n + 1)$th row of Pascal's Triangle. Since $n = 5$, use the 6th row of the Triangle, which has the values 1, 5, 10, 10, 5, and 1. The x^5 term is the first term; $a_0 = 1$. The x^5 term is therefore $1(2x)^5(-1)^0 = 32x^5$. The coefficient of the x^5 term is 32.

Long division for polynomials.

Long division for polynomials is similar to long division of integers. For example, when dividing 385 by 12, you first determine how many times 12 goes into 38 (and write 3 as the corresponding digit of the quotient). Then you subtract 36 from 38, giving 2, and the 5 is brought down to form 25, and so on. With polynomial division, the first term written for the quotient is equal to the first term of the dividend divided by the first term of the divisor. For example, if $5x^2 + 10x + 3$ is being divided by $x - 2$, the first term for the quotient is $\frac{5x^2}{x} = 5x$. $5x$ times $x - 2$ is $5x^2 - 10x$, and then $5x^2 - 10x$ is subtracted from $5x^2 + 10x$, yielding $20x$; the 3 is then brought down to form $20x + 3$. This process continues until the remainder is determined.

Find the remainder when $2b^2 + 3b + 2$ is divided by $2b + 1$.

The remainder when $2b^2 + 3b + 2$ is divided by $2b + 1$ can be found by long division. To divide polynomials using long division, find the first term of the quotient by dividing $2b^2$ by $2b$, which gives b. Multiply this by the divisor to get $2b^2 + b$, and then subtract this result from the first two terms of the dividend to obtain $2b$. Then bring down the $+2$ to form $2b + 2$, and continue in this way. The complete division is shown below.

When the degree of the result after a subtraction is less than that of the divisor, the result is the remainder. So, the remainder is 1, and $2b^2 + 3b + 2$ divided by $2b + 1$ is equal to $b + 1 + \frac{1}{2b+1}$.

(Note: synthetic division cannot be used in this case, since the divisor is not a linear factor.)

Rewrite the rational expression $\frac{3x^3+2x^2}{x}$ by inspection.

The rational expression has a monomial for a denominator. This means that when each term of the numerator is divided by the denominator, the result of each division can be found by applying properties of exponents. In particular, the property $\frac{x^n}{x^m} = x^{n-m}$ can be used to rewrite each term as shown:

$$\frac{3x^3 + 2x^2}{x} = \frac{3x^3}{x} + \frac{2x^2}{x} = 3x^2 + 2x$$

The polynomial $3x^2 + 2x$ is equivalent to the original rational expression. Note that the only exception is the value $x = 0$, because the original rational expression is undefined for $x = 0$.

Add the expressions $\frac{1}{x+1} + \frac{x}{x+1}$ and simplify the result.

To add rational expressions, first obtain a common denominator. Then add the numerators, and keep the same denominator. Since the denominator of each expression is $x + 1$, the expressions can be added directly:

$$\frac{1}{x + 1} + \frac{x}{x + 1} = \frac{1 + x}{x + 1}$$

- 19 -

The expressions $1 + x$ and $x + 1$ are equivalent. By dividing the numerator and denominator by $x + 1$, the expression can be further simplified:

$$\frac{1+x}{x+1} = \frac{x+1}{x+1} = 1$$

The sum of the rational expressions is equal to 1. This is true for all values of x except $x = -1$, since the original expressions are undefined for $x = -1$.

What is the least common denominator of $\frac{3x}{x^2-x-6}$ and $\frac{2x}{x^2-6x+9}$?

To determine the least common denominator, or LCD, of two rational expressions, factor the denominators completely. The LCD is equal to the product of the greatest occurring power of each unique factor.

$x^2 - x - 6 = (x - 3)(x + 2)$
$x^2 - 6x + 9 = (x - 3)^2$

The unique factors are $(x + 2)$ and $(x - 3)$. The greatest occurring power of $(x - 3)$ is 2. Therefore the LCD of the two expressions is
$(x + 2)(x - 3)^2$.

Multiply the expressions $\frac{1-x}{x^2+2x+1}$ and $\frac{5}{x^2-1}$. Simplify the result.

To multiply two rational expressions, multiply the numerators to obtain the new numerator, and multiply the denominators to obtain the new denominator:

$$\frac{1-x}{x^2+2x+1} \cdot \frac{5}{x^2-1} = \frac{5(1-x)}{(x^2+2x+1)(x^2-1)}$$

To simplify the result, factor the numerator and denominator completely. The factor $1 - x$ in the numerator can be rewritten as $-(x - 1)$, and the common factor $(x - 1)$ in the numerator and denominator can be cancelled:

$$\frac{5(1-x)}{(x^2+2x+1)(x^2-1)} = \frac{-5(x-1)}{(x+1)(x+1)(x+1)(x-1)} = \frac{-5}{(x+1)^3}$$

Note that this expression is equivalent to the original product for all x except $x = \pm1$, since the original expressions are undefined for these values.

Rational expressions are closed under subtraction using closure properties of polynomials.

Rational expressions are closed under subtraction if the difference of any two rational expressions results in a rational expression. Consider two rational expressions $\frac{a(x)}{b(x)}$ and $\frac{c(x)}{d(x)}$, where $a(x)$, $b(x)$, $c(x)$, and $d(x)$ are polynomials. Their difference can be written as follows:

$$\frac{a(x)}{b(x)} - \frac{c(x)}{d(x)} = \frac{a(x) \cdot d(x) - b(x) \cdot c(x)}{b(x) \cdot d(x)}$$

Since polynomials are closed under multiplication, the products in the right side of the equation (including the denominator) are all polynomials. Since polynomials are closed under subtraction, the numerator is also a polynomial. So, the expression is a ratio of polynomials and is therefore a rational expression.

Prove that polynomials are not closed under division.

Polynomials are additions, subtractions and/or multiplication (but not division by variables) of variable expressions containing only non-negative integer exponents. To prove that polynomials are not closed under division, use a counterexample. Assume that polynomials are closed under division. This means the quotient $(x + 1) \div x = \frac{x+1}{x} = 1 + \frac{1}{x} = 1 + x^{-1}$ would have to be a polynomial. This expression, however, is not a polynomial, because the term x^{-1} contains a negative exponent (or would have to be written as the division by x). All terms of a polynomial must be of the form ax^n, where a is a real number and n is a non-negative integer. Although there are *some* quotients of polynomials that are polynomials, closure requires this to be true for *all* polynomials.

If $p(x)$ is a polynomial and $\frac{p(x)}{x-3}$ leaves a reminder of –6, what is $p(3)$?

By the Remainder Theorem, for a polynomial $p(x)$ and a real number a, the remainder when $p(x)$ is divided by $(x - a)$ is $p(a)$. In the given equation, $p(x)$ is divided by the binomial $x - 3$, and leaves a reminder of –6. This means that the value of $p(3)$ is –6. Note that the theorem can be applied without needing to know the actual terms of the polynomial $p(x)$.

What are the zeros of the polynomial $(2x – 1)(x^2 – 9)$?

The zeros of the polynomial can be determined by factoring. The expression $x^2 – 9$ is a difference of squares, and factors as $(x – 3)(x + 3)$. The factored form of the full polynomial is therefore $(2x – 1)(x – 3)(x + 3)$. Set each of the linear factors equal to zero and solve for x:

$2x - 1 = 0$	$x - 3 = 0$	$x + 3 = 0$	
$2x = 1$	$x = 3$	$x = -3$	$x = \frac{1}{2}$

The zeros of the polynomial are $\frac{1}{2}$, 3, and –3.

Prove that the product of two consecutive even or odd integers is equal to 1 less than the square of their mean.

Let n represent the first of two consecutive even or odd integers. Then the following consecutive integer is given by the expression $n + 2$. The mean of the two numbers is $n + 1$, since $\frac{n+n+2}{2} = \frac{2n+2}{2} = n + 1$. One less than the square of this expression is written as $(n + 1)^2 – 1$. Show that this expression is equal to the product of the two consecutive even or odd integers by factoring the expression as a difference of squares:

$(n + 1)^2 – 1 = (n + 1 – 1)(n + 1 + 1) = (n + 0)(n + 2) = n(n + 2)$

What is the constant term in the expansion of $(-2 - 4m)^5$?

The Binomial Theorem gives the expansion of the expression $(x + y)^n$, where x and y are real numbers and n is a positive integer. The theorem can be written as follows:

$$(x+y)^n = a_0 x^n y^0 + a_1 x^{n-1} y^1 + a_2 x^{n-2} y^2 + \ldots + a_{n-1} x^1 y^{n-1} + a_n x^0 y^n$$

where the coefficients $a_0, a_1, \ldots, a_n$ are given by the $(n + 1)^{\text{th}}$ row of Pascal's Triangle. For the expression $(-2 - 4m)^5$, let $x = -2$ and $y = 4m$ in the equation above. The first term, $a_0 x^n y^0$, must represent the constant term in this case, since the variable y is raised to the power of zero. Also, the first term in each row of Pascal's Triangle is one, so a_0 is 1. The constant term is therefore $1(-2)^5 = -32$.

Simplify the rational expression $\frac{x-1}{1-x^2}$.

To simplify a rational expression, factor the numerator and denominator completely. Factors that are the same and appear in the numerator and denominator have a ratio of 1. The denominator, $1 - x^2$, is a difference of squares. It can be factored as $(1 - x)(1 + x)$. The factor $1 - x$ and the numerator $x - 1$ are opposites, and have a ratio of -1. Rewrite the numerator as $-1(1 - x)$. So, the rational expression can be simplified as follows:

$$\frac{x-1}{1-x^2} = \frac{-1(1-x)}{(1-x)(1+x)} = \frac{-1}{1+x}$$

(Note that since the original expression is defined for $x \neq \{-1, 1\}$, the simplified expression has the same restrictions.)

Alison knows that rational expressions are closed under division, assuming a nonzero divisor. She then claims that since all polynomials are rational expressions, polynomials are also closed under division, assuming a nonzero divisor. Find her error.

Alison is correct that rational expressions are closed under division, assuming a nonzero divisor. She is also correct in saying that all polynomials are rational expressions, since the polynomial could be written with a denominator of 1, such as $3x^2 + 4 = \frac{3x^2+4}{1}$. However, closure of rational expressions only guarantees that dividing one rational expression by another results in a rational expression. Polynomials are a subset of the rational expressions, but the ratio of two polynomials is only a polynomial if the divisor is a nonzero constant. Since there are divisors of polynomials that do not yield polynomial quotients, polynomials are not closed under division.

Simplify the quotient: $\frac{x-2}{3x} \div \frac{x^2-4}{6x^2}$.

To simplify the quotient, first rewrite it as a product by taking the reciprocal of the divisor. Then completely factor the numerators and denominators, and simplify by recognizing identical factors in the numerator and the denominator have a ratio of 1:

$$\frac{x-2}{3x} \div \frac{x^2-4}{6x^2} =$$
$$\frac{x-2}{3x} \cdot \frac{6x^2}{x^2-4} =$$
$$\frac{x-2}{3x} \cdot \frac{2x(3x)}{(x-2)(x+2)} =$$
$$\frac{2x}{x+2}$$

Creating Equations

The cost to produce x items is given by the equation $c = 8000 + 30x$. How many items are produced if the average cost per item is \$46?

The average cost per item is equal to the total cost of the items divided by the number of items produced. The cost to produce x items is given by the equation $c = 8000 + 30x$, so the average cost A is given by the rational equation $A = \frac{c}{x} = \frac{8000+30x}{x}$. Since this average cost is \$46, substitute 46 for A in the equation and solve for x:

$$A = \frac{8000 + 30x}{x}$$
$$46 = \frac{8000 + 30x}{x}$$
$$46x = 8000 + 30x$$
$$8000 = 16x$$
$$x = 500$$

500 items are produced when the average cost per item is \$46.

Ray has test scores of 78, 90, and 83. What score can he receive on a 4ᵗʰ test to have an average of at least 85 for the four tests?

Ray's average will be the sum of all the test scores, divided by the number of test scores, which is 4. Let x represent the score he receives on the 4ᵗʰ test. Then the expression $\frac{78+90+83+x}{4}$ gives the average on all four tests. Since Ray is looking for the score that will give an average of *at least* 85, write an inequality using the 'greater than or equal to' symbol:

$$\frac{78+90+83+x}{4} \geq 85$$
$$251 + x \geq 340$$
$$x \geq 89$$

Ray must receive a score of 89 or greater on the 4ᵗʰ test to bring his average up to at least 85.

If Sally squares the number representing her age, the result is 14 more than 5 times her age. What is Sally's age?

Let a represent Sally's age. The square of Sally's age is therefore given by the expression a^2. The word *times* means multiply, so an expression for 5 times Sally's age is $5a$. The square of her age, a^2, is 14 more than this expression $5a$. This leads to the equation $a^2 - 14 = 5a$. Solve this equation by factoring:

$a^2 - 14 = 5a$
$a^2 - 5a - 14 = 0$
$(a - 7)(a + 2) = 0$
$a = 7$ or $a = -2$

Sally cannot possibly be –2 years old, so discard the solution $a = -2$. Sally must be 7 years old.

A town's population increased exponentially from 40,000 to 76,000 over a 3 year period. On average, what was the percent increase in population per year?

The town's population increased exponentially, so the population P can be modeled by the equation $P = P_0(1 + r)^t$, where P_0 is the initial population, r is the annual rate of growth, and t is the number of years. Substitute the given values and solve for r:

$$76,000 = 40,000(1 + r)^3$$
$$1.9 = (1 + r)^3$$
$$\sqrt[3]{1.9} = 1 + r$$
$$r = \sqrt[3]{1.9} - 1 \approx 0.239$$

Therefore, on average, the town population increased about 23.9% per year.

A tractor rental requires an $800 deposit, and tractors can be rented for $42 per hour. The balance of the deposit is returned after the rental. Write an equation that gives the money m returned after the tractor is rented for h hours. Assume that $h <$ 12.

The tractor can be rented for $42 per hour. The word *per* indicates multiplying the cost by the duration, so that if h represents the number of hours, the expression $42h$ represents the total cost to rent the tractor. The equation that gives the money returned m is therefore $m = 800 - 42h$. Note that this equation is only valid for a number of hours that does not make the cost exceed the deposit of $800. For $h < 12$, the equation is valid because $42 \cdot 12 = 504$ and $504 is less than $800.

Fred buys some CDs for $12 each. He also buys two DVDs. If Fred spends $60, write an equation that relates the number of CDs and the average cost of a DVD.

Let c represent the number of CDs that Fred buys, and let d represent the average cost of one of the DVDs that Fred buys. The cost per item times the number of items will give the part of the total cost that each kind of item contributes. The expression $12c$ gives the cost of the CDs, and the expression $2d$ gives the cost of the DVDs. So, the equation $12c + 2d = 60$ relates the number of CDs and the average cost of a DVD. Note that even though the variables have different units, the unit for each of the three terms in the equation is dollars.

A basketball player scores field goals worth 2 points and three-pointers worth 3 points. Sketch a graph showing how a player might score 36 points.

Let x represent the number of field goals made and y represent the number of three-pointers made. The equation $2x + 3y = 36$ expresses the total score of 36 points since every field goal (x) is worth 2 points and every three-pointer (y) is worth 3. The graph is only valid in the first quadrant, since the number of field goals or three-points must be greater than or equal to zero. Also, only integer solutions are valid, not every point on the line. For example, the bullet on the graph below shows a possible solution $(x, y) = (12, 4)$, or 12 field goals and 4 three-pointers.

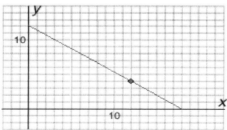

Describe what a constraint on a two-variable inequality is.

A two-variable equation shows a relationship between two quantities. A constraint is another equation or inequality that places restrictions on one or both of the variables. For example, let p and r represent the number of pounds of peanuts and raisins, respectively, in a trail mix. A possible constraint on these variables is given by the inequality $p + r < 4$, which means the total number of pounds must be less than 4. A further constraint on this inequality could be given by $2r \leq 3p$, which can be interpreted as requiring the ratio of raisins to peanuts be less than or equal to 3:2.

Write a quadratic equation based on the graph. Describe a possible relationship that is represented by the graph.

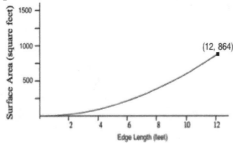

The graph represents a quadratic equation. Since it passes through the origin and opens upward, the equation is of the form $y = ax^2$. To determine the value of a, use the point (12, 864) to substitute for x and y:

$y = ax^2$

$864 = a(12)^2$

$864 = 144a$

$a = 6$

The equation for the graph is therefore $y = 6x^2$. Based on the descriptions for the axes of the graph, one possible relation between x and y is that x is the edge length of a cube (in feet), and y is the surface area of the cube (in square feet).

A delivery company requires the length plus the girth of a package to be less than 110 inches. The length is the measurement of the longest dimension, and the girth is the distance around the package, perpendicular to the length. Write an inequality representing this constraint for the package shown.

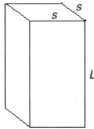

The length is the measurement of the longest dimension, which is labeled L in the diagram. The girth is the distance around the package, perpendicular to the length. Since the base is square and has side length s, the girth is given by the expression $4s$. Assuming both variables represent lengths in inches, the length L plus the girth $4s$ of the must be less than 110 inches. Write an inequality using the less than symbol: $L + 4s < 110$.

A cab company charges \$6 to enter a cab, and then \$.80 per mile. What is the range of miles traveled for a ride that costs between \$14 and \$22?

Let m represent the number of miles of a ride in the cab. The total cost is the \$6 to enter the cab plus the cost associated with the mileage. Since the company charges \$.80 per mile, the expression $6 + 0.8m$ gives the total cost for a ride that is m miles. The inequality $14 < 6 + 0.8m < 22$ represents this cost being between \$14 and \$22. Solve the inequality for m:

$14 < 6 + 0.8m < 22$

$14 - 6 < 6 - 6 + 0.8m < 22 - 6$

$8 < 0.8m < 16$

$$\frac{8}{0.8} < \frac{0.8m}{0.8} < \frac{16}{0.8}$$
$$10 < m < 20$$

The range of miles is between 10 and 20 miles. A 10-mile or 20-mile ride would cost exactly $14 or $22, respectively.

Explain how to isolate *h* in the formula *V* = π*r*²*h* + *lwh*.

In the formula $V = \pi r^2 h + lwh$, h appears in both terms on the right side of the equation. Factor out h:

$$V = \pi r^2 h + lwh$$
$$V = h(\pi r^2 + lw)$$

The variable h is now a factor in the product $h(\pi r^2 + lw)$. To isolate h, divide each side of the equation by the other factor, $\pi r^2 + lw$:

$$V = h(\pi r^2 + lw)$$
$$\frac{V}{\pi r^2 + lw} = h$$

The diagram at right shows a rectangle inside an equilateral triangle with side length 10 units. One side of the rectangle is part of a side of the triangle. Find the maximum area of the rectangle.

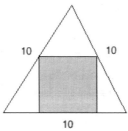

Place the figure on the coordinate plane as shown below. By the Pythagorean Theorem, then, the height of the triangle is $5\sqrt{3}$ units ($10^2 - 5^2 = 75 = \sqrt{75}^2 = \sqrt{25 \cdot 3}^2 = (5\sqrt{3})^2$. The equation of the line that represents the right side of the triangle is $y = -x\sqrt{3} + 5\sqrt{3}$, since the slope is $\frac{\Delta y}{\Delta x} = \frac{0 - 5\sqrt{3}}{5} = -\sqrt{3}$, and the y-intercept is $5\sqrt{3}$. The area of the rectangle is then given by $A = xy = x(-x\sqrt{3} + 5\sqrt{3}) = -x^2\sqrt{3} + 5x\sqrt{3}$. This equation represents a parabola that opens down, with maximum value at the vertex.

The x-value of the vertex of a general parabola is given by –b/2a, and is therefore $\frac{-5\sqrt{3}}{-2\sqrt{3}} = \frac{5}{2}$, so the maximum area (the value of the area function A at that x-value, is therefore equal to:

$-\left(\frac{5}{2}\right)^2 \sqrt{3} + 5\left(\frac{5}{2}\right)\sqrt{3} = \frac{-25\sqrt{3}}{4} + \frac{25\sqrt{3}}{2} = \frac{25\sqrt{3}}{4}$ square units

- 27 -

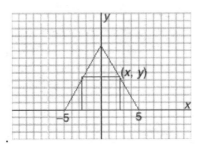

Solve the equation $\frac{1}{R_1} + \frac{1}{R_2} = 2$ for R_1.

To solve a rational equation for which the variable of interest in in the denominator, multiply the equation by the LCD, or least common denominator. The LCD of this equation is R_1R_2. The rest of the algebra is shown here:

$$\frac{1}{R_1} + \frac{1}{R_2} = 2$$
$$R_1R_2\left(\frac{1}{R_1} + \frac{1}{R_2}\right) = 2R_1R_2$$
$$R_2 + R_1 = 2R_1R_2$$
$$R_2 = 2R_1R_2 - R_1$$
$$R_2 = R_1(2R_2 - 1)$$
$$R_1 = \frac{R_2}{2R_2 - 1}$$

Rearrange the formula $I = P(1+r)^t$ by solving for P.

In the formula $I = P(1+r)^t$, I is equal to the product of the two expressions P and $(1+r)^t$. The exponent t does not apply to the variable P. To solve for P means to isolate P on one side of the equation, with no P appearing on the other side of the equation. To do this, divide each side by $(1+r)^t$:

$$I = P(1+r)^t$$
$$P = \frac{I}{(1+r)^t}$$

Write the linear equation $AX + By = C$ solved for y. State any restrictions.

The equation $AX + By = C$ is the standard form of a linear equation in two variables. To solve for y, isolate y on one side of the equation, and divide the equation by the coefficient of y:

$$Ax + By = C$$
$$By = -Ax + C$$
$$y = -\frac{A}{B}x + \frac{C}{B}$$

The restriction on the transformed equation is that $B \neq 0$. This is because division by zero is undefined.

A farm stand sells vegetables and dairy products. One third of the sales from dairy products plus half of the sales from vegetables should exceed the monthly payment P for the farm. Show variables and write an inequality

Let d represent the sales from dairy products, and v represent the sales from vegetables. One third of the sales from dairy products is given by the expression $\frac{d}{3}$. One half of the sales from vegetables is given by the expression $\frac{v}{2}$. The sum of these expressions should exceed the monthly payment for the farm, represented by P. An inequality expressing this situation is $\frac{d}{3} + \frac{v}{2} > P$.

Sam can write 8 invitations in 20 minutes. With Jane's help, together they can write 30 invitations in 45 minutes. About how many more invitations per hour can Sam write than Jane?

The rate at which Sam can write invitations can be readily expressed in invitations per minute: $\frac{8 \, invitations}{20 \, minutes} = \frac{8}{20} \frac{invitations}{minute} = \frac{2}{5} \frac{invitations}{minute}$.

Convert this to invitations per hour: $\frac{2}{5} \frac{invitations}{minute} \cdot \left(\frac{60 \, minutes}{1 \, hour} \right) = 24 \frac{invitations}{hour}$.

Similarly, 30 invitations in 45 minutes is equivalent to 40 invitations per hour. If Jane writes x invitations per hour, then $24 + x = 40$. Subtract 24 from each side to get $x = 16$. Sam can write 24 – 16 or 8 more invitations per hour than Jane.

Dina will meet her friend at the library in t minutes. She must first bicycle back home 3 miles, leave the bike, and then walk 0.5 miles to the library. Dina can bicycle 3 times as fast as she can walk. If Dina walks w miles per hour, write an equation relating t and w.

The equation $d = rt$ can be rewritten as $t = \frac{d}{r}$. An expression for the time needed to walk is $\frac{0.5}{w}$, where w represents the rate at which Dina walks. Similarly, an expression for the time needed to bicycle is $\frac{3}{3w} = \frac{1}{w}$, where $3w$ represents the rate at which Dina bicycles, which is 3 times her walking rate w. The total time that Dina has to walk and bicycle is t minutes. The sum of the two expressions for time must therefore equal t. An equation relating t and w is $\frac{0.5}{w} + \frac{1}{w} = t$, or $\frac{1.5}{w} = t$.

Write an equation that gives the radius r of a cylinder in terms of its height h and volume V.

The formula for the volume of a cylinder with radius r and height h is $V = \pi r^2 h$. To solve for r, first isolate r^2 by dividing each side of the equation by πh. Then take the square root of each side, so the equation has only r on one side.

$$V = \pi r^2 h$$
$$\frac{V}{\pi h} = r^2$$
$$\sqrt{\frac{V}{\pi h}} = r$$

- 29 -

(The values of r, V, and h are all positive, so a plus-or-minus sign ($\pm$) is not needed when taking the square root.)

Reasoning with Equations & Inequalities

Solve $3x - 2 = -5$ by first assuming the solution exists. Explicitly justify each step.

Assume that the solution exists, and that each side of the equation represents the same real number. In this case, that real number is –5, since the right side of the equation is –5. Adding 2 to each side results in two more equal numbers. So, the equation can be transformed as follows:
$3x - 2 = -5$
$3x - 2 + 2 = -5 + 2$
$3x = -3$

The same approach can be taken with the new equation. Since each side of the equation represents the same real number, divide each side by 3:

$$3x = -3$$
$$\frac{3x}{3} = \frac{-3}{3}$$
$$x = -1$$

The solution of the equation is $x = -1$.

Tom says the equation $3x = 5x$ has no solution. Find his error.

Tom made an error, because the correct (and only) solution is $x = 0$. Tom may have incorrectly thought that 3 times a number can't possibly equal 5 times the same number, or perhaps he divided each side by the variable x. A correct method of solving the equation would be to assume there is a solution, so that each side equals the same real number. Subtract $3x$ from each side, yielding $0 = 2x$, each side of which equals some real number as well, since $3x$ was a real number. Dividing each side by 2 yields $x = 0$, which is the correct solution.

Find the solution of the equation $x^2 = 36$. Justify your solution method.

One method of solution is to assume there is a solution, so that x^2 and 36 each represent the same real number. Subtract 36 from each side, so that $x^2 - 36 = 0$. The expression on the left side can be factored, and the equation rewritten as $(x + 6)(x - 6) = 0$. If a product of two numbers is equal to zero, then one (or the other) of the numbers must be zero. This leads to the two equations $x + 6 = 0$ and $x - 6 = 0$. Assuming these equations have solutions, add (or subtract) 6 from each side to arrive at the two solutions, $x = -6$ or $x = 6$.

Solve $\frac{6}{x} = \frac{9}{10}$. Determine how each step follows from the equality of numbers.

Assume that the solution exists, and that $\frac{6}{x}$ and $\frac{9}{10}$ equal the same real number. Since $\frac{9}{10}$ is positive, and a positive number divided by a positive number is positive, the value of x must be positive. Multiply each side of the equation by x to get $6 = \frac{9x}{10}$, where each side again

- 30 -

represents the same real number. Then multiply each side by $\frac{10}{9}$, to arrive at the solution $\frac{60}{9} = x$.

What is an extraneous solution is, and why they may arise when solving a rational or radical equation.

An extraneous solution is the solution of an equation that arises during the process of solving an equation, which is <u>not</u> a solution of the original equation. When solving a rational equation, each side is often multiplied by x or an expression containing x. Since the value of x is unknown, this may mean multiplying by zero, which will make any equation the true statement $0 = 0$. Similarly, when solving a radical expression, each side of the equation is often squared, or raised to some power. This can also change the sign of unknown expressions. For example, the equation $3 = -3$ is false, but squaring each side gives $9 = 9$, which is true.

Solve the rational equation $\frac{2}{x} - 2 = x - 1$.

To solve the rational equation, multiply each side of the equation by the LCD, which is x. This will transform the rational equation into a quadratic equation that can be solved by factoring:

$$\frac{2}{x} - 2 = x - 1$$
$$x\left(\frac{2}{x} - 2\right) = x(x - 1)$$
$$2 - 2x = x^2 - x$$
$$x^2 + x - 2 = 0$$
$$(x + 2)(x - 1) = 0$$
$$x = -2, x = 1$$

Both $x = -2$ and $x = 1$ check out in the original equation. The solution is $x = \{-2, 1\}$.

Solve the radical equation $\sqrt{x - 1} + 3 = x$.

To solve the radical equation, isolate the radical $\sqrt{x - 1}$ on one side of the equation. Then square both sides and solve the resulting quadratic equation:

$$\sqrt{x - 1} + 3 = x$$
$$\sqrt{x - 1} = x - 3$$
$$\left(\sqrt{x - 1}\right)^2 = (x - 3)^2$$
$$x - 1 = x^2 - 6x + 9$$
$$x^2 - 7x + 10 = 0$$
$$(x - 5)(x - 2) = 0$$
$$x = 2, x = 5$$

Only $x = 5$ checks out in the original equation; $\sqrt{2 - 1} + 3 \overset{?}{\Leftrightarrow} 2 \xrightarrow{yields} \sqrt{1} + 3 = 4 \neq 2!$

The solution, then, is just $x = \{5\}$.

Solve $x + 1 = \sqrt{x + 1}$. Check for extraneous solutions.

To solve the radical equation, square both sides and solve the resulting quadratic equation by factoring:

$$x + 1 = \sqrt{x + 1}$$
$$(x + 1)^2 = \left(\sqrt{x + 1}\right)^2$$
$$x^2 + 2x + 1 = x + 1$$
$$x^2 + x = 0$$
$$x(x + 1) = 0$$
$$x = -1, x = 0$$

To check whether either solution is extraneous, substitute into the original equation:

$x + 1 = \sqrt{x + 1}$ $\qquad\qquad$ $x + 1 = \sqrt{x + 1}$
$-1 + 1 = \sqrt{-1 + 1}$ $\qquad\qquad$ $0 + 1 = \sqrt{0 + 1}$
$0 = 0$ $\qquad\qquad\qquad\qquad$ $0 = 0$

Both solutions are valid. The solution is $x = \{-1, 0\}$.

Find the solution of the inequality
  $-4x + 2 \leq -10$.

To solve the inequality, isolate the variable x on one side. When multiplying or dividing by negative numbers, change the inequality symbol from $\leq$ to $\geq$, or vice versa:

$-4x + 2 \leq -10$
$-4x + 2 - 2 \leq -10 - 2$
$-4x \leq -12$

$$\frac{-4x}{-4} \geq \frac{-12}{-4}$$
$$x \geq 3$$

The solution of the inequality is $x \geq 3$. (Note that when $x = 3$, both sides of the inequality equal -10. Also, when $x = 4$, the inequality is $-14 \leq -10$, which is true. Therefore the solution is correct.)

A softball player's average is the number of hits divided by the number of at-bats. Gene currently has 20 hits in 75 at-bats. If he can get 30 more at-bats, how many hits must he get to have an average of 0.300 or better?

Let h represent the number of additional hits Gene gets in the 30 at-bats. His total number of hits will be $20 + h$, and his total number of at-bats will be $75 + 30 = 105$. The quotient of these two expressions represents Gene's average. Write a greater-than-or-equal-to inequality for this situation:

$$\frac{20 + h}{105} \geq 0.300$$
$$20 + h \geq 31.5$$
$$h \geq 11.5$$

Since there is no such thing as half a hit, Gene needs 12 or more hits in the next 30 at-bats to have an average of 0.300 or better.

A cab company charges $8 to enter the cab, and then $.42 per mile. If the ride cost $19.76, how long was the trip, in miles?

Let m represent the number of miles for a ride in the cab. The total cost is the $8 to enter the cab, plus $.42 per mile. If c represents the total cost for a ride of m miles, an equation for the total cost is
$c = 8 + 0.42m$. Substitute 19.76 for c in the equation and solve for m:

$8 + 0.42m = 19.76$
$0.42m = 11.76$

$$\frac{0.42m}{0.42} = \frac{11.76}{0.42}$$
$$m = 28$$

A ride that cost $19.76 was 28 miles long.

Solve the linear equation $ax + b = c$, where a, b, and c are real numbers. State any restrictions on the values of a, b, and c.

The equation can be solved the same way as if the parameters a, b, and c were real numbers. Isolate x on one side of the equation:

$$ax + b = c$$
$$ax = c - b$$
$$\frac{ax}{a} = \frac{c - b}{a}$$
$$x = \frac{c - b}{a}$$

The solution is $x = \frac{c-b}{a}$. Since division by zero is undefined, the value of a must be nonzero. However, if the value of a were zero, the original equation would not be a one-variable equation, but would simply read $b = c$.

Rewrite $x^2 + 4x = 2$ in the form $(x - p)^2 = q$.

To rewrite $x^2 + 4x = 2$ in the form $(x - p)^2 = q$, complete the square. Begin by adding the square of one half the coefficient of x to each side. In this case, the coefficient is 4, so add ($\frac{1}{2}$ · 4)^2 = 4 to both sides, and rewrite the trinomial as a squared binomial:

$$x^2 + 4x = 2$$
$$x^2 + 4x + 4 = 2 + 4$$
$$x^2 + 4x + 4 = 6$$
$$(x + 2)^2 = 6$$

This equation is in the form $(x - p)^2 = q$, with $p = -2$ and $q = 6$.

**Complete the square in the equation
$3x^2 - 5x = 2$.**

To complete the square, first divide by 3 so that the leading coefficient (the coefficient of x^2) is 1. Then add the square of one half the coefficient of x to each side of the equation, and rewrite the trinomial as a squared binomial:

$$3x^2 - 5x = 2$$
$$x^2 - \frac{5}{3}x = \frac{2}{3}$$
$$x^2 - \frac{5}{3}x + \left(\frac{5}{6}\right)^2 = 2 + \left(\frac{5}{6}\right)^2$$
$$x^2 - \frac{5}{3}x + \frac{25}{36} = \frac{72}{36} + \frac{25}{36} = \frac{97}{36}$$
$$\left(x + \frac{5}{6}\right)^2 = \frac{97}{36}$$

Derive the quadratic formula by completing the square in the general quadratic equation $ax^2 + bx + c = 0$.

The quadratic formula gives the solutions to the equation $ax^2 + bx + c = 0$ in terms of the parameters a, b, and c. To derive the formula by completing the square:

$a\left(x^2 + \frac{b}{a}x\right) = c$ Subtract c from each side, and factor out a.

$a\left(x^2 + \frac{b}{a}x + \frac{b^2}{4a^2}\right) = \frac{b^2}{4a} - c$ Complete the square and add $\left(\frac{1}{2} \cdot \frac{b}{a}\right)^2 = \frac{b^2}{4a}$ to both.

$\left(x + \frac{b}{2a}\right)^2 = \frac{b^2}{4a^2} - \frac{c}{a}$ Rewrite the trinomial as a perfect square and divide both sides by a.

$x + \frac{b}{2a} = \pm\frac{\sqrt{(b^2-4ac)}}{2a}$ Take the square root of each side, simplifying the denominator.

$x = \frac{-b \pm \sqrt{b^2-4ac}}{2a}$ Solve for x and simplify.

Compare the quadratic forms $a(x - m)(x - n) = 0$ and $(x - p)^2 = q$. What are the solutions of each equation?

The quadratic equation $a(x - m)(x - n) = 0$ is in factored form. Since the right side of the equation is zero, the factors make it easy to find the solutions: the two equations $x - m = 0$ and $x - n = 0$ give the solutions $x = m$ and $x = n$. The equation $(x - p)^2 = q$ has the form of a quadratic after completing the square, which means the left side is a squared binomial. Taking the square root of each side and then adding p to each side of the equation gives the solutions $x = p \pm \sqrt{q}$.

What is the general form of a complex number?

The general form of a complex number is $a + bi$, where a and b are real numbers. The imaginary number i is equal to the square root of –1: $i = \sqrt{-1}$. Therefore the number i itself is a complex number, with $a = 0$ and $b = 1$. Other examples of complex numbers include $-12i$ and $\sqrt{3} + 4i$. Note that all real numbers are also complex numbers: if $b = 0$, then $a + bi = a + 0i = a$, which is a real number.

Solve $4x^2 = 100$ by inspection.

To solve an equation by inspection means to solve using fairly obvious mental math, without performing calculations on paper or with a calculator. Dividing each side of the equation by 4 gives $x^2 = 25$. The two square roots of 25 are –5 and 5, so the solution of the equation is $x = -5$ or $x = 5$. A check of each solution (by substituting into the original equation) can seem self-evident:

$4x^2 = 100$ $4x^2 = 100$
$4(-5)^2 = 100$ $4(5)^2 = 100$
$4(25) = 100$ $4(25) = 100$
$100 = 100$ $100 = 100$

Write the quadratic formula. Apply it to solve the equation $2x^2 = 5x - 1$.

The quadratic formula is $x = \frac{-b \pm \sqrt{b^2 - 4ac}}{2a}$. It gives the solution of the quadratic equation $ax^2 + bx + c = 0$. The equation $2x^2 = 5x - 1$ can be written in this form as $2x^2 - 5x + 1 = 0$. Substitute into the quadratic formula with $a = 2$, $b = -5$, and $c = 1$:

$$x = \frac{-b \pm \sqrt{b^2 - 4ac}}{2a}$$

$$x = \frac{-(-5) \pm \sqrt{(-5)^2 - 4(2)(1)}}{2(2)}$$

$$x = \frac{5 \pm \sqrt{17}}{4}$$

The solutions of the equation are $x = \frac{5+\sqrt{17}}{4}$ and $x = \frac{5-\sqrt{17}}{4}$.

Bethany claims the solutions of $(x - 2)(x + 3) = -4$ are $x = -3$ and $x = 2$. Correct her error.

Bethany applied the zero product property to an equation that does not equal zero. Although her values of x make the left side of the equation zero, the right side is –4. To correct her error, she should first multiply the binomials, and then write the equation so that the right side is zero:

$(x - 2)(x + 3) = -4$
$x^2 - 2x + 3x - 6 = -4$
$x^2 + x - 6 = -4$
$x^2 + x - 2 = 0$
$(x + 2)(x - 1) = 0$
$x = -2$ or $x = 1$
The solution is $x = \{-2, 1\}$.

Solve the system $\begin{cases} \frac{x}{2} + \frac{y}{3} = -1 \\ \frac{x}{5} - \frac{y}{3} = 1 \end{cases}$. **Describe your solution method.**

To solve the system, multiply each equation by the least common denominator, or LCD. This will eliminate the fractions, and transform the system into one with integer coefficients.

$$\begin{cases} \left(\frac{x}{2} + \frac{y}{3} = -1\right)6 \\ \left(\frac{x}{5} - \frac{y}{3} = 1\right)15 \end{cases}$$

$$\begin{cases} 3x + 2y = -6 \\ 3x - 5y = 15 \end{cases}$$

Subtracting the equations results in the equation $7y = -21$, so $y = -3$. Substitute -3 for y into $3x + 2y = -6$ to get $3x = 0$, so $x = 0$. The solution of the system is $(0, -3)$.

Without solving either system, explain why the systems below have the same solution. Then verify this fact.

$$\begin{cases} x + y = 4 \\ 2x - y = -1 \end{cases} \qquad \begin{cases} x + y = 4 \\ 3x = 3 \end{cases}$$

When comparing the two systems, it is clear that the first equation of each system is the same. If an equation of one system is a linear combination of the equations of the other system, then the systems are equivalent and therefore have the same solution. A linear combination is the sum of two equations, with either equation possibly multiplied by a real number. Adding the two equations of the first system results in the equation $3x = 3$. This is the 2nd equation of the other system, so the systems are equivalent and have the same solution. The solution is $(x, y) = (1, 3)$ and satisfies both systems.

Show that if (a, b) is the solution to the system on the left below, then it is also the solution to the system on the right. In the system on the right, one equation was replaced with the sum of that equation and a multiple of the first equation.

$$\begin{cases} 3x+8y=2 \\ 2x-5y=-7 \end{cases} \qquad \begin{cases} 3x+8y=2 \\ 3x+8y+k(2x-5y)=2-7k \end{cases}$$

The solution of the original system is (a, b). Substituting these values for x and y in the equations gives the following true statements:

$$3a + 8b = 2$$
$$2a - 5b = -7$$

To show that (a, b) is the solution of the system on the right, show that (a, b) makes both equations true. The first equation $3x + 8y = 2$ is true, because it is the same equation as the other system and $3a + 8b = 2$. Substituting a and b for x and y in the second equation gives $3a + 8b + k(2a - 5b) = 2 - 7k$. Using the two true equations above, substitute 2 for $3a + 8b$ and -7 for $2a - 5b$ gives $2 + k(-7) = 2 - 7k$, which is an identity and true for any value of k.

Solve the system $\begin{cases} x - 4y = 3 \\ 2x + y = -3 \end{cases}$

The first equation of the system is $x - 4y = 3$. This equation can easily be solved for x, resulting in the equation $x = 4y + 3$. Substitute this expression for x into the other equation and solve for y:
$2x + y = -3$
$2(4y + 3) + y = -3$
$8y + 6 + y = -3$
$9y = -9$
$y = -1$

Substitute –1 for y in the equation $2x + y = -3$ gives $2x = -2$, and $x = -1$. The solution of the system is therefore $(-1, -1)$.

Use a graph to approximate the solution of the system $\begin{cases} -x + y = 9 \\ 2x + y = 5 \end{cases}$ **to the nearest integer values of x and y.**

The solution to a linear system is the intersection of the graphs of the system. The equations can be sketched by using the x- and y- intercepts of each line. For example, for $-x + y = 9$, the x- and y- intercepts are $(-9, 0)$ and $(0, 9)$, respectively. The intercepts for the other equation are determined similarly.

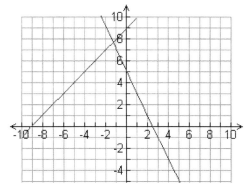

The intersection point is in the second quadrant. To the nearest integer values of x and y, the solution is $(-1, 8)$.

Describe the graph of a linear system with no solution.

If a linear system has no solution, there is no value of x and y that satisfies both equations of the system. Graphically, this means that the lines that represent each equation of the system will never intersect. Lines that never intersect are by definition parallel. Parallel lines have the same slope, so it can often be determined that a system has no solution without graphing or solving algebraically. For example, if the equations of the system are $y = -2x + 3$ and $y = -2x - 5$, the system has no solution. The equations represent distinct parallel lines.

At what point or points does the line $y = -x + 2$ intersect a circle with radius 2 and center at the origin?

The equation of a circle centered at the origin with radius r is $x^2 + y^2 = r^2$. For a radius of 2, this becomes $x^2 + y^2 = 4$. Substitute the expression $-x + 2$ for y in the equation of the circle, and solve for x:

$x^2 + y^2 = 4$
$x^2 + (-x + 2)^2 = 4$
$x^2 + x^2 - 4x + 4 = 4$
$2x^2 - 4x = 0$
$2x(x - 2) = 0$
$x = 0, x = 2$

If $x = 0$, then $y = -(0) + 2 = 2$. If $x = 2$, the $y = -(2) + 2 = 0$. The points of intersection, then, are $(0, 2)$ and $(2, 0)$.

Solve the system $\begin{cases} 3x - y = 6 \\ y = 4 - x^2 \end{cases}$**, and find any intersection points.**

The first equation of the system can be rewritten as $y = 3x - 6$. Substitute the expression $3x - 6$ for y in the quadratic equation:

$y = 4 - x^2$
$3x - 6 = 4 - x^2$
$x^2 + 3x - 10 = 0$
$(x + 5)(x - 2) = 0$
$x = -5, x = 2$

If $x = -5$, then $y = 3(-5) - 6 = -21$. If $x = 2$, then $y = 3(2) - 6 = 0$. The points of intersection are $(-5, -21)$ and $(2, 0)$.

A system consists of a linear equation and a quadratic equation. How many solutions are possible? Compare with a linear system.

For a system that consists of a linear equation and a quadratic equation, it is possible to have 0, 1, or 2 solutions. This is different than a linear system, which has 0 solutions, 1 solutions, or infinitely many solutions. When a linear solution has infinitely many solutions, the two equations in the system are equivalent. A line may never intersect a parabola (0 solutions), or may be tangent to the parabola (1 solution), or may intersect the parabola in two points (2 solutions). Since solving a linear/quadratic system leads to a quadratic equation, it is not possible to have more than 2 solutions; that is, no line can intersect a parabola at more than 2 points.

Solve the system $\begin{cases} y = 4 - x^2 \\ y - 3 = 0 \end{cases}$ **by graphing.**

The equation $y = 4 - x^2$, which can be written as $y = -x^2 + 4$, represents a parabola that opens downward with vertex at $(0, 4)$. The equation $y - 3 = 0$ can be written as $y = 3$, the equation of a horizontal line passing through the point $(0, 3)$. The graph of the equations is shown below.

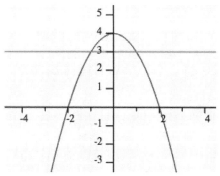

There are two points of intersection of the graphs, $(-1, 3)$ and $(1, 3)$. These are the solutions to the system; both points check out algebraically.

What is a matrix? How can a matrix represent several variables as a vector?

A matrix is a rectangular array of real numbers. These numbers can represent coefficients of a linear system. For example, consider the system $\begin{cases} x + 3y = 1 \\ x - y = 2 \end{cases}$. The coefficients can be represented using the matrix $\begin{bmatrix} 1 & 3 \\ 1 & -1 \end{bmatrix}$. Similarly, a matrix can represent a vector variable, which can represent several non-vector variables. Using the same example, the matrix $\begin{bmatrix} x \\ y \end{bmatrix}$ represents the vector variable $\langle x, y \rangle$, which represents x and y in the linear system.

Represent the system $\begin{cases} 2x - 3y = 11 \\ 6x - y = 20 \end{cases}$ **using a matrix equation.**

To write the system with a matrix equation, first define matrices for the coefficients of the variables, the variables, and the constants.

Coefficient matrix: $\begin{bmatrix} 2 & -3 \\ 6 & -1 \end{bmatrix}$

Variable matrix: $\begin{bmatrix} x \\ y \end{bmatrix}$

Constant matrix: $\begin{bmatrix} 11 \\ 20 \end{bmatrix}$

The product of the coefficient matrix and the variable matrix equals the constant matrix. This can be written as a matrix equation as follows:

$$\begin{bmatrix} 2 & -3 \\ 6 & -1 \end{bmatrix} \begin{bmatrix} x \\ y \end{bmatrix} = \begin{bmatrix} 11 \\ 20 \end{bmatrix}$$

Write the linear system represented by the matrix equation.
$$\begin{bmatrix} 3 & -7 \\ 1 & 5 \end{bmatrix} \begin{bmatrix} x \\ y \end{bmatrix} = \begin{bmatrix} 10 \\ -2 \end{bmatrix}$$

By multiplying the matrices on the left, a 2 by 1 matrix is formed. Each entry of this matrix is equal to the corresponding entry in the matrix $\begin{bmatrix} 10 \\ -2 \end{bmatrix}$. Multiplying the first row of $\begin{bmatrix} 3 & -7 \\ 1 & 5 \end{bmatrix}$ by the column of the matrix $\begin{bmatrix} x \\ y \end{bmatrix}$ gives the expression $3x - 7y$. Multiplying the second row of $\begin{bmatrix} 3 & -7 \\ 1 & 5 \end{bmatrix}$ by the column of the matrix $\begin{bmatrix} x \\ y \end{bmatrix}$ gives the expression $x + 5y$. These two equations are equal to 10 and –2, respectively. The linear system is therefore $\begin{cases} 3x - 7y = 10 \\ x + 5y = -2 \end{cases}$

Represent the system $\begin{cases} 2x - 3z = -1 \\ 6x - y = 2 \\ 2y + z = 4 \end{cases}$ **using a matrix equation.**

The equations describe a three-variable linear system. Since each equation only has two variable terms, the coefficient of the missing term is 0 in each equation. So, for the first row of the coefficient matrix, the entries are 2, 0, and –3, since there is no y-term in the first equation. That is, the first equation could be written as $2x + 0y - 3z = -1$. A matrix equation for the system is shown below:
$$\begin{bmatrix} 2 & 0 & -3 \\ 6 & -1 & 0 \\ 0 & 2 & 1 \end{bmatrix} \begin{bmatrix} x \\ y \\ z \end{bmatrix} = \begin{bmatrix} -1 \\ 2 \\ 4 \end{bmatrix}$$

What is the inverse of a matrix? Which matrices have an inverse?

An inverse of a matrix A is the matrix A^{-1} such that $A(A^{-1}) = I$. The matrix I is the identity matrix, which has the value 1 on the main diagonal, and 0 elsewhere. Only square matrices (same number of rows as columns) have an inverse. Additionally, the determinant of the square matrix must not be zero for the matrix to have an inverse. As example, the inverse of the matrix $\begin{bmatrix} 3 & 1 \\ 5 & 2 \end{bmatrix}$ is $\begin{bmatrix} 2 & -1 \\ -5 & 3 \end{bmatrix}$ as illustrated below:

$$\begin{bmatrix} 3 & 1 \\ 5 & 2 \end{bmatrix} \begin{bmatrix} 2 & -1 \\ -5 & 3 \end{bmatrix} = \begin{bmatrix} 6\text{-}5 & -3+3 \\ 10\text{-}(\text{-}10) & -5+6 \end{bmatrix} = \begin{bmatrix} 1 & 0 \\ 0 & 1 \end{bmatrix}$$

What is the inverse of the matrix $\begin{bmatrix} 5 & 7 \\ 3 & 4 \end{bmatrix}$**?**

The inverse of a 2 by 2 matrix $A = \begin{bmatrix} a & b \\ c & d \end{bmatrix}$ is given by the following matrix:
$$\frac{1}{\det A} \begin{bmatrix} d & -b \\ -c & a \end{bmatrix}$$

The notation $\det A$ represents the determinant of the matrix A. For the 2 by 2 matrix $A = \begin{bmatrix} a & b \\ c & d \end{bmatrix}$, $\det A = ad - bc$. Note that since the inverse involves the reciprocal of the determinant, if the determinant is 0, the inverse does not exist. The determinant of $\begin{bmatrix} 5 & 7 \\ 3 & 4 \end{bmatrix}$ is $5(4) - 3(7) = 20 - 21 = -1$, and the inverse is therefore $\frac{1}{-1}\begin{bmatrix} 4 & -7 \\ -3 & 5 \end{bmatrix} = \begin{bmatrix} -4 & 7 \\ 3 & -5 \end{bmatrix}$.

Use a graphing calculator to find the inverse of $\begin{bmatrix} -1 & 2 & 3 \\ 2 & 1 & 1 \\ 3 & 0 & -2 \end{bmatrix}$.

```
MATRIX[A] 3 x3
[ -1      2      3      ]
[ 2       1      1      ]
[ 3       0      -2     ]


3,3=-2
```

To find the inverse of the matrix, select to edit a 3 by 3 matrix on the calculator. You may have to enter the dimensions first. Then, enter each value for each row of the matrix. Check that the matrix is entered correctly:

The matrix shown is named A. Next, calculate the inverse, A^{-1}. In the second screen shot on the right, the entries are displayed as fractions.

Solve the system $\begin{cases} 2x - 3y = -2 \\ x + 4y = 10 \end{cases}$ **by using an inverse matrix.**

```
[ .4283714286  .0
Ans▶Frac
        [ -2/7   4/7    -1/7 ]
        [  1     -1      1   ]
        [ -3/7   6/7    -5/7 ]
■
```

To solve the system using an inverse matrix, first write the corresponding matrix equation for the system.

$$\begin{bmatrix} 2 & -3 \\ 1 & 4 \end{bmatrix}\begin{bmatrix} x \\ y \end{bmatrix} = \begin{bmatrix} -2 \\ 10 \end{bmatrix}$$

Multiply each side of the matrix equation from the left by the inverse of the matrix $\begin{bmatrix} 2 & -3 \\ 1 & 4 \end{bmatrix}$,

which is $\frac{1}{11}\begin{bmatrix} 4 & 3 \\ -1 & 2 \end{bmatrix} = \begin{bmatrix} \frac{4}{11} & \frac{3}{11} \\ -\frac{1}{11} & \frac{2}{11} \end{bmatrix}$. The result is shown below.

$$\begin{bmatrix} 1 & 0 \\ 0 & 1 \end{bmatrix}\begin{bmatrix} x \\ y \end{bmatrix} = \begin{bmatrix} \frac{4}{11} & \frac{3}{11} \\ -\frac{1}{11} & \frac{2}{11} \end{bmatrix}\begin{bmatrix} -2 \\ 10 \end{bmatrix}$$

$$\begin{bmatrix} x \\ y \end{bmatrix} = \begin{bmatrix} 2 \\ 2 \end{bmatrix}$$

The solution of the system is (2, 2).

How can you show the solutions of the equation $x + y = 10$ graphically?

The solutions of a two-variable equation are all the ordered pairs that make the equation true. For the equation $x + y = 10$, all of the points (x, y) that satisfy the equation can be shown in the coordinate plane. For example, $(3, 7)$ is a solution of the equation, as is $(-2, 12)$. All of the solutions will fall on a straight line that passes through these two points, given by the equation $y = 10 - x$. The ordered pair $(-856, 866)$ is also a solution, although it may not be visible on the graph of the equation. There are infinitely many solutions, and the line extends in both directions without end.

Must a graph in the coordinate plane have an equation with two variables in it? If not, give an example.

A graph in the coordinate plane is used to show the relationship between two variables. For example, the graph of the equation $y = 2x$ shows all the points such that the y-value is twice the x-value. The equation does not, however, have to have two variables in it. For example, the equation $y = 2$ is a horizontal line that passes through the point $(0, 2)$. For any x-value, the value of y is 2. There is still a relationship, but the value of y does not depend on the value of x.

Describe how to graphically determine the solution of $3x + 4 = x^2$.

A one-variable equation can be solved graphically by considering each side of the equation as the expression for a function of y. By graphing the two equations in the coordinate plane, the x-value of the intersection point(s), if there are any, represent the solution(s) of the equation. The graphs of $y = 3x + 4$ and $y = x^2$ are shown below, and intersect at $(-1, 1)$ and $(4, 16)$. Therefore the solution to the equation is $x = \{-2, 4\}$.

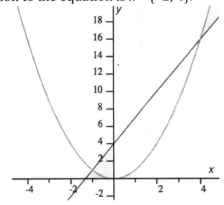

Use a table to determine if $f(x) = 3x^2$ and $g(x) = 8x + 3$ intersect. Use integer values of x from –1 to 5.

Set up a table that shows x, $f(x)$, and $g(x)$. The values for x in the table range from –1 to 5, and the values of $f(x)$ and $g(x)$ are the functions evaluated at the particular value of x.

x	$f(x)$	$g(x)$
–1	3	–5
0	0	3
1	3	11
2	12	19
3	27	27
4	48	35
5	75	43

The table reveals that $f(3) = g(3) = 27$. This means that the functions intersect at the point (3, 27). Also, in the interval from $x = -1$ to $x = 0$, $f(x)$ changes from being greater than $g(x)$ to less than $g(x)$. This means that the functions intersect at another x-value between –1 and 0, although the table does not show this value.

Find an approximate solution to $3^x = -(x + 2)$. Use a graphing calculator.

The equation $3^x = -(x + 2)$ cannot be solved for x. An approximate solution can be found by graphing the equations $y = 3^x$ and $y = -(x + 2)$ on a graphing calculator. The intersection points, if there are any, will have an x-coordinate that is a solution to the equation. The graphs intersect at approximately (–2.0996, 0.0996). This is the only intersection point, since the linear function is decreasing and the exponential function is increasing. The approximate solution, then, of the equation is $x = -2.0996$. Another solution is to graph the equation $y = 3^x + x + 2$ and determine where it crosses the x-axis.

What is the process of successive approximations for finding the solution of the equation $f(x) = g(x)$? Use $\ln x = -x^2$ as an example.

The process of successive approximations involves making a guess, or an approximation, for a solution to an equation. Then make another guess that is close to the original guess, and determine whether the result makes each side of the equation closer to being equal. For example, a reasonable first guess for the solution to $\ln x = -x^2$ is $x = 0.5$. This gives –0.6931 and –0.25, and the guess $x = -0.6$ yields –0.5108 and –0.36. Since $x = -0.6$ is better, next guess $x = -0.7$, which yields –0.3567 and–0.49, only a slight improvement. Perhaps guess $x = -0.65$ next, which yields –0.4308 and –0.4225 which are equal to the tenths place. Therefore, $x = -0.65$ is an approximate solution accurate to the tenths place. Further guesses might yield even better approximations.

Sketch the graph of $y \geq -2x + 4$ in the coordinate plane.

To sketch the graph of $y \geq -2x + 4$, begin by graphing the corresponding linear equation $y = -2x + 4$. Draw the line as a solid line, since the greater-than-or-equal-to sign indicates that the line itself is part of the solution. The test point (0, 0), when substituted into the inequality, gives $0 \geq 4$, which is FALSE. Therefore, the half-plane that represents the solution region is the side of the line that does not contain (0, 0). Shade this region, which is above the line, as shown below.

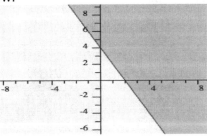

Graph the solution of the system $\begin{cases} x \leq y - 1 \\ 2x \geq y \end{cases}$.

To sketch the graph of the system, graph the equations $y = x + 1$ and $y = 2x$. The lines for $y = 2x$ and $y = x + 1$ should be solid, since the inequality symbols include equality. Shade the half-plane that represents the solution for each inequality. The shaded areas intersect in a triangular region in the first quadrant, as shown in the graph. This represents the solution of the system. Note that the boundary of the solution region is included in the solution.

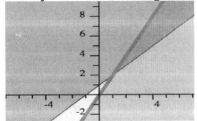

What system of inequalities describes the points in the 3rd quadrant of the coordinate plane?

The coordinate plane is divided into 4 quadrants. The points in each quadrant can be described the signs of the coordinates of the points:
1st quadrant: both coordinates positive
2nd quadrant: y-coordinates positive, x-coordinates negative
3rd quadrant: both coordinates negative
4th quadrant: x-coordinate positive, y-coordinate negative
The x-coordinates are negative, so $x < 0$. Similarly, the y-coordinates are negative, so $y < 0$. A system of inequalities that describes the points is $\begin{cases} x < 0 \\ y < 0 \end{cases}$.

When is the boundary line of the graph of a linear inequality in two variables part of the solution?

The boundary line of a linear inequality in two variables is the line that represents the corresponding equation of the inequality. For example, in both inequalities $y < 3x + 5$ and $y \geq 3x + 5$, the boundary line is given by the equation $y = 3x + 5$. When the inequality has the symbol < or >, the boundary line is not part of the solution. This is indicated by drawing a dashed line for the equation. When the inequality has the symbol ≤ or ≥, the boundary line is part of the solution. This is indicated by drawing a solid line for the equation.

Construct a viable argument to show the solution to the equation $|1 - x| = |x - 1|$ is all real numbers.

Assuming there is a solution to the equation, there are two possibilities. Either $1 - x = x - 1$, or $1 - x = -(x - 1)$. In other words, the expressions inside absolute value signs are either equal or opposite in value. Assume that $1 - x = x - 1$ has a solution, and that the expressions equal the same real number. Then adding $x + 1$ to each side will give two expressions equal to a new same real number. Doing this results in the equation $2 = 2x$, and dividing by 2 gives $1 = x$. Assume also that $1 - x = -(x - 1)$ has a solution, or equivalently $1 - x = -x + 1$. Adding x to each side gives $1 = 1$, which is always true. Therefore x can equal any real number.

The reciprocal of a number is 0.45 more than the number. Find the number.

Let n represent the unknown number. Then the reciprocal of this number, assuming the number is not zero, is given by the expression $\frac{1}{n}$. This number is 0.45 more than the original number, or $\frac{1}{n} = 0.45 + n$.

$$\frac{1}{n} = 0.45 + n$$
$$n\left(\frac{1}{n}\right) = n(0.45 + n)$$
$$1 = 0.45n + n^2$$

This equation could be solved using the quadratic formula, but also through factoring:

$$100n^2 + 45n - 100 = 0$$
$$20n^2 + 9n - 20 = 0$$
$$(4n + 5)(5n - 4) = 0$$
$$n = -\frac{5}{4} \text{ or } n = \frac{4}{5}$$

There are two possible values of n, $-\frac{5}{4}$ and $\frac{4}{5}$.

Solve the equation $2(3 - (4 - x) - 3x) = 4$.

To solve the equation, use the Distributive Property. First, distribute the subtraction that is inside the parentheses:
$2(3 - (4 - x) - 3x) = 4$

$2(3 - 4 + x - 3x) = 4$

Next, simplify the expression inside the parentheses by combining like terms:
$2(3 - 4 + x - 3x) = 4$
$2(-1 - 2x) = 4$

Distribute one more time, and then isolate x:
$$2(-1 - 2x) = 4$$
$$-2 - 4x = 4$$
$$-4x = 6$$

- 45 -

$$x = -\frac{3}{2}$$

Ron completes the square of the expression $3x^2 - 10x$ by writing the equivalent expression $3(x-5)^2 - \frac{25}{3}$. Is Ron correct?

Ron is not correct. This is evident by noting that while the original expression does not have a constant term, Ron's answer will have the constants 75 and $\frac{25}{3}$ in it, which are not opposites so their sum is not zero. This breaks the equality the method of completing the square preserves. Ron should have proceeded as follows:

$$3x^2 - 10x =$$
$$3\left(x^2 - \frac{10}{3}x\right) =$$
$$3\left(x^2 - \frac{10}{3}x + \left(\frac{1}{2}\cdot\frac{10}{3}\right)^2\right) - 3\left(\frac{1}{2}\cdot\frac{10}{3}\right)^2 =$$
$$33\left(x^2 - \frac{10}{3}x + \left(\frac{10}{6}\right)^2\right) - 3\left(\frac{10}{6}\right)^2 = 3\left(x^2 - \frac{10}{3}x + \frac{25}{9}\right) - \frac{25}{3} =$$
$$3\left(x - \frac{5}{3}\right)^2 - \frac{25}{3}$$

Show that the quadratic formula and factoring give the same solution set for the equation $x^2 - 3x + 2 = 0$.

To factor the equation, find two numbers with a product of 2 and a sum of –3. The numbers are –1 and –2, so $x^2 - 3x + 2 = (x-1)(x-2)$, and the equation becomes $(x-1)(x-2) = 0$, and the solutions are $\{1, 2\}$. The quadratic formula, with $a = 1$, $b = -3$, and $c = 2$, gives:

$$x = \frac{-b \pm \sqrt{b^2 - 4ac}}{2a} =$$
$$\frac{3 \pm \sqrt{(-3)^2 - 4(1)(2)}}{2(1)} =$$
$$\frac{3 \pm \sqrt{1}}{2}$$
$$\therefore x = \frac{3+1}{2}, \frac{3-1}{2}$$

The two expressions are equal to 2 and 1, so the solution is the same.

Solve the linear system $\begin{cases} x - y = -3 \\ 2x + 6 = 2y \end{cases}$

The second equation can be simplified by dividing by 2. This gives the equation $x + 3 = y$. The first equation can be rewritten as $x + 3 = y$. Since these are the same equation, there are infinitely many solutions. To verify this, substitute $x + 3$ for y in the first equation to create an equation with only x as a variable:

$$x - y = -3$$
$$x - (x + 3) = -3$$
$$x - x - 3 = -3$$
$$-3 = -3$$

The equation that results is always true. This means that the two equations that make up the system are the same equation. There are therefore infinitely many solutions, and the solution can be written $\{(x, y) \mid x - y = -3\}$. (Graphically, this solution describes a line.)

Solve the system $\begin{cases} x - y^2 = 2 \\ x + y = 4 \end{cases}$

Solve the first equation for x. This gives $x = y^2 + 2$, and the expression $y^2 + 2$ can be substituted into the second equation, which can then be solved for y:

$x + y = 4$
$y^2 + 2 + y = 4$
$y^2 + y - 2 = 0$
$(y + 2)(y - 1) = 0$
$y = -2$ or $y = 1$

If $y = -2$, then $x = 6$. If $y = 1$, then $x = 3$. There are two solutions of the system, $(6, -2)$ and $(3, 1)$. Each solution makes both equations of the system true.

Write the linear system represented by the matrix equation.
$$\begin{bmatrix} 1 & 0 & -1 \\ 0 & 4 & 2 \\ -1 & 3 & 3 \end{bmatrix} \begin{bmatrix} x \\ y \\ z \end{bmatrix} = \begin{bmatrix} 1 \\ -2 \\ 5 \end{bmatrix}$$

By multiplying the matrices on the left, a 3 by 1 matrix is formed. Each entry of this matrix is equal to the corresponding entry in the matrix $\begin{bmatrix} 1 \\ -2 \\ 5 \end{bmatrix}$. Multiplying the first row of $\begin{bmatrix} 1 & 0 & -1 \\ 0 & 4 & 2 \\ -1 & 3 & 3 \end{bmatrix}$ by the column matrix $\begin{bmatrix} x \\ y \\ z \end{bmatrix}$ gives the expression $x - z$. Multiplying the second row of $\begin{bmatrix} 1 & 0 & -1 \\ 0 & 4 & 2 \\ -1 & 3 & 3 \end{bmatrix}$ by the column matrix $\begin{bmatrix} x \\ y \\ z \end{bmatrix}$ gives the expression $4y + 2z$. Multiplying the third row of $\begin{bmatrix} 1 & 0 & -1 \\ 0 & 4 & 2 \\ -1 & 3 & 3 \end{bmatrix}$ by the column matrix $\begin{bmatrix} x \\ y \\ z \end{bmatrix}$ gives the expression $-x + 3y + 3z$. These

- 47 -

three equations are equal to 1, –2, and 5, respectively. The linear system is therefore

$$\begin{cases} x - z = 1 \\ 4y + 2z = -2 \\ -x + 3y + 3z = 5 \end{cases}$$

The inverse of the matrix $\begin{bmatrix} a & -4 \\ 7 & -2 \end{bmatrix}$ does not exist. What is the value of a?

In order for the inverse of the matrix $\begin{bmatrix} a & -4 \\ 7 & -2 \end{bmatrix}$ to not exist, its determinant must be zero. The determinant of a 2 by 2 matrix $\begin{bmatrix} a & b \\ c & d \end{bmatrix}$ is given by the expression $ad - bc$. Write an equation that represents this situation:

$-2(a) - 7(-4) = 0$
$-2a = -28$
$a = 14$

The value of a is 14. For any other value of a, the matrix would have an inverse.

Find two exact solutions of $\frac{1}{x^2+1} = 2^x$ using a graphing calculator. Verify the solutions are true.

The solutions can be found by graphing the equations $y = \frac{1}{x^2+1}$ and $y = 2^x$ on a graphing calculator. The intersection points, if there are any, will have x-coordinates that are solutions to the equation. The graphs appear to intersect at the points $(0, 2)$ and $(-1, 0.5)$. Therefore the two solutions of the equation are $x = 0$ and $x = -1$. Substitute to verify the solutions:

$$\frac{1}{x^2+1} = 2^x \qquad\qquad \frac{1}{(-1)^2+1} = 2^{-1}$$
$$\frac{1}{0^2+1} = 2^0 \qquad\qquad \frac{1}{1+1} = \frac{1}{2}$$
$$1 = 1 \qquad\qquad\qquad \frac{1}{2} = \frac{1}{2}$$

Interpreting Functions

A function is a relation between two sets, the *domain* and the *range*, such that each element of the domain is associated with exactly one element of the range.

There are other ways this definition can be phrased. A less technical wording is that a function is a relation that associates each possible value of one variable, x, with a unique value of a second variable, y.

Note that it is *not* necessarily the case that each element of the *range* is associated with exactly one element of the *domain* (or, under the other definition, that each value of y is associated with a unique value of x). However, a relation for which this condition does hold is *invertible*—in this case, interchanging the domain and the range of the function gives rise to another function (the original function's *inverse*).

Linear, quadratic, polynomial, and rational functions

A *linear* function is a function the graph of which is a straight line. The expression for a linear function includes x (possibly multiplied by some constant coefficient, and possibly added to some other constant), but does not include x^2 or any higher powers of x. The following, for example, are all linear functions: $f(x) = x$, $f(x) = 1 - 2x$, $f(x) = \frac{3}{4}x + 3$.

The expression for a *quadratic* function includes a term containing x^2 (again possibly multiplied by some constant coefficient), but no term contains x^3 or any higher powers of x. The following, for example, are all quadratic functions: $f(x) = x^2 + x + 1$, $f(x) = 3x^2 - 2$, $f(x) = -\frac{1}{2}x^2$.

The expression for a *polynomial* function is a sum of one or more powers of x, possibly multiplied by constant coefficients. (Note that $1 = x^0$ is a power of x.) All linear and quadratic functions are polynomials; so are the following: $f(x) = 3x^7$, $f(x) = 2x^3 - 2x^2 + 5x - 6$, $f(x) = x^{2000} - x^{169}$.

A *rational function* is a ratio of polynomials. Examples include $\frac{x^2-1}{x}$, $\frac{1}{3x^3+2x^2+x}$, and $\frac{x^4+3}{x^2-2}$.

Determine how you can tell from looking at a graph whether the graph represents a function

The simplest way to tell by visual inspection whether a graph represents a function is a procedure sometimes known as the "vertical line test". Imagine a vertical line scanning across the graph. If, at any point, the line intersects more than one point on the graph, the graph does *not* represent a function. Otherwise, it does.

For example, consider the following graphs.

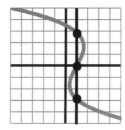 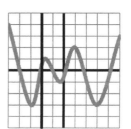

The vertical line in the image on the left intersects the graph in three points. Therefore, the graph on the left does *not* represent a function. On the right, however, no matter where we place the vertical line, it will never intersect more than one point. Therefore, the graph on the right represents a function.

Finding the domain of the function

Given a function expressed in a table like the one below, determine how you can find the domain of the function.

x	0	3	2	1	8	10	6	7
f(x)	2	8	6	8	2	3	4	5

The *domain* of a function $f(x)$ is the set of all input values for which the function is defined. For a function expressed in a table like the one in this example, it's simple to find the domain, because every point in the function—that is, every input-output pair—is given explicitly. To find the domain, we just list all the x values: in this case, that would be $\{0, 3, 2, 1, 8, 10, 6, 7\}$, or, putting them in ascending order, $\{0, 1, 2, 3, 6, 7, 8, 10\}$. (Putting the values in ascending order isn't strictly necessary, but generally makes the set easier to read.)

Note that we don't have to worry about the possibility of an input value being repeated: by definition of a function, no input value can be matched to more than one output value.

Given a function expressed in analytic form such as $f(x) = \sin x$, $g(x) = \sqrt{x+1}$, or $h(x) = \frac{x}{x^2-1}$, explain how you can find the domain of the function.

The *domain* of a function $f(x)$ is the set of all possible input values of the function—that is, of every possible value of x for which the function is defined. Some functions, such as $f(x) = \sin x$, are defined for any real value of x; in this case, the domain of $f(x)$ is $(-\infty, \infty)$, that is, it includes all real numbers. There are functions, however, for which that isn't true. For instance, consider $g(x) = \sqrt{x+1}$. The square root of a negative number is not defined (at least as a real number), so in order for $g(x)$ to be defined we must have $x + 1 \geq 0$, so $x \geq -1$. The domain of $g(x)$ is thus $[-1, \infty)$. Similarly, $h(x) = \frac{x}{x^2-1}$ is not defined when the denominator is zero, which is true when $x = \pm1$. The domain therefore includes all real numbers *except* 1 and –1, which we can write as $(-\infty, -1) \cup (-1, 1) \cup (1, \infty)$.

Finding the range of a function

Given a function expressed in a table like the one below, determine how you can find the range of the function.

x	-1	4	2	1	0	3	8	6
f(x)	3	0	3	−1	−1	2	4	6

The *range* of a function $f(x)$ is the set of all possible output values of the function—that is, of every possible value of $f(x)$, for any value of x in the function's domain. For a function expressed in a table like the one in this example, it's simple to find the range, because every point in the function—that is, every input-output pair—is given explicitly. To find the range, we just list all the values of $f(x)$; in this case, that would be $\{3, 0, 3, -1, -1, 2, 4, 6\}$. Note that some of these values appear more than once. This is entirely permissible for a function; while each value of x must be matched to a unique value of $f(x)$, the converse is not true. We don't need to list each value more than once, so eliminating duplicates, the range is $\{3, 0, -1, 2, 4, 6\}$, or, putting them in ascending order,

{−1, 0, 2, 3, 4, 6}. (Putting the values in ascending order isn't strictly necessary, but generally makes the set easier to read.)

Given a function expressed in analytic form such as $f(x) = x^3$, $g(x) = x^2 - 2x + 4$, or $h(x) = 1/x$, explain how you can find the range of the function.

For a continuous function, we can find the range by just finding the maximum and minimum values of the function; the range comprises all the points in between. Some functions have no maximum or minimum; this is the case, for instance, with $f(x) = x^3$. At the left, the function decreases indefinitely, and on the right, it increases indefinitely. The range therefore includes all real numbers, $(-\infty, \infty)$. Other functions may have a maximum, but no minimum, or vice versa. The quadratic function $g(x) = x^2 - 2x + 4$ has a minimum at $(1,3)$, but no maximum, so its range is $[3, \infty)$.

For a discontinuous function, we must examine each part separately. $h(x) = 1/x$ has a discontinuity at $x = 0$. On the left side, the function has no minimum, but has an asymptotic maximum of 0 (asymptotic because it approaches 0 but never actually reaches it); the range of this side is $(-\infty, 0)$. Similarly, the right side has a range of $(0, \infty)$. The total range of the function is the union of these two ranges, hence $(-\infty, 0) \cup (0, \infty)$.

Example
> Suppose f(x) = x^2 + 1 and g(x) = x − 1. How would you find each of the following
>
> $f(3)$ $g(3)$ $f(y^2)$ $g(z + 1)$
>
> In function notation, "$f(3)$" can be thought of as a shorthand for "$f(x)$ when $x = 3$". To evaluate the function at this point, just replace the x in the expression for the function with the number. If $f(x) = x^2 + 1$, then to find $f(3)$ we just replace each x in "$x^2 + 1$" with 3. So $f(3) = 3^2 + 1$, which we can simplify to 10. Similarly, $g(3) = 3 - 1 = 2$.
>
> The same principle holds when instead of a number, there is a variable or an expression within the parentheses. To find $f(y^2)$, where $f(x) = x^2 + 1$, we replace each x in "$x^2 + 1$" with "y^2" (or "(y^2)"—including parentheses may make it easier to keep track of the substitution). This yields $(y^2) = (y^2)^2 + 1 = y^4 + 1$. Similarly,
> $g(z + 1) = (z + 1) - 1 = z$.

Example
> Describe in words what a statement such as f(x) = x^2 + 1 means
>
> This kind of statement defines a particular function; it tells how to match up each point in the domain with a point in the range. The possible values of x comprise the domain—this can usually be assumed to include all real numbers unless specified otherwise, or unless there are some points for which the expression on the right side of the equation is undefined. Each value of x is then matched with a (not necessarily unique) value of $f(x)$ (or y); all the values of $f(x)$ that are matched to values of x comprise the range.

In the case of the statement $f(x) = x^2 + 1$, this defines a function in which each real number x is matched to the number $x^2 + 1$. For instance, $x = 0$ corresponds to $f(0) = 0^2 + 1 = 1$, when $x = 1$ $f(1) = 1^2 + 1 = 2$, and so forth. Note that $f(x)$ in this case can never be less than 1, so the range of this function is $[1, \infty)$.

Real-world situations that can be modeled by statements that use function notation

A statement using function notation can model any situation in which one quantity depends uniquely on one or more other quantities. For example, the area of a rectangle can be expressed as a function of its width and height. The maximum vertical distance a projectile travels can be expressed as a function of its initial vertical speed. An object's position, the amount of money in a bank account, or any other quantity that changes over time can be expressed as a function of time.

A relationship *cannot* be modeled with a function, however, if it involves two quantities neither of which is uniquely determined by the other—that is, if each quantity may have multiple values corresponding to the same value of the other. For example, we could *not* write a function to represent the relationship between peoples' height in inches and their weight in pounds. There are people of the same height with different weights, and people of the same weight but different heights.

Defining a function recursively

To define a function recursively is to give the value of the function for a given input value in terms of the function's values for other input values—for example, to define $f(x)$ in terms of $f(x - 1)$. A function cannot be defined *purely* recursively; it's necessary to define the function absolutely for at least one point to give a starting point for the recursion.

For example, the factorial function, $f(n) = n! = n(n - 1)(n - 2) \ldots (2)(1)$, can be defined recursively as follows: $f(1) = 1$, otherwise $f(n) = n \cdot f(n - 1)$. The domain of this function is the positive integers. (Technically, the factorial function is also defined at $n = 0$, where $0! = 1$, but that's not important for this example.) Then, for example, $f(3) = 3 \cdot f(2) = 3 \cdot 2 \cdot f(1) = 3 \cdot 2 \cdot 1$.

Sequence

A sequence is a function in which the domain is confined to the integers, or some subset of the integers. Very often, the subset in question is the positive integers, in which case the sequence can be thought of as an ordered list of the elements of the range, with $f(n)$ identified directly with the nth element of the sequence. Such sequences are often written in list form; the sequence $f(n) = \frac{n^2 + n}{2}$, where $f(1) = 1$, $f(2) = 3$, $f(3) = 6$, and so on, can simply be written as $1, 3, 6, 10, 15, \ldots$

Sequences are often defined recursively, with the first few elements of the sequence defined explicitly and with $f(n)$ otherwise defined in terms of $f(n - 1)$ or in general of function values for smaller versions of n. Many functions can be equivalently defined explicitly or recursively. For instance, the sequence above, $f(n) = \frac{n^2 + n}{2}$, can also be defined as $f(1) = 1$ and $f(n) = f(n - 1) + n$.

Fibonacci sequence

The Fibonacci sequence is a sequence in which the first two terms are 1 and each succeeding term is the sum of the preceding two terms: 1, 1, 2, 3, 5, 8, 13, 21... Written algebraically, $f(1) = f(2) = 1$, and thereafter $f(n) = f(n-1) + f(n-2)$. (There are some variations in its definition; sometimes the domain starts at 0 instead of 1, for instance, or the first term may be defined as 0 instead of 1.)

The Fibonacci sequence is the most common and perhaps the simplest sequence that is recursively defined in terms of more than one earlier term in the sequence (rather than each term being only defined in terms of the immediately preceding term). It also arises in many real-world phenomena.

<u>Example</u>

Given a function definition such as $(x) = x^2 - 9$, determine how you would find the function's x and y intercepts

To find the y intercept, simply find $f(0)$. The y intercept is by definition the point where the function crosses the y-axis, which means it's the function's value when $x = 0$. For the example function definition, $f(x) = x^2 - 9$, $f(0) = 0^2 - 9 = -9$. So the y intercept is $(0, -9)$. Since no function can have multiple y values associated with a single value of x, a function cannot have more than one y intercept.

To find the x intercepts, we need to find where the function crosses the x-axis, so we have to find the value(s) of x, if any, for which $f(x) = 0$. There may be more than one such value. In the case of the example function, $f(x) = x^2 - 9$, this means $0 = x^2 - 9$. Solving for x, we get $x^2 = 9$, so $x = \pm 3$. So this function has two x intercepts, $(-3, 0)$ and $(3, 0)$.

All functions do not necessarily have x and y intercepts

No, not all functions necessarily have x and y intercepts. To have a y intercept, a function must be defined at $x = 0$. This is not true of all functions: $f(x) = \sqrt{x-1}$, for instance, does not have a y intercept, because $f(0) = \sqrt{-1}$ is not defined in the real numbers. For a function $f(x)$ to have an x intercept, there must be one or more values of x such that $f(x) = 0$. This, again, is not true of all functions. For instance, for $f(x) = x^2 + 1$, there is no value of x for which $f(x) = 0$, since we cannot find a real value of x that satisfies the equation $x^2 + 1 = 0$. This function has no x intercept.

It is possible for a function to have neither an x nor a y intercept. One simple example is $f(x) = 1/x$. Since $1/0$ is undefined, this function does not have a y intercept. Since there is no finite value of x satisfying $1/x = 0$, this function does not have an x intercept.

"Relative maximum" and "relative minimum" of a function

A "relative maximum" of a function is a point at which the function has a higher value than any other point in its immediate vicinity. More technically, a relative maximum is a point $(x,$

y) such that if we choose a sufficiently small interval around *x*, $f(x) > f(x')$ for any other point *x'* within the interval.

A relative minimum is just the opposite: a point at which the function has a *lower* value than any other point in its immediate vicinity, or, more technically, a point (x, y) such that if we choose a sufficiently small interval around *x*, $f(x) < f(x')$ for any other point *x'* within the interval.

A function may have multiple relative maxima and relative minima, or it may have none. A linear function such as $y = x$, for instance, has no relative maxima or minima, while $y = \sin(x)$ has infinitely many of each.

Finding a relative maximum or minimum from a graph

At a relative maximum, the graph goes from increasing to decreasing, forming a "peak" on the graph which is generally easy to spot visually. Similarly, at a relative minimum, the graph goes from decreasing to increasing, forming a "trough". On the graph below, for instance, points A and C are relative maxima, and point B is a relative minimum.

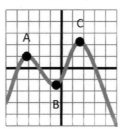

Note that point A is a relative maximum, but not an absolute maximum; the function has a higher value at point C. Similarly, point B is a relative minimum, but not an absolute minimum; the function has a lower value at the left and right ends of the graph than it does at point B. Point C, however, is both a relative and an absolute maximum; nowhere on the graph does the function have a higher value than at point C.

Determining how you can tell over what intervals a function is increasing or decreasing

If the function is presented in graph form, it's easy to tell by inspection where it's increasing and where it's decreasing. Where the slope of the graph is positive—where the graph goes from lower left to upper right—the function is increasing. Where the slope is negative—where the graph goes from upper left to lower right—the function is decreasing. In the graph below, for example, the graph is increasing over the intervals $(-\infty, -3)$ and $(0, 3)$, and decreasing over the intervals $(-3, 0)$ and $(3, \infty)$.

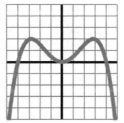

If the function is presented explicitly, such as $f(x) = x^2 - x^4$, we can graph the function and then find the appropriate intervals as above, but we can also, for instance, find the relative maxima and minima; an interval with a minimum on the left and a maximum on the right is increasing, and one with a maximum on the left and minimum on the right is decreasing.

If a function is given symbolically, name some features we can find that may be useful in sketching its graph

Sketching a graph without the aid of technology is facilitated by first determining some key properties of the function. If the function has horizontal asymptotes, we can use these as guidelines for the function's end behavior. If it doesn't have horizontal asymptotes, we can often determine the end behavior by other means. A function's vertical asymptotes likewise indicate its behavior near the corresponding values of x.

Also useful in determining the shape of a function are the relative maxima and minima, and the intervals over which the function is increasing or decreasing. The x and y intercepts provide a few points we know the function passes through. If the function has any symmetries or periodicity, these are also helpful in plotting it. Of course, if all else fails, we can also just pick a few x values at random, solve for $f(x)$ at those points, and plot those points to get a feel for the function's shape.

Periodic functions

A function is *periodic* if it comprises successive repetitions of an identical shape. That is, a periodic function is unchanged if displaced by some constant P. This constant—the length of the repeating portion—is called the function's *period*. Periodicity can be defined in a more precise, mathematical form: a function $f(x)$ is periodic if $f(x + P) = f(x)$ for all x. (If this is true for P, it's also true for all multiples of P, but the function's period is defined as the smallest possible value of P for which the relation holds.)

For instance, the function $f(x) = \sin(x)$ is periodic with a period of 2π, since $\sin(x + 2\pi) = \sin(x)$ for all x. (It's also true that, for instance, $\sin(x + 4\pi) = \sin(x)$, and $\sin(x + 6\pi) = \sin(x)$, but there is no positive value of P *smaller* than 2π satisfying $\sin(x + P) = \sin(x)$.)

Symmetrical functions

A function is symmetrical if it remains unchanged under certain kinds of transformations. While there are many kinds of transformations and many kinds of symmetries, for functions the type of transformation most often considered is reflection. Particularly important are reflections through the y-axis and reflections through the origin.

A function is symmetrical under a reflection through the y-axis if it stays the same when "flipped over" around the y-axis into its mirror image—mathematically, $f(x) = f(-x)$. Such a function is by definition *even*. A function is symmetrical under a reflection through the origin if it stays the same when each point is reflected to the opposite side of the origin— mathematically, $f(x) = -f(-x)$. Such a function is by definition *odd*.

A periodic function is also symmetrical, not necessarily under reflection, but under an appropriate *translation*. The function is unchanged when translated (moved) horizontally by a distance equal to the function's period.

Function's *end behavior*

A function's *end behavior* refers to its tendency at the extreme right and left sides of the graph—that is, what happens to the function as x tends toward $\pm\infty$. There are essentially three possibilities: either $f(x)$ increases without limit ($f(x)$ goes to ∞), $f(x)$ decreases without limit ($f(x)$ goes to $-\infty$), or $f(x)$ tends toward some finite value (a horizontal asymptote). The behavior may be different at the two sides: while $f(x) = x^2$ goes to ∞ on both sides, $g(x) = x^3$ goes to ∞ on the right side and to $-\infty$ on the left, and $h(x) = e^{-x}$ goes to ∞ on the left and tends toward the horizontal asymptote $y = 0$ on the right.

When writing a function to represent a quantitative relationship given in a word problem, explain how to determine the function's domain

Sometimes the domain is given explicitly; if given the earnings of a company between 1980 and 2000, then if you write this as a function of the company's earnings over time in years, the domain would run from 1980 to 2000.

When not given explicitly, the domain must be deduced by considering logically within what limits the function applies. Often this involves noting that the function and/or its argument must be non-negative. For instance, suppose a word problem says that a builder wishes to use 100 feet of fence to enclose three sides of a rectangle, and asks for the rectangle's length as a function of its width. Such a function could be written as $f(x) = 100 - 2x$, where x is the width and $f(x)$ the length. Clearly, the width cannot be negative, so we must have $x \geq 0$. Nor can the length be negative, so we must have $f(x) \geq 0$, i.e. $100 - 2x \geq 0$, so $x \leq 50$. Therefore, the domain is $0 \leq x \leq 50$.

Determining the domain of a function from its graph

The *domain* of a function is the set of x values for which the function is defined. This can be seen from the graph by observing for what values of x the function is drawn. Essentially, if a vertical line drawn through the graph at a particular value of x intercepts the graph of the function, then the function is defined at that point. If a vertical line intercepts the function no matter where it is drawn, then the domain contains all real numbers.

If this is not the case, then special considerations apply at the endpoints of intervals over which the function is defined. A function is never defined at a vertical asymptote. If $f(x)$ is finite at the endpoint of the interval, however, then the endpoint is drawn either as a filled circle to indicate that it is included in the function, or a hollow circle if not. Of the two graphs below, for instance, the left has a domain of $[-2, \infty)$, and the right of $(-2, \infty)$.

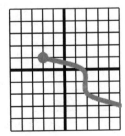
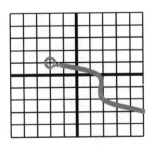

<u>Example</u>

Determine the domains of each of the functions shown below

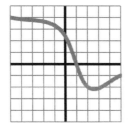 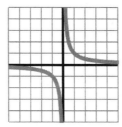 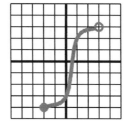

The domain of a function can be seen from its graph by observing what values along the x-axis have part of the function directly above or below them. Often the domain comprises all real numbers, $(-\infty, \infty)$. This is the case for the sample function shown on the left: the function extends unbroken from the left edge of the graph to its right edge; there is no x value for which it is not defined. For a function with a vertical asymptote, the x value corresponding to that asymptote is not part of the domain. The middle example function has a vertical asymptote at $x = 0$, so its domain is $(-\infty, 0) \cup (0, \infty)$.

Other functions are only defined over particular intervals. In this case, a solid circle at the end of the interval means that end point is included in the function's domain, and a hollow circle means it isn't. The example function on the right, then, is defined at $x = -2$ but not at $x = 3$; its domain is $[-2, 3)$.

<u>Example</u>

Calculating a function's average rate of change over a specific interval when the function is given as a table

x	0	2	4	6	8	10	12	14	16
$f(x)$	-100	-54	-26	-10	0	10	26	54	100

The function's average rate of change over the interval $[x_1, x_2]$ can be calculated as $\frac{f(x_2)-f(x_1)}{x_2-x_1}$. For the sample table, for instance, if we want to determine the function's rate of change during the entire interval represented in the table, then $x_1 = 0$ and $x_2 = 16$. By reference to the table, $f(x_1) = f(0) = -100$, and $f(x_2) = f(16) = 100$. Thus, the function's rate of change is equal to $\frac{100-(-100)}{16-0} = \frac{200}{16} = 12.5$. If on the other hand we only want to find the rate of change between 0 and 4, then $x_1 = 0$, $x_2 = 4$, $f(x_1) = f(0) = -100$, and $f(x_2) = f(4) = -26$. The rate of change is then $\frac{-26-(-100)}{4-0} = \frac{74}{4} = 18.5$. If we are asked for the rate of change in the interval $[6, 10]$, then $x_1 = 6$, $x_2 = 10$, $f(x_1) = f(6) = -10$, and $f(x_2) = f(10) = 10$. The rate of change is then $\frac{10-(-10)}{10-6} = \frac{20}{4} = 5$.

- 57 -

<u>Example</u>

Calculating a function's average rate of change over a specific interval when the function is given algebraically, such as $f(x) = x^2 + 1$

The function's average rate of change over the interval $[x_1, x_2]$ can be calculated as $\frac{f(x_2)-f(x_1)}{x_2-x_1}$. For the sample function, for instance, suppose we're asked to find the function's average rate of change between 0 and 10. Then $x_1 = 0$ and $x_2 = 10$. To find $f(x_1)$ and $f(x_2)$, we simply evaluate the function at these two points: $f(x_1) = f(0) = 0^2 + 1 = 1$, and $f(x_2) = f(10) = 10^2 + 1 = 101$. The function's average rate of change in this interval is therefore $\frac{101-1}{10-0} = \frac{100}{10} = 10$.

If we're asked to find the function's average rate of change over the interval $[-4, 2]$, then $x_1 = -4$, $x_2 = 2$, $f(x_1) = f(-4) = (-4)^2 + 1 = 17$, and $f(x_2) = f(2) = 2^2 + 1 = 5$. The average rate of change is therefore $\frac{5-17}{2-(-4)} = \frac{-12}{6} = -2$. If we're asked to find the average rate of change over the interval $[-5, 5]$, then $x_1 = -5$, $x_2 = 5$, $f(x_1) = f(-5) = (-5)^2 + 1 = 26$, and $f(x_2) = f(5) = 5^2 + 1 = 26$. The average rate of change is therefore $\frac{26-26}{5-(-5)} = \frac{0}{10} = 0$.

Estimating a function's average rate of change over a specific interval when the function is given graphically, like the graph below

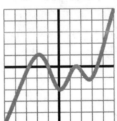

A function's average rate of change over an interval $[a, b]$ contained in the function's domain is the change in the value of $f(x)$ in that interval relative to the change in x. In other words, mathematically, it can be expressed as $\frac{f(b)-f(a)}{b-a}$. To estimate the average rate of change over an interval for a function given graphically, then, we have to estimate the coordinates of the endpoints of the desired interval and then put the appropriate values into that expression and carry out the calculation. For example, consider the sample function over the entire interval shown on the graph, $[-5, 5]$. At the left end is passes through the point $(-5, -5)$, and at the right end $(5, 5)$; the average rate of change is therefore $\frac{f(5)-f(-5)}{5-(-5)} = \frac{5-(-5)}{10} = \frac{10}{10} = 1$. If we instead consider the interval $[-2, 0]$, the left endpoint is about $(-2, 1)$ and the right about $(0, -2)$; the average rate of change over the interval $[-2, 0]$ is then $\frac{f(0)-f(-2)}{0-(-2)} = \frac{-2-1}{2} = \frac{-3}{2} = -\frac{3}{2}$. The average rate of change over the interval $[-5, 0]$ is $\frac{f(0)-f(-5)}{0-(-5)} = \frac{-2-(-5)}{5} = \frac{3}{5}$.

Graphing a linear function given in slope-intercept form, such as $f(x) = 3x + 1$

There are several ways to graph a linear function. For a function given in slope-intercept form, like this example, it's usually easiest to use the slope and the y intercept. The slope-intercept form of a linear function takes the form $y = mx + b$, where m is the slope and b the y intercept. (If the x has no coefficient, the slope is 1.) For the sample function $f(x) = 3x + 1$ (i.e. $y = 3x + 1$), the slope is 3 and the y-intercept is 1. Therefore, we can plot the point $(0,1)$, and then draw a line through that point with the appropriate slope: for every 1 unit to the right, the line goes 3 units up. If the slope is negative, then instead of up and to the right, it goes down and to the right (or, equivalently, up and to the left). A graph of the sample function therefore looks as follows:

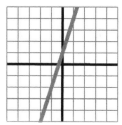

Graphing a linear function given in standard form, such as $2x - 3y = 12$

There are several ways to graph a linear function. If the function is given in standard form, $Ax + By = C$, like this example, then it's usually easiest to use the x and y intercepts. Consider the example equation, $2x - 3y = 12$. When $x = 0$, we get $-3y = 12$, so $y = -4$; this is the y intercept. When $y = 0$, we get $2x = 12$, so $x = 6$; this is the x intercept. We now know the points $(0, -4)$ and $(6, 0)$ are on the graph, so we can plot these two points and draw a straight line through them. A graph of the sample function therefore looks as follows:

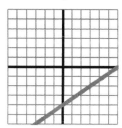

Graphing a quadratic function, such as $f(x) = 2(x - 4)^2 + 3$

If a quadratic function is in *vertex form*, $a(x - h)^2 + k$, we can see at a glance the coordinates of the vertex: they are simply (h, k). In this case, $h = 4$ and $k = 3$, so the vertex is at (4,3). We can use the coefficient a to see the direction of the opening: if $a > 0$, the graph opens upward, while if $a < 0$ it opens downward. Here $a = 2 > 0$, so this graph opens upward. After that, the only remaining feature to distinguish the quadratic function is its width. We can get a feel for this by simply plotting a few other points. The x intercepts are good choices, but some quadratic functions have no x intercepts, like this one: the equation $0 = 2(x - 4)^2 + 3$ has no real solutions. However, we can still choose other values to plot: $f(3) = 2(3 - 4)^2 + 3 = 5$ and $f(5) = 2(5 - 4)^2 + 3 = 5$, so we can plot the points (3,5) and (5,5). Our final graph in this case looks like this:

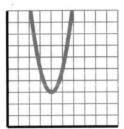

Piecewise-defined function

A *piecewise-defined function* is a function that has different definitions on two or more different intervals. The following, for instance, is one example of a piecewise-defined function:

$$f(x) = \begin{cases} x^2, & x < 0 \\ x, & 0 \leq x \leq 2 \\ (x - 2)^2, & x > 2 \end{cases}$$

To graph this function, we'd simply graph each part separately in the appropriate domain. Our final graph would look like this:

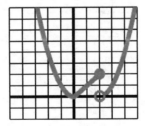

Note the filled and hollow dots at the discontinuity at $x = 2$. This is important to show which side of the graph that point corresponds to. Because $f(x) = x$ on the closed interval $0 \leq x \leq 2$, $f(2) = 2$. The point (2,2) is therefore marked with a filled circle, and the point (2,0), which is the endpoint of the rightmost $(x - 2)^2$ part of the graph but *not actually part of the function*, is marked with a hollow dot to indicate this.

Graphing a square root function, such as $f(x) = -2\sqrt{4x + 4}$

All square root functions have a characteristic shape (essentially, the shape of half a quadratic function rotated ninety degrees). They vary, however, in their dimensions and displacement. If we rewrite the given function as $f(x) = -2\sqrt{4(x + 1)}$, we can see by inspection how it differs from the "plain" square root function $f(x) = \sqrt{x}$: it is shifted one unit to the left (because of the $x + 1$), flipped over vertically (because of the sign of the coefficient -2), stretched vertically by a factor of 2, and squashed horizontally by a factor of 4. Alternately, we can just plot a few points to get a feel for the graph's shape: for instance, $f(-1) = -2\sqrt{-4 + 4} = 0$, $f(0) = -2\sqrt{0 + 4} = -4$, and $f(1) = -2\sqrt{4 + 4} = -4\sqrt{2} \approx -5.66$. Our final graph looks like this:

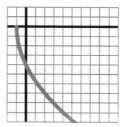

Graphing a cube root function such as $f(x) = 3\sqrt[3]{x} - 2$

All cube root functions have a characteristic shape (somewhat like a stretched-out S—note that unlike that of the square root, the domain of the cube root function encompasses all real numbers). They vary, however, in their dimensions and displacement. In the case of the given function, $3\sqrt[3]{x} - 2$, we can see by inspection how it differs from the "plain" cube root function $f(x) = \sqrt[3]{x}$: it is stretched vertically by a factor of 3 (because of the coefficient 3), and shifted two units downward (because of the -2). We can just draw a cube root function modified accordingly. Alternately, we can just plot a few points to get a feel for the graph's shape: for instance, $f(0) = 3\sqrt[3]{0} - 2 = -2$, $f(1) = 3\sqrt[3]{1} - 2 = 1$, $f(8) = 3\sqrt[3]{8} - 2 = 4$, and so on. Our final graph looks like this:

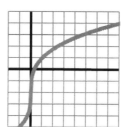

- 61 -

Graphing an absolute value function such as $f(x) = 2|x + 1| - 3$

The key to graphing an absolute value function is to recognize that its behavior depends on whether the expression within the absolute value sign is positive or negative, and to graph these parts separately. In the case of the function $f(x) = 2|x + 1| - 3$, the point at which the behavior changes is when $x + 1 = 0$, i.e. when $x = -1$. When $x \geq -1$, $|x + 1| = x + 1$, and the function reduces to the linear function $f_+(x) = 2(x + 1) - 3 = 2x - 1$. When $x \leq -1$, $|x + 1| = -(x + 1)$, and the function reduces to $f_-(x) = 2\big(-(x + 1)\big) - 3 = -2x - 5$. So we can graph $y = -2x - 5$ to the left of $x = -1$ and $y = 2x - 1$ to the right, yielding the following graph:

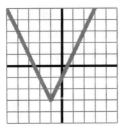

Graphing a step function such as $f(x) = 2 \left\llbracket \frac{1}{3}(x - 1) \right\rrbracket$

The double brackets indicate a step function. For a step function, all values inside the double brackets are rounded down to the nearest integer. The graph of the function $f_0(x) = \llbracket x \rrbracket$ appears as shown on the graph on the left below. In this case, we can see by inspection how the given $f(x) = 2 \left\llbracket \frac{1}{3}(x - 1) \right\rrbracket$ differs from $f_0(x)$. The coefficient of 2 shows that it's stretched vertically by a factor of 2 (so there's a vertical distance of 2 units between successive "steps"). The coefficient of $\frac{1}{3}$ in front of the x shows that it's stretched horizontally by a factor of 3 (so each "step" is three units long), and the $x - 1$ shows that it's displaced one unit to the right. The final graph, then, is on the right below.

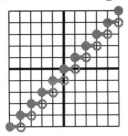 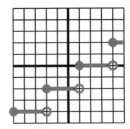

Determining the end behavior of a polynomial function

The "end behavior" of a function is what happens to the function when $|x|$ is very large. For a polynomial function, there are only two possibilities: either the function continues increasing indefinitely (it "goes to infinity"), or the function continues *decreasing* indefinitely (it "goes to negative infinity").

To see which is true, we need only look at the largest-order term of the polynomial, that is, the term with the largest exponent. To find the behavior of the function as $x \to \infty$ (at the right end), we just look at the coefficient of that term: if it's positive, the function goes to infinity; if it's negative, the function goes to negative infinity. The behavior of the function as $x \to -\infty$ (at the left end) is only slightly more complicated. If the exponent is even, the same

- 62 -

rule holds as for the right end. If the exponent is odd, they're reversed: if the coefficient is positive, the function goes to negative infinity, and if it's negative, the function goes to positive infinity.

Graphing a polynomial such as $\frac{1}{4}x^4 - \frac{9}{4}x^2$

To graph a polynomial, like most other functions, there are a few key characteristics we can observe. First, we can observe the end behavior, which depends only on the largest order term. To find the y intercept, we evaluate the function at $x = 0$. To find the x intercepts, the points where the polynomial equals zero, is a little harder, but often we can factor the function and set each factor equal to zero. Depending on the polynomial, there may be other characteristics we can find, such as the local maxima and minima.

For the given example, since the highest order term has an even order and a positive coefficient, the polynomial goes to positive infinity at both ends. The y intercept is at $\frac{1}{4}(0^4) - \frac{9}{4}(0^2) = 0$. We can factor the polynomial as $\frac{1}{4}x^4 - \frac{9}{4}x^2 = \frac{1}{4}x^2(x^2 - 9) = \frac{1}{4}x^2(x + 3)(x - 3)$, so it has x intercepts at $x = 0, 3,$ and -3. Its graph looks like this:

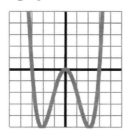

Example

> Identifying the zeroes of a polynomial such as $x^3 - 3x^2 - 4x$ or $x^3 + 2x^2 - 2x - 4$

> We can find the zeroes of a polynomial by factoring it. Cubics and higher polynomials can be difficult to factor, but there are special cases that can be readily factored. In the first sample polynomial here, for instance, $x^3 - 3x^2 - 4x$, it's clear that every term of the polynomial is divisible by x. We can therefore factor out the x to get $x(x^2 - 3x - 4)$. This now leaves a quadratic factor, which can be further factored to yield $x(x + 1)(x - 4)$. The zeroes of the polynomial are therefore 0, -1, and 4.

> In the second polynomial, $x^3 + 2x^2 - 2x - 4$, there's no such divisor that goes into every term. If we compare the first two terms with the last two, however, we note that both *pairs* of terms are divisible by $x + 2$. We can then write the polynomial as $x^2(x + 2) - 2(x + 2)$, or $(x^2 - 2)(x + 2)$, and further factoring the first term, $(x + \sqrt{2})(x - \sqrt{2})(x + 2)$. The zeroes of this polynomial are -2 and $\pm\sqrt{2}$.

Finding the horizontal asymptote of a rational function

A rational function is a ratio of polynomials, and the horizontal asymptote is a horizontal line that the rational function tends toward as x approaches $\pm\infty$. To find the horizontal

- 63 -

asymptote, first compare the orders of the numerator and the denominator—that is, the largest exponents appearing in them. If the numerator has a larger order than the denominator (as in $\frac{x^2-1}{x}$ or $\frac{x^4+x+2}{x^2-x}$), then the function has no horizontal asymptote. If the numerator has a smaller order the denominator (as in $\frac{x}{x^2-1}$ or $\frac{x^2+x+1}{x^5}$), then the function has a horizontal asymptote at $y = 0$.

If the orders of the numerator and denominator are equal (as in $\frac{2x^2+2}{x^2+2x+1}$ or $\frac{3x-4}{4x-3}$), then the horizontal asymptote is $y = y_0$, where y_0 is the ratio of the coefficients of the highest-order terms. For instance, the rational function $\frac{2x^2+2}{x^2+2x+1}$ has a horizontal asymptote at $y = \frac{2}{1} = 2$; $\frac{3x-4}{4x-3}$ has a horizontal asymptote at $y = \frac{3}{4}$.

Determining whether a rational function has a horizontal asymptote, a slant asymptote, or neither

To determine the end behavior of a rational function, it is only necessary to compare the orders of the numerator and the denominator—that is, the largest exponents appearing in them. If the order of the numerator is less than or equal to the order of the denominator, then the function has a horizontal asymptote. If the order of the numerator is one more than the order of the denominator, then the function has a slant asymptote. If the order of the numerator exceeds the order of the denominator by two or more, then the function has neither a horizontal nor a slant asymptote.

For instance, consider the rational function $\frac{3x^3+4x^2-2}{5x^7-5}$. The order of the numerator is 3; the order of the denominator is 7. Since $3 \leq 7$, this function has a horizontal asymptote (at $y = 0$). In the rational function $\frac{2x^4-x^2+3}{x^3-x}$, the order of the numerator is 4 and the order of the denominator is 3. Since $4 = 3 + 1$, this function has a slant asymptote.

Finding the vertical asymptotes of a rational function

Generally, a rational function has a vertical asymptote where the denominator is equal to zero, making the function undefined at that point (since the result of dividing by zero is undefined). For instance, consider the function $\frac{x^2+4x+4}{x^3-1}$. $1^3 - 1 = 0$, so this function has a vertical asymptote at $x = 1$.

There is one important exception to the above rule, however. If there is a common term to the numerator and denominator of the rational function, then it has vertical asymptotes only where the denominator is zero *after canceling common terms*. For instance, the function $f(x) = \frac{x^2-2x+1}{x^2+x-2}$ is undefined at $x = 1$, since $1^2 + 1 - 2 = 0$. However, $\frac{x^2-2x+1}{x^2+x-2} = \frac{(x-1)(x-1)}{(x-1)(x+2)}$; canceling the common term yields $\frac{x-1}{x+2}$. So $f(x)$ has a vertical asymptote at $x = -2$, but *not* at $x = 1$. (This doesn't change the fact that $f(x)$ is *undefined* at $x = 1$, but it can be undefined there without having a vertical asymptote.)

Determining the end behavior of a rational function such as $f(x) = \frac{3x^2+2x-3}{6x^3-2x^2+1}$ **or** $g(x) = \frac{-7x^7+1}{2x^2-x+3}$

To determine the end behavior of a rational function, it's only necessary to consider the leading terms of the numerator and denominator—the terms with the largest exponents. If the leading term of the denominator has a larger exponent, then $f(x)$ goes to zero as x goes to $\pm\infty$. We can then take the ratio of these leading terms, which will result in a single term of which the end behavior should be clear. For example, consider the first example, $f(x) = \frac{3x^2+2x-3}{6x^3-2x^2+1}$. The leading term of the numerator is $3x^2$, and the leading term of the denominator is $6x^3$. The latter has a larger exponent, so this function goes to zero as x goes to $\pm\infty$. In the second function, $g(x) = \frac{-7x^7+1}{2x^2-x+3}$, the leading term of the numerator is $-7x^7$, and the leading term of the numerator is $2x^2$. The ratio is $\frac{-7x^7}{2x^2} = -\frac{7}{2}x^5$, which goes to ∞ as x goes to $-\infty$ and $-\infty$ as x goes to ∞.

Finding the zeroes of a rational function such as $f(x) = \frac{x^2+3x+2}{x^3+x+1}$ **or** $g(x) = \frac{x^4-x^2}{x^3-2x^2+1}$.

A rational function $R(x)$ is a ratio of two polynomials, which we can write as $\frac{P(x)}{Q(x)}$. The rational function has a zero at any point $x = x_0$ for which the numerator $P(x_0)$ is equal to zero and the denominator $Q(x_0)$ is *not* equal to zero. If $Q(x_0) = 0$, then $R(x_0)$ is undefined.

In the first sample function, $f(x) = \frac{x^2+3x+2}{x^3+x+1}$, the numerator $P(x) = x^2 + 3x + 2$ has zeroes at $x = -1$ and $x = -2$. Neither of these is a zero of the denominator $Q(x) = x^3 + x + 1$: $Q(-1) = -1$, and $Q(-2) = -9$. So both of these are zeroes of $f(x)$.

In the second sample function, $g(x) = \frac{x^4-x^2}{x^3-2x^2+1}$, the numerator $P(x) = x^4 - x^2 = x^2(x^2 - 1)$ has zeroes at $x = 0$ and $x = \pm1$. Before concluding that these are zeroes of $g(x)$, though, we have to check whether they're zeroes of the denominator $Q(x) = x^3 - 2x^2 + 1$. $Q(-1) = -2$, $Q(0) = 1$, and $Q(1) = 0$. This means $x = 1$ is *not* a zero of $g(x)$, so the zeroes of $g(x)$ are $x = -1$ and $x = 0$.

<u>Example</u>

Given a trigonometric function of the form $f(x) = A\sin(Bx + C) + D$ (such as $f(x) = 2 + \frac{3}{2}\sin\left(\pi x + \frac{\pi}{2}\right)$), determine how you would find the function's period, amplitude, and midline and use them to graph the function

In the function $f(x) = A\sin(Bx + C) + D$, the amplitude is simply equal to A, and the midline is $y = D$. The period is only a little more complicated; the period is equal to $2\pi/B$. For instance, consider the example function $f(x) = 2 + \frac{3}{2}\sin\left(\pi x + \frac{\pi}{2}\right)$. Here $A = \frac{3}{2}$, $B = \pi$, $C = \frac{\pi}{2}$, and $D = 2$, so the midline is at $y = 2$, the amplitude is $\frac{3}{2}$, and the period is $2\pi/\pi = 2$.

To graph this equation, we center the sine wave on the midline and extend it to a height above and below the midline equal to the amplitude—so this graph would have a minimum value of $2 - \frac{3}{2} = \frac{1}{2}$ and a maximum of $2 + \frac{3}{2} = \frac{7}{2}$. The period (here equal to 2) is the distance between successive peaks or troughs. As for the last value, C, this is related to the *phase shift*, which is equal to $-\frac{C}{B}$ (in this case $-\frac{1}{2}$) and can be thought of as a starting point where $f(x) = D$ (the midline) and increasing. So the function above would be graphed as follows:

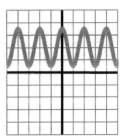

<u>Example</u>

Find the x and y intercepts, if any, of an exponential function of the form $f(x) = Ae^{bx} + C$

To find the y intercept, we just evaluate the function at $x = 0$. This gives $f(0) = Ae^{b \cdot 0} + C = Ae^0 + C = A(1) + C = A + C$. For instance, if $f(x) = \frac{1}{2}e^{3x} - 4$, $f(0) = \frac{1}{2}e^{3 \cdot 0} - 4 = \frac{1}{2}(1) - 4 = -\frac{7}{2}$. This function has a y intercept at $(0, -\frac{7}{2})$.

To find the x intercept, we have to find a value of x for which $f(x) = 0$. Thus, $Ae^{bx} + C = 0$, so $Ae^{bx} = -C$, and $e^{bx} = -\frac{C}{A}$. From here, we have to take the logarithm of both sides, so $bx = \ln\left(-\frac{C}{A}\right)$, and $x = \frac{1}{b}\ln\left(-\frac{C}{A}\right)$. (Note that the logarithm of a negative number is undefined, so this has a solution only if $-\frac{C}{A} > 0$, i.e. $\frac{C}{A} < 0$. Otherwise, there is no x intercept.) If $f(x) = \frac{1}{2}e^{3x} - 4$, then to find the x intercept we use $\frac{1}{2}e^{3x} - 4 = 0$, so $\frac{1}{2}e^{3x} = 4$, $e^{3x} = 8$, and hence $3x = \ln 8$ and $x = \frac{\ln 8}{3} \approx 0.693$.

<u>Example</u>

Determine the end behavior of an exponential function such as $f(x) = 2e^{2x}$ or $g(x) = -e^{-x}$

The exponential function $y = e^x$ goes to zero as x goes to $-\infty$ and goes to ∞ as x goes to ∞. Multiplying either the exponent or the full exponential by a positive coefficient doesn't change this behavior, so this is the end behavior of $f(x) = 2e^{2x}$: it goes to zero on the left and goes to ∞ on the right.

Negative coefficients, on the other hand, do make a difference. A negative coefficient in the exponent interchanges the left and right side behavior, while a negative coefficient in front of the entire function makes the function go to negative infinity on the right instead of positive infinity. The function $g(x) = -e^{-x}$ has negative coefficients in *both* places, so it goes to $-\infty$ as x goes to $-\infty$, and goes to zero as x goes to ∞.

<u>Example</u>

Determine the end behavior of a logarithmic function such as $f(x) = \ln(-x)$ or $g(x) = -\frac{1}{2}\log_{10}(x + 2)$

Regardless of the base, the logarithmic function $y = \log(x)$ goes to ∞ as x goes to ∞. The domain of $y = \log(x)$ is $(0, \infty)$, so we don't need to consider what happens as x goes to $-\infty$, but as x approaches the vertical asymptote at $x = 0$, $\log(x)$ goes to $-\infty$.

The function $f(x) = \ln(-x)$ has a negative coefficient in front of the x, which means the function is reflected from left to right. This function, therefore, goes to ∞ as x goes to $-\infty$, and on the right $f(x)$ goes to $-\infty$ as x approaches the vertical asymptote at $x = 0$.

The $x + 2$ in the function $g(x) = -\frac{1}{2}\log_{10}(x + 2)$ means the function is shifted two units to the left—which means, in particular, that the vertical asymptote is shifted two units to the left. The negative coefficient in front of the function means the entire graph is flipped vertically. Therefore, $g(x)$ goes to $-\infty$ as x goes to ∞, and goes to ∞ as x approaches the vertical asymptote at $x = -2$.

<u>Example</u>

Given a tangent function such as $f(x) = 2\tan(3x - 4) + 1$, determine how you would find the function's period and midline and use them to graph the function

In the function $f(x) = A\tan(Bx + C) + D$, the midline is $y = D$, and the period is π/B. Larger values of A stretch the tangent vertically, but since the range of the tangent includes all real numbers, the tangent doesn't have an amplitude in the same sense as the sine and cosine do. If A is negative, the function is flipped vertically. C is related to the *phase shift*, ϕ, which is equal to $-C/B$, and is the amount by which the function is displaced horizontally.

For instance, consider the example function $f(x) = 2\tan(3x - 4) + 1$. Here $A = 2$, $B = 3$, $C = -4$, and $D = 1$, so the midline is at $y = 1$, the period is $\pi/3 \approx 1.05$, and the phase shift is $-\left(-\frac{4}{3}\right) = \frac{4}{3}$. To graph this equation, we start at the point (ϕ, D)—in this case, $\left(\frac{4}{3}, 1\right)$—and we draw the tangent shape centered on this point, with a width equal to the period. We then repeat this shape to both sides at regular intervals. The result is as follows:

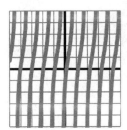

What it means to "complete the square" of a quadratic function, and what purpose it serves

A quadratic function in the "vertex form" $f(x) = a(x - h)^2 + k$ readily shows the coordinates of the vertex, (h, k). However, quadratic functions are often given in "standard form", $f(x) = ax^2 + bx + c$, which doesn't show the coordinates of the vertex directly. Completing the square is one way to convert the function from standard form to vertex form.

To complete the square, we first factor out the a from the first two terms: $f(x) = a\left(x^2 + \frac{b}{a}x\right) + c$. Now, we have to find a linear expression which, squared, yields a quadratic the first two terms of which match the terms in parentheses. This is probably most easily shown with an example: if $f(x) = 2x^2 + 8x + 6 = 2(x^2 + 4x) + 6$, then a suitable linear expression is $x + 2$, because $(x + 2)^2 = x^2 + 4x + 4$. Therefore, we have $f(x) = 2(x + 2)^2 + h$. All we have to do now is find a value for h that matches the original equation. Expanding, we have
$f(x) = 2x^2 + 8x + 8 + h$, so we require $8 + h = 6$, thus $h = -2$, and $f(x) = 2(x + 2)^2 - 2$.

Factoring a quadratic function such as $f(x) = x^2 + x - 6$, $g(x) = x^2 - 16$, or $h(x) = 2x^2 + 3x - 7$

Factoring a quadratic function of the form $ax^2 + bx + c$ means finding two factors $(px + q)$ and $(rx + s)$ such that $(px + q)(rx + s) = ax^2 + bx + c$. Since $(px + q)(rx + s) = prx^2 +$

- 68 -

$(ps + qr)x + qs$, we're looking specifically for p, q, r, s such that $pr = a$, $ps + qr = b$, and $qs = c$. The matter is much simpler if $a = 1$; then we need only find q and s such that $q + s = b$ and $qs = c$. For instance, for the first example, $f(x) = x^2 + x - 6$, $b = 1$ and $c = -6$, so we need to find two numbers that add to 1 and multiply to –6. –2 and 3 qualify, so $f(x)$ can be factored to $(x - 2)(x + 3)$. When the quadratic function has the form $x^2 - c$, we don't even need to do that much work; we know the function's factors are $(x + \sqrt{c})$ and $(x - \sqrt{c})$. So $g(x) = x^2 - 16$ factorizes to

$(x + \sqrt{16})(x - \sqrt{16}) = (x + 4)(x - 4)$.

Sometimes a quadratic function can't readily be factored by any of these systems. In this case, one can resort to the *quadratic formula*: $x = \frac{-b \pm \sqrt{b^2 - 4ac}}{2a}$. Note that when you use the quadratic formula to solve the equation $0 = ax^2 + bx + c$ what you are really solving is $0 = x^2 + \frac{b}{a}x + \frac{c}{a}$; therefore, when using the quadratic formula to find the factors of $ax^2 + bx + c$ you must include the coefficient a as one of your factors. In the case of our third sample function, $h(x) = 2x^2 + 3x - 7$, this gives us $x = \frac{-3 \pm \sqrt{3^2 - 4(2)(-7)}}{2 \cdot 2} = \frac{-3 \pm \sqrt{65}}{4} = -\frac{3}{4} \pm \frac{\sqrt{65}}{4}$, and the factorization is $2\left(x + \frac{3}{4} - \frac{\sqrt{65}}{4}\right)\left(x + \frac{3}{4} + \frac{\sqrt{65}}{4}\right)$.

Finding the extreme values of a quadratic function such as $f(x) = x^2 - 6x + 3$

A quadratic function of the form $ax^2 + bx + c$ has only a single extreme value, at its vertex. Whether this is a maximum or a minimum depends on whether the graph opens upward or downward. This in turn depends on the sign of the coefficient a: if a is positive, then the graph opens upward and the vertex is a minimum, while if a is negative, the graph opens downward and the vertex is a maximum.

In the case of the sample function $f(x) = x^2 - 6x + 3$, the coefficient $a = 1 > 0$, so the vertex is a minimum. To find the coordinates of the vertex, we can put the function in *vertex form*, $f(x) = a(x - h)^2 + k$. We can do this by completing the square: $(x - 3)^2 = x^2 - 6x + 9$, so $f(x) = (x - 3)^2 - 6$. The vertex is at the coordinates (h, k)—in this case, $(3, -6)$.

Symmetry of a quadratic function such as $f(x) = 3(x - 2)^2 + 5$

Any quadratic function is symmetrical through a vertical line passing through the vertex. When the quadratic function is in vertex form, $f(x) = a(x - h)^2 + k$, the coordinates of the vertex can be readily seen from the equation; they are simply (h, k). The axis of symmetry is then $x = h$; the function is unchanged when reflected through this line. If $h = 0$, then the axis of symmetry is the line $x = 0$, which is the y axis; the function is then symmetrical with respect to reflections through the y axis, which means it is an even function. Quadratic functions with $h \neq 0$ are neither even nor odd.

In the case of the sample function given here, $f(x) = 3(x - 2)^2 + 5$, $h = 2$ and $k = 5$. This function, therefore, is symmetrical with respect to reflections through the line $x = 2$.

Example

Given an exponential equation such as $f(x) = 200 \cdot (1.2)^{3x}$, show how you can determine whether it represents exponential growth or exponential decay

If the coefficient of the exponent is positive (as it is in the sample function given), then the function represents exponential growth if the base of the exponent is greater than 1, and exponential decay if the exponent is less than 1. The sample function therefore represents exponential growth, since the base, 1.2, is greater than 1. An example of a function that would represent exponential decay would be $g(x) = 13 \cdot (0.9)^{2.5x}$, since here the base, 0.9, is less than one.

If the coefficient in the exponent is negative, then this rule of thumb is reversed. Thus, for instance,
$h(x) = 10 \cdot (1.1)^{-2x}$ represents exponential decay, since the coefficient (−2) is negative, and the base (1.1) is greater than 1; $k(x) = 7 \cdot (0.8)^{-1.5x}$ is exponential growth, since the exponent (−1.5) is negative, and the base (0.8) is less than 1.

Example

Finding the percent rate of change of an exponential function such as $f(t) = 70 \cdot (1.4)^{1.05t}$

The percent rate of change is the amount by which a function changes per unit of time, expressed as a percentage. This can be calculated as $\frac{f(t+1)-f(t)}{f(t)}$.
For the sample function, $f(t) = 70 \cdot (1.4)^{1.05t}$, this calculation gives
$\frac{70 \cdot (1.4)^{1.05(t+1)} - 70 \cdot (1.4)^{1.05t}}{70 \cdot (1.4)^{1.05t}} = \frac{70 \cdot (1.4)^{1.05(t+1)}}{70 \cdot (1.4)^{1.05t}} - 1 = (1.4)^{(1.05(t+1)-1.05t)} - 1 = 1.4^{1.05} - 1 \approx 0.424 = 42.4\%$ per unit of time. Note that the time, t, cancels from the calculation, and therefore the rate of change does not depend on t. This is a characteristic of exponential functions; they have a constant percent rate of change.

The answer we obtained for the sample function can be generalized: in general, the percent rate of change of an exponential function $f(t) = a \cdot b^{ct}$ is equal to $b^c - 1$. Note that if $b^c < 1$, then the percent rate of change is negative. For instance, consider $g(t) = 2 \cdot \left(\frac{1}{2}\right)^t$. The percent rate of change is $\left(\frac{1}{2}\right)^1 - 1 = -\frac{1}{2} = -50\%$. This makes sense, because if $b^c < 1$ then the function represents exponential decay; the function is decreasing, so the percent rate of change is indeed negative.

Important properties of exponents, and explain how they could be used in a problem

One important property of exponents is the property that $x^a x^b = x^{a+b}$. This could come into play in a problem in which we have a product of two exponentials, and it simplifies the problem to combine them into one. Conversely, we can use it to simplify an expression with a sum in the exponent, such as $3 \cdot 2^{x+4}$; this simplifies to $3 \cdot 2^x 2^4 = 3 \cdot 2^x \cdot 16 = 48 \cdot 2^x$.

Often given separately is the property $x^a/_{x^b} = x^{a-b}$, but this is really a special case of the previous property where $b < 0$, and applies under similar circumstances.

Another important property of exponents is the property that $(x^a)^b = x^{ab}$. This can be used to simplify expressions in which an exponential is raised to a power, or to simplify an expression with a product in the exponent into a single exponent: for example, $3^{3x} = (3^3)^x = 27^x$.

Given two functions, one represented algebraically and one graphically, determine how you can find which has the larger maximum

One way to compare the features of two functions represented in different ways is to convert them both to the same manner of representation. If one function is represented algebraically and the other graphically, we can graph the first function on the same axis as the second, enabling us to compare their maxima visually by just observing which one extends farther in the positive y direction.

It's also possible to compare their maxima without converting them to the same representation, by simply finding the maximum of each function and comparing them. If the function expressed algebraically is one for which we can find the maximum analytically (for example, a quadratic function), we can compare that value directly with the maximum estimated from the graphed function by observing the y coordinate of its highest peak.

Given two functions, one of which is given algebraically and the other in a verbal description, determine how you could find which has the larger maximum

When given two functions in different formats, one way to compare their properties is to convert both functions to the same format. If one of the functions is given in the form of a verbal description, we can write an algebraic expression to represent the described relationship. For instance, if we're told that a function represents the area of a rectangular field for which the total distance around three sides is 40 meters (implying that, if we write l as the length and w as the width, $l + 2w = 40$), we can write the relationship between the area and the width algebraically as $A = l \cdot w = (40 - 2w)w$. Or, using the more familiar f and x, $f(x) = (40 - 2x)x = -2x^2 + 40x$. Completing the square gives us $f(x) = -2(x - 10)^2 + 200$. This function has a maximum when $x = 10$, at which point $f(x) = 200$. We can likewise find the maximum of the other function given algebraically, and we can now compare the maxima directly.

Given two functions, one of which is given graphically and one in a table, determine how you can find which has the larger y intercept

When given two functions in different formats, one way to compare their properties is to convert both functions to the same format. If one of the functions is given as a table, we can graph that function and then compare it to the graph directly. Conversely, we could determine the values of the graphed function at the x values given in the table and therefore express both functions in tabular format.

It's also sometimes possible to compare properties of the functions even without converting them to the same format, and in the case of finding the y intercept this isn't difficult (assuming that the y intercept of the second function is actually given in the table). We can find the y intercept of the graphed function by seeing where the graph crosses the y-axis, find the y intercept of the table function by seeing what value of the function corresponds to an x value of 0, and compare these values directly.

Building Functions

<u>Example</u>

Given a description of a relationship, such as a statement that the population of a particular area is 2000 in the year 1980 and doubles every 10 years thereafter, determine how you can write an explicit expression to describe that relationship

The first step in writing an expression to describe a relationship is to pinpoint the variables involved in the expression. In the sample case, the statement describes how the population changes over time, we will write the population P as a function of time, t.

Next, we look for telltale signs that tell us what kind of function we are dealing with. Here, the population increases by a fixed proportion over a specific unit of time, a hallmark of an exponential relationship. Therefore, the expression will take the form $P(t) = P_0 A^{ct}$. More specifically, since we're given the population at 1980 as a starting point, we can simplify matters by setting the exponent proportional to the number of years since 1980: $P(t) = P_{1980} A^{c(t-1980)}$.

Finally, we use the given data to put in numbers. When $t = 1980$, $P(t) = 2000$, so $P_{1980} = 2000$. Incorporating the other information gives us $P(t) = 2000 \cdot 2^{(t-1980)/10}$.

Determine what kinds of relationships lend themselves to being written as recursively defined functions

A recursively defined function is generally a *sequence*; that is, its domain consists of a subset of the integers (usually, though not always, the positive integers). Furthermore, the value of the function for a given value of x must be defined in terms of its value for smaller values of x. Often this means $f(x)$ is defined in terms of $f(x - 1)$, though it may also be defined in terms of even smaller values. Finally, we need to have $f(x_0)$ explicitly defined for the smallest value or values of x_0 to give us a starting point.

For example, consider the following relationship: A pile of stones starts with three stones, and then every day its size is doubled and then one stone is removed. On day one, then, the size of the pile is $f(1) = 3$. On day x thereafter, we have the relationship $f(x) = 2f(x - 1) - 1$. This is a valid recursive definition.

Example

Suppose $f(x) = x^2 - 1$ and $g(x) = x - 1$. How would you find each of the following

$$(f + g)(x) \qquad\qquad (f - g)(x) \qquad\qquad (f \cdot g)(x)$$
$$(f/g)(x)$$

To combine functions using arithmetic operations, we need only apply the appropriate arithmetic operation to the function's expression. So $(f + g)(x) = f(x) + g(x) = (x^2 - 1) + (x - 1) = x^2 + x - 2$. $(f - g)(x) = (x^2 - 1) - (x - 1) = x^2 - x$. $(f \cdot g)(x) = (x^2 - 1)(x - 1) = x^3 - x^2 - x + 1$.

Finally, $(f/g)(x) = (x^2 - 1)/(x - 1)$. Here we have to be a little more careful. $(x^2 - 1) = (x + 1)(x - 1)$, so it's tempting to cancel out the $(x - 1)$ terms and state simply that $(f/g)(x) = \frac{(x+1)(x-1)}{x-1} = x + 1$. However, this doesn't hold when $x = 1$: $(f/g)(1) = (1^2 - 1)/(1 - 1) = 0/0$, which is undefined, and *not* equal to $1 + 1$. It's more accurate, therefore, to state that $(f/g)(x) = x + 1$ when $x \neq 1$, but is undefined when $x = 1$.

Example

Determine under what circumstances a relationship might be modeled by an arithmetic operation of two functions

A relationship might be modeled by an arithmetic operation of two functions if it represents a sum, product, difference, or quotient of two processes each modeled by a different function. For example, consider the following: A man has $1000 in one bank account that generates 4% interest, compounded annually, and $2000 in another bank account that generates 3% annual interest, continually compounded. We want to find the total amount of money he has in the bank after t years.

Applying the compound interest formula, $A = P\left(1 + \frac{r}{n}\right)^{nt}$, we find that the amount of money he has in the first account is equal to $f(t) = 1000(1.04)^t$. For continually compounded interest, the formula is $A = Pe^{rt}$, so the amount he has in the second account is equal to $g(t) = 2000e^{0.03t}$. The *total* amount of money he has in the bank is then simply the arithmetic sum of these two: $h(t) = f(t) + g(t) = 1000(1.04)^t + 2000e^{0.03t}$.

<u>Example</u>

Given two functions $f(x)$ and $g(x)$, show how you would determine the domain of each of the following

$(f + g)(x)$ $\qquad\qquad$ $(f - g)(x)$ $\qquad\qquad$ $(f \cdot g)(x)$
$(f/g)(x)$

In order for an arithmetic operation of two functions to be defined for a given x, each of the two functions themselves must also be defined at that x. In other words, in order to be in the domain of $(f + g)(x)$, $(f - g)(x)$, $(f \cdot g)(x)$, or $(f/g)(x)$, a particular number must be in the domain of both $f(x)$ and $g(x)$. For instance, if $f(x) = \ln(x + 1)$ and $g(x) = \sqrt{2-x}$, since the domain of $f(x)$ is $(-1, \infty)$ and the domain of $g(x)$ is $(-\infty, 2]$, the domain of $(f + g)(x)$ is the intersection of those two domains, namely $(-1, 2]$.

For $(f/g)(x)$, we also have to take into account the fact that we can't divide by zero. Therefore, any values x for which $g(x) = 0$ are excluded from the domain of $(f/g)(x)$. For the sample $f(x)$ and $g(x)$ given above, for instance, the domain of $(f/g)(x)$ would be not $(-1, 2]$ but $(-1, 2)$, since $g(2) = 0$.

Function composition

Function composition is a process in which the "output" of one function is used as the "input" of another. The composition of two functions $f(x)$ and $g(x)$ can be written as $(f \circ g)(x)$ or as $f(g(x))$.

<u>How to evaluate the composition of two functions</u>
This means we find the value of $f(x')$ at $x' = g(x)$. In other words, to evaluate the function composition $(f \circ g)(x)$ at $x = x_0$, we first find $y_0 = g(x_0)$ and then find $f(y_0)$, which is our final answer. For example, if $f(x) = x^2 + 1$ and $g(x) = x - 1$, then to find $(f \circ g)(3)$, we first find $g(3) = 2$, and then find $f(2) = 5$. So $(f \circ g)(3) = 5$. We can also rewrite the composition of two functions explicitly as a single function by substituting the expression for one function into the other. For instance, for the above functions, $(f \circ g)(x) = f(x - 1) = (x - 1)^2 + 1 = x^2 - 2x + 2$.

Example

Suppose $f(x) = x^2 - x$ and $g(x) = \frac{x}{x+1}$. How you would find each of the following

$$(f \circ g)(3) \qquad\qquad g(f(-1)) \qquad\qquad (f \circ f)(2)$$
$$f\left(g(f(1))\right)$$

All of these expressions indicate function composition, though they use different notations: the notation $(f \circ g)(x)$, for instance, is equivalent to $f(g(x))$. To evaluate a function composition, we can first evaluate the "inner" function expression, and then put that in as the input to the "outer" function. For instance, to evaluate $(f \circ g)(3)$, we first evaluate $g(3) = \frac{3}{3+1} = \frac{3}{4}$, and then $f(g(3)) = f\left(\frac{3}{4}\right) = \left(\frac{3}{4}\right)^2 - \frac{3}{4} = \frac{9}{16} - \frac{12}{16} = -3/16$. Similarly, $g(f(-1)) = g((-1)^2 - (-1)) = g(1 + 1) = g(2) = \frac{2}{2+1} = 2/3$, and $f(f(2)) = f(2^2 - 2) = f(2) = 2^2 - 2 = 2$.

The last expression here can be evaluated similarly; it only takes an extra step: $f\left(g(f(1))\right) = f\left(g(1^2 - 1)\right) = f(g(0)) = f\left(\frac{0}{0+1}\right) = f(0) = 0^2 - 0 = 0$. In principle, we could apply the same procedure to a composition of any number of functions, such as $(f \circ g \circ g \circ f \circ g)(4)$.

Example

Suppose $f(x) = x^2 + 1$ and $g(x) = x - 1$. How would you write each of the following as a single function?

$$f(g(x)) \qquad\qquad (g \circ f)(x) \qquad\qquad (g \circ g)(x)$$
$$g\left(f(g(x))\right)$$

All of these expressions indicate function composition, though they use different notations: the notation $(g \circ f)(x)$, for instance, is equivalent to $g(f(x))$. To rewrite a function composition as a single expression, we substitute the expression for one function in for x in the expression for the other. To find $f(g(x))$, for instance, we replace each x in the expression for $f(x)$—that is, $x^2 + 1$—with the expression for $g(x)$ —$(x - 1)$. This gives us $f(g(x)) = f(x - 1) = (x - 1)^2 + 1 = x^2 - 2x + 1 + 1 = x^2 - 2x + 2$. Similarly, $(g \circ f)(x) = g(f(x)) = (x^2 + 1) - 1 = x^2$, and $(g \circ g)(x) = g(g(x)) = (x - 1) - 1 = x - 2$.

The final expression, $g\left(f(g(x))\right)$, looks complex but requires the same procedure, just done in two steps. We've already found $f(g(x)) = x^2 - 2x + 2$. To find $g\left(f(g(x))\right)$, then, we just substitute this into the expression for $g(x)$: $g\left(f(g(x))\right) = g(x^2 - 2x + 2) = (x^2 - 2x + 2) - 1 = x^2 - 2x + 1$.

Under what circumstances a relationship might be modeled by a composition of two functions

A relationship might be modeled by a composition of two functions if it represents a process that depends on the output of another process. For example, consider the following: The population of a town increases exponentially according to the formula $P(t) = 1500e^{0.2t}$, where t is the time in years from a fixed starting year. On average, each person in the town eats 800 kilograms of food per year. We want to find the total amount of food eaten by the entire population of the town in year t.

The relationship between the total amount of food eaten in a year and the population of the town is straightforward: $f(x) = 800x$, where x equals the population. However, x is itself a function: specifically, it's $P(t)$, as given above. Therefore, the total amount of food, as a function of t, is $f(P(t)) = f(1500e^{0.2t}) = 800 \cdot 1500e^{0.2t} = 1200000e^{0.2t}$.

Example

    Given two functions $f(x)$ and $g(x)$, show how you would determine the domain and range of $(f \circ g)(x)$

    The notation $(f \circ g)(x)$ indicates function composition; this can also be written as $f(g(x))$. $(f \circ g)(x)$ can be evaluated at a point $x = x_0$ by first finding $g(x_0)$ and then putting that as the "input" for $f(x)$. In order for a value x_0 to be in the domain of $(f \circ g)(x)$, then, it's necessary first that x_0 be in the domain of $g(x)$ and second that $g(x_0)$ be in the domain of $f(x)$. For instance, if $f(x) = \sqrt{x}$ and $g(x) = x - 2$, then $x = 1$ is not in the domain of $(f \circ g)(x)$, even though it *is* in the domain of $f(x)$ and $g(x)$, since $g(1) = -1$ is not in the domain of $f(x)$.

    Similarly, for a value $y = y_0$ to be in the range of $(f \circ g)(x)$, it's necessary not only that y_0 is in the range of $f(x)$, but that there is at least one value y' in the range of $g(x)$ such that $f(y') = y_0$.

<u>Example</u>

Given an arithmetic sequence expressed recursively, such as $a_1 = 2$, $a_n = a_{n-1} + 3$, explain how to write this sequence in an explicit (nonrecursive) form

An arithmetic sequence is one with a constant difference between consecutive terms: each term is equal to the preceding term plus (or minus) some constant number. An arithmetic sequence can be uniquely characterized by two specific numbers: the first element of the sequence a_1, and the sequence's common difference d. The latter is the difference between two consecutive terms of the sequence; d is positive if the sequence is increasing and negative if the sequence is decreasing.

An arithmetic sequence can be defined recursively by specifying a_1 and then giving the relationship between consecutive terms, $a_n = a_{n-1} + d$. It can also be defined explicitly with the expression $a_n = a_1 + d(n-1)$ (or, equivalently, $a_n = (a_1 - d) + dn$).

Here, we have a recursive definition; by inspecting it, we see that $a_1 = 2$ and $d = 3$. We can simply put those values into the explicit expression to get $a_n = 2 + 3(n-1)$ (or, equivalently, $a_n = -1 + 3n$).

<u>Example</u>

Given a geometric sequence expressed recursively, such as $a_1 = 3$, $a_n = 2a_{n-1}$, determine how to write this sequence in an explicit (nonrecursive) form

A geometric sequence is one with a constant ratio between consecutive terms: each term is equal to the preceding term multiplied (or divided) by some constant number. A geometric sequence can be uniquely characterized by two specific numbers: the first element of the sequence a_1, and the sequence's common ratio r. The latter is the ratio between two consecutive terms of the sequence; r is greater than one if the sequence is increasing and less than one if the sequence is decreasing. (If r is negative, the terms of the sequence alternate between positive and negative.)

A geometric sequence can be defined recursively by specifying a_1 and then giving the relationship between consecutive terms, $a_n = r \cdot a_{n-1}$. It can also be defined explicitly with the expression $a_n = a_1 \cdot r^{n-1}$ (or, equivalently, $a_n = (a_1/r) \cdot r^n$).

Here, we have a recursive definition; by inspecting it, we see that $a_1 = 3$ and $r = 2$. We can simply put those values into the explicit expression to get $a_n = 3 \cdot 2^{n-1}$ (or, equivalently, $a_n = \frac{3}{2} \cdot 2^n$).

<u>Example</u>

> Given an arithmetic sequence defined explicitly, such as $a_n = 3 + 4n$, determine how you can write this sequence in a recursive form
>
> An arithmetic sequence is a sequence in which each term differs from the previous amount by a fixed amount. An arithmetic sequence can be uniquely specified by this fixed difference, d, and the first term, a_1. The sequence can be expressed either explicitly, in the form $a_n = a_1 + d(n-1)$, or recursively, in the form $a_n = a_{n-1} + d$ (after specifying the first term).
>
> In this case, being given the sequence in explicit form, we can find a_1 and d by inspection: $a_n = 3 + 4n = 3 + 4(1 + n - 1) = 3 + 4 + 4(n - 1) = 7 + 4(n - 1)$. So, comparing this to the general equation $a_n = a_1 + d(n-1)$, we find $a_1 = 7$ and $d = 4$. We can therefore write the sequence recursively as follows: $a_1 = 7, a_n = a_{n-1} + 4$.

<u>Example</u>

> Given a geometric sequence defined explicitly, such as $a_n = 3\left(\frac{2}{3}\right)^n$, determine how you can write this sequence in a recursive form
>
> A geometric sequence is a sequence in which each term differs from the previous amount by a fixed ratio. A geometric sequence can be uniquely specified by this fixed ratio, r, and the first term, a_1. The sequence can be expressed either explicitly, in the form $a_n = a_1 r^{n-1}$, or recursively, in the form $a_n = r \cdot a_{n-1}$ (after specifying the first term).
>
> In this case, being given the sequence in explicit form, we can find a_1 and r by inspection: $a_n = 3\left(\frac{2}{3}\right)^n = 3\left(\frac{2}{3}\right)^{1+n-1} = 3\left(\frac{2}{3}\right)\left(\frac{2}{3}\right)^{n-1} = 2\left(\frac{2}{3}\right)^{n-1}$. So, comparing this to the general equation $a_n = a_1 r^{n-1}$, we find $a_1 = 2$ and r$=\frac{2}{3}$. We can therefore write the sequence recursively as follows: $a_1 = 2, a_n = \frac{2}{3}a_{n-1}$.

Situations modeled by arithmetic sequences

An arithmetic sequence is a good model for any situation that involves a quantity that increases at equal intervals by a constant difference. That is, if the quantity is only defined relative to the positive integers (or technically at any other discrete, evenly spaced intervals), and the difference between the quantity corresponding to any two consecutive integers is the same, then it can be modeled by an arithmetic sequence.

Consider, for instance, the following situation: a large jar initially contains five marbles, and every day three more marbles are added to it. This fits the criteria described above: the quantity is defined relative to the positive integers (number of days), and the difference between the quantity corresponding to consecutive integers (the number of marbles on consecutive days) is constant (three). We can model this situation by the arithmetic sequence
$f(n) = 5 + 3(n - 1)$.

Situations modeled by geometric sequences

A geometric sequence is a good model for any situation that involves a quantity that increases at fixed intervals by a fixed ratio. That is, if the quantity is only defined relative to the positive integers (or technically at any other discrete, evenly spaced intervals), and the ratio of the quantity corresponding to any two consecutive integers is the same, then it can be modeled by a geometric sequence.

Consider, for instance, the following situation: the score for completing level one of a video game is 100, and the score for completing each level afterward is double the score for the previous level. This fits the criteria described above: the quantity is defined relative to the positive integers (levels), and the ratio between the quantity corresponding to consecutive integers (the scores for completing two consecutive levels) is constant (two). We can model this situation by the geometric sequence $f(n) = 100 \cdot 2^{n-1}$.

Example

Graphing of a function $f(x)$ compares with the graph of $f(x) + k$ for some constant k. What about the graph of $f(x + k)$

If we replace $f(x)$ by $(x) + k$, this means the y coordinate of each point on the graph increases by k. This means the graph will be displaced vertically by a value of k: for instance, the graph of $y = x^2 + 1$ will be one unit higher than the graph of $y = x^2$. If k is negative, then the graph will be lowered.

Replacing $f(x)$ by $f(x + k)$ effectively means the x coordinate of each point on the graph *decreases* by k. (Consider that $f((x - k) + k) = f(x)$, so evaluating $f(x)$ at $x = x_0$ yields the same value as evaluating $f(x + k)$ at $x = x_0 - k$.) This means the graph will be displaced horizontally to the left by a value of k: for instance, the graph of $y = (x + 1)^2$ will be one unit to the left of the graph of $y = x^2$. If k is negative, the graph will be displaced to the right.

Example

Graphing of a function $f(x)$ compares with the graph of $kf(x)$ for some constant k. What about the graph of $f(kx)$

If we replace $f(x)$ by $kf(x)$, this means the y coordinate of each point on the graph is multiplied k. This means the graph will be stretched vertically by a factor of k: for instance, the graph of $y = 2x^2$ will be stretched by a factor of 2 in the vertical direction relative to the graph of $y = x^2$. If k is less than one, then the graph will be compressed; if k is negative, it will be inverted vertically (in addition to the stretch or compression).

Replacing $f(x)$ by $f(kx)$ effectively means the x coordinate of each point on the graph is *divided* by a factor of k. This means the graph will be compressed horizontally by a factor of k (or, if $k < 1$, stretched horizontally by a factor of $1/k$): for instance, the graph of $y = (2x)^2$ will be compressed horizontally by a factor of two relative to the graph of $y = x^2$. If k is negative, the graph will be inverted horizontally (in addition to the stretch or compression).

- 79 -

Determining from inspection of a graph whether the graph represents an odd or even function

An *odd function* is one for which $f(-x) = -f(x)$. This means that when the x coordinate is inverted, so is the y coordinate. The left half of the graph (to the left of the y-axis) will therefore be an inverted version of the right half (to the right of the y-axis). Rotating the graph by $180°$ inverts both the x and the y coordinates, so an odd function is symmetrical with respect to $180°$ rotations around the origin.

An *even function* is one for which $f(-x) = f(x)$. This means that when the x coordinate is inverted, the y coordinate does not change. The left half of the graph is therefore a mirror image of the right half. Reflecting the graph through the y-axis inverts the x coordinate without changing the y coordinate, so an even function is symmetrical with respect to reflections through the y-axis.

A graph that exhibits neither symmetry is neither even nor odd.

Determining whether a function given algebraically is even or odd

A function $f(x)$ is *even* if it is unchanged when x is replaced by $-x$. It is *odd* if the sign of the function is changed when x is replaced by $-x$. In other words, for an even function, $f(-x) = f(x)$; for an odd function, $f(-x) = -f(x)$. We can therefore check whether a function is even or odd by evaluating $f(-x)$ and checking whether (perhaps after some suitable algebraic manipulation) it is equal to $f(x)$ or $-f(x)$.

For instance, consider the function $f(x) = x^2 + 1$. $f(-x) = (-x)^2 + 1 = x^2 + 1 = f(x)$. $f(-x) = f(x)$, so this function is even. Now consider $g(x) = x^3 + \frac{1}{x}$. $g(-x) = (-x)^3 + \frac{1}{-x} = -x^3 - \frac{1}{x} = -\left(x^3 + \frac{1}{x}\right) = -g(x)$. $g(-x) = -g(x)$, so this function is odd. Finally, consider $h(x) = x - 1$. $h(-x) = -x - 1 = -(x + 1)$. This is equal to neither $h(x)$ nor $-h(x)$, so this function is neither even nor odd.

<u>Example</u>

Given an expression for a function such as $f(x) = x^3 + 1$ or $g(x) = \frac{x}{x-1}$, determine how to find the function's inverse

One algorithm for finding the inverse of the function is as follows: Solve the equation of the function for x—that is, manipulate the equation to get x by itself on one side of the equation. This equation now shows the inverse function of $f(x)$; to write it explicitly as an inverse, change the x to $f^{-1}(x)$ and change each instance of $f(x)$ on the other side of the equation to x.

For instance, we can rewrite our first equation, $f(x) = x^3 + 1$, as $x^3 = f(x) - 1$, so $x = \sqrt[3]{f(x) - 1}$. Writing this explicitly as an inverse function, we can change the x to $f^{-1}(x)$ and the $f(x)$ to x to get $f^{-1}(x) = \sqrt[3]{x - 1}$. Our second example, $g(x) = \frac{x}{x-1}$, takes a little more work: multiplying both sides by $x - 1$ gives $(x - 1)g(x) = x$, which we can rearrange to $xg(x) - x = g(x)$, and finally to $x = \frac{g(x)}{g(x)-1}$. Replacing the x by $g^{-1}(x)$ and the $g(x)$ by x yields $g^{-1}(x) = \frac{x}{x-1}$: this function is its own inverse.

<u>Example</u>

Given a function such as $f(x) = 3x^3 - 4$, determine how you could solve an equation such as $f(x) = 20$

To solve an equation such as $f(x) = 20$, we're not asked to evaluate the function. Rather, we're asked to find a value for x at which the function evaluates to a given value. While in some cases it may be possible to solve such an equation through trial and error, a more reliable method is to use inverse functions (if $f(x)$ is invertible, which is the case here). If we find the inverse $f^{-1}(x)$ of $f(x)$, then we can apply that inverse function to both sides, yielding $f^{-1}(f(x)) = f^{-1}(20)$, which is to say $x = f^{-1}(20)$.

For our sample equation, $f(x) = 3x^3 - 4$, we can find the inverse algebraically. If $y = 3x^3 - 4$, then $3x^3 = y + 4$, $x^3 = \frac{y+4}{3}$, and finally $x = \sqrt[3]{(y+4)/3}$. So $f^{-1}(x) = \sqrt[3]{(x+4)/3}$. We can now find $f^{-1}(20)$: $f^{-1}(20) = \sqrt[3]{(20+4)/3} = \sqrt[3]{24/3} = \sqrt[3]{8} = 2$.

Under what circumstances an equation of the form $f(x) = C$ will have a unique solution

An equation of the form $f(x) = C$ may have one solution, multiple solutions, or no solution. For example, $x + 1 = 1$ has one solution; $x^2 = 1$ has two solutions; $\sin x = 1$ has infinitely many solutions; and $e^x + 2 = 1$ has no solutions.

In order for $f(x) = C$ to have any solutions at all, C must be in the range of $f(x)$. (Note that 1 is not in the range of $f(x) = e^x + 2$.) However, this doesn't guarantee that the solution is unique. If the function $f(x)$ is invertible, then $f(x) = C$ is guaranteed to have a unique solution for all values of C in the range of $f(x)$. If not, then for at least some values of C the solution of $f(x) = C$ will not be unique. For instance, if $f(x) = x^3 - x$, then $f(x) = 0$ has three solutions, since $f(0) = f(1) = f(-1) = 0$, but $f(x) = 6$ has the unique solution $x = 2$.

<u>Example</u>

Given two functions expressed algebraically, explain how to determine whether they are inverses

The simplest way to determine algebraically whether two functions are inverses is to evaluate their composition. If $(f \circ g)(x) = x$ and $(g \circ f)(x) = x$, then $g(x) = f^{-1}(x)$ and vice versa; these two functions are inverses.

For example, consider $f(x) = x^3 + 1$ and $g(x) = \sqrt[3]{x - 1}$. $(f \circ g)(x) = f(\sqrt[3]{x-1}) = (\sqrt[3]{x-1})^3 + 1 = (x-1) + 1 = x$, and $(g \circ f)(x) = g(x^3 + 1) = \sqrt[3]{(x^3 + 1) - 1} = \sqrt[3]{x^3} = x$. These two functions, therefore, are inverses. Some functions are their own inverses. Consider $h(x) = \frac{x}{x-1}$: $(h \circ h)(x) = h\left(\frac{x}{x-1}\right) = \frac{x/(x-1)}{x/(x-1)-1} = \frac{x}{x-(x-1)} = \frac{x}{1} = x$. So $h^{-1}(x) = h(x)$.

Example

If $f(g(x)) = x$ for all x in the domain of $g(x)$, and $g(f(x)) = x$ for all x in the domain of $f(x)$, what does this imply about the relationship between $f(x)$ and $g(x)$

If $f(g(x)) = x$ and $g(f(x)) = x$ for all x in the appropriate domains, then this means that $f(x)$ and $g(x)$ are inverse functions, i.e. $f^{-1}(x) = g(x)$ and $g^{-1}(x) = f(x)$. This means that if $f(x_0) = y_0$, then $g(y_0) = x_0$, and vice versa.

Inverse functions are useful because they can be used to solve equations of the form $f(x) = C$. We can get the solution by simply taking the inverse function of both sides: $f^{-1}(f(x)) = f^{-1}(C)$, but $f^{-1}(f(x)) = x$, so $x = f^{-1}(C)$. For example, the exponential function e^x and the logarithm $\ln x$ are inverses, so we can use the exponential to solve logarithmic functions, and vice versa: if $e^x = 3$, then $\ln e^x = \ln 3$, so $x = \ln 3$.

Example

Given a function represented by a table like the one below, determine how you can find the function's inverse

x	0	1	2	3	4	5	6	7
$f(x)$	4	5	0	2	7	1	6	3

To change a function into its inverse, essentially all we need to do is to interchange its domain and range. Therefore, when the function is given in table form, we can just switch the two rows, as follows:

x	4	5	0	2	7	1	6	3
$f^{-1}(x)$	0	1	2	3	4	5	6	7

Putting the domain in ascending order (which isn't technically necessary, but makes the table easier to refer to) gives:

X	0	1	2	3	4	5	6	7
$f^{-1}(x)$	2	5	3	7	0	1	6	4

So, for instance, $f^{-1}(0) = 2$, and $f^{-1}(1) = 5$ —as we would expect, since $f(2) = 0$ and $f(5) = 1$.

Describe how the graph of a function compares to the graph of its inverse

To convert an invertible function $f(x)$ into its inverse, we interchange the domain and range. This means that the point (x, y) in $f(x)$ maps into the point (y, x) in $f^{-1}(x)$. On a graph, this is equivalent to reflecting the point through the line $y = x$, i.e. flipping it over diagonally, from upper left to lower right. Since this transformation applies to each point, it also applies to the function as a whole: we can get the graph of $f^{-1}(x)$ from the graph of $f(x)$ by just flipping the whole graph over through the diagonal line $y = x$. For example, if the graph of $f(x)$ is the graph shown on the left below, then flipping it over diagonally yields the graph on the right, which is the graph of $f^{-1}(x)$.

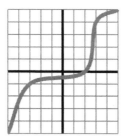 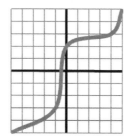

Example

Given a graph of an invertible function $f(x)$ and a value x_0, determine how you can read the value $f^{-1}(x_0)$ from the graph

While it's possible to turn the graph of $f(x)$ into a graph of $f^{-1}(x)$ by simply flipping it over diagonally through the line $y = x$, it's also possible to read values of $f^{-1}(x)$ off the graph of $f(x)$ directly. Just as we can read the value of $f(x_0)$ from a graph by finding the point where the graph intersects the line $x = x_0$ and observing the y coordinate of that point, so we can read the value of $f^{-1}(x_0)$ by the inverse process: We can find the point where the graph intersects the line $y = x_0$, and then read off the point's x-coordinate. The diagram below illustrates this procedure:

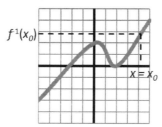

Determine how you can tell from the graph of a function whether the function has an inverse

A function has an inverse if and only if each point in the range corresponds to a unique point in the domain. This is similar to the definition of a function itself—in a function, each point in the domain corresponds to a unique point in the range. Therefore, we can use similar guidelines to identify invertible functions. One simple way to tell whether a graph represents a function is the "vertical line test"; we observe whether there exists any vertical line that intersects the graph in more than one point. Similarly, we can check whether a function is invertible from its graph by using a sort of "horizontal line test": we check whether there exists any *horizontal* line that intersects the function in more than one point. If so, then the y coordinate corresponding to that line is matched up with more than one x coordinate, which means that the function is *not* invertible. If no such horizontal line exists, then the function is invertible.

Example

Given a non-invertible function such as $f(x) = x^2 + 1$ or $g(x) = x^3 - x$, determine how you could produce an invertible function by restricting the domain

What makes these functions non-invertible is that there are certain y values that correspond to more than one x value. For instance, $f(1) = f(-1) = 2$, and $g(-1) = g(0) = g(1) = 0$. However, this only occurs because the graph is increasing in some parts of the domain and decreasing in others. If we restrict the domain to regions where the function is only increasing or decreasing, within these regions each y corresponds to a unique x, so this restricted function is invertible.

Our first example, $f(x) = x^2 + 1$, decreases from $-\infty$ to 0, and increases from 0 to ∞. Restricting the domain to either the interval $(-\infty, 0]$ or $[0, \infty)$ produces an invertible function. Finding exactly where $g(x) = x^3 - x$ transitions between increasing and decreasing is difficult without calculus, but we don't need to know the precise transition points; we can choose a smaller interval over which it's clearly increasing or decreasing. For instance, if we graph $g(x)$, we can see it's clearly increasing for all $x > 1$, so we can get an invertible function by restricting its domain to $[1, \infty)$.

Example

Why is it incorrect (or at least incomplete) to say that the functions $f(x) = x^2$ and $g(x) = \sqrt{x}$ are inverses

At first, it might seem obvious that $f(x) = x^2$ and $g(x) = \sqrt{x}$ are inverses. After all, if we take the function composition $f(g(x))$, we find $f(g(x)) = f(\sqrt{x}) = (\sqrt{x})^2 = x$. However, one characteristic of inverse functions is that the domain of the inverse function is the same as the range of the original function, and vice versa. In this case, the range of $f(x)$ is indeed equal to the domain of $g(x)$: $[0, \infty)$. But the domain of $f(x)$ is not equal to the range of $g(x)$: the former is $(-\infty, \infty)$ but the latter only $[0, \infty)$. And, indeed, while $f(g(x)) = x$, we can find points for which $g(f(x)) \neq x$. For example, $g(f(-1)) = g((-1)^2) = g(1) = \sqrt{1} = 1$.

The root of the problem is that the function $f(x)$ is not invertible. There are elements in the range that match up to multiple points in the domain, such as $f(1) = f(-1) = 1$. If we make a new function $f_+(x)$ by restricting the domain of $f(x)$ to the interval $[0, \infty)$, then indeed $g(x) = f_+^{-1}(x)$.

- 84 -

Example

Is it possible that $f(g(x)) = x$ for all x in the domain of $g(x)$, but $g(f(x)) \neq x$ for some x in the domain of $f(x)$

Yes, it's possible that $f(g(x)) = x$ for all x in the domain of $g(x)$ without the same being true for $g(f(x))$. A simple example is $f(x) = x^2$ and $g(x) = \sqrt{x}$. For all x in the domain of $g(x)$, $f(g(x)) = f(\sqrt{x}) = (\sqrt{x})^2 = x$. However, this isn't true for $g(f(x))$: consider $g(f(-1)) = g((-1)^2) = g(1) = \sqrt{1} = 1 \neq -1$.

The reason that occurs is because in this case $f(x)$ is not an invertible function; there are multiple values of x that correspond to the same value of $f(x)$. Accordingly, there can be no function for which $f(g(x)) = x$ and $g(f(x)) = x$, because then the functions would be inverses. If we restrict $f(x)$ to the interval $[0, \infty)$, to produce a new function $f_2(x)$, then $f_2(x)$ is invertible, $f_2(g(x)) = x$, and $g(f_2(x)) = x$.

Example

Given a logarithmic equation such as $3 \log_2 2x = 15$, determine how you could solve for x.

To solve a logarithmic equation where the variable appears in the argument of the logarithm, we have to use the fact that the exponential function is the inverse of the logarithmic. First, we rearrange the expression to get the logarithmic expression on a side by itself. After that, we can cancel the logarithm by taking the exponential function of both sides (with the same base as the logarithm). From that point on, solving the equation is a matter of simple algebra.

For instance, we can divide by three both sides of our sample equation, $3 \log_2 2x = 15$, to get $\log_2 2x = \frac{15}{3} = 5$. We can now cancel the logarithm with an exponential: $2^{\log_2 2x} = 2^5$, or, simplifying the left hand side, $2x = 2^5$. So $x = \frac{2^5}{2} = \frac{32}{2} = 16$.

Relationship between exponential functions and logarithms

Exponential functions and logarithms are inverse functions. More specifically, an exponential function of a particular base is the inverse of a logarithmic function of the same base. For instance, e^x and $\ln x$ are inverse functions. 10^x and $\log_{10} x$ are inverse functions. And, in general, a^x and $\log_a x$ are inverse functions.

How we can use this relationship to solve problems

This relationship is often useful for solving problems, because we can use it to cancel an exponential or logarithmic function on one side of an equation. For example, given an equation of the form $a^x = C$, we can solve for x by taking the logarithm of both sides: $\log_a(a^x) = \log_a C$, which, since a^x and $\log_a x$ are inverse functions, reduces to $x = \log_a C$. Conversely, given an equation of the form $\log_a x = C$, we can solve for x by taking the exponential of both sides: $a^{\log_a x} = a^C$, which reduces to $x = a^C$.

Describe under what circumstances you would use a logarithmic function to solve a problem

The logarithm is the inverse of the exponential, and so can be used to cancel an exponential function. This is useful if a problem involves an exponential equation in which the variable to be solved for is in the exponent; we can then use the logarithmic equation to get the variable out of the exponent. For instance, we can solve the equation $10^x = 20$ by simply taking the logarithm, base 10, of both sides: $\log_{10}(10^x) = \log_{10}(20)$, thus $x = \log_{10} 20$.

More complex equations may require some algebraic manipulation: from $2e^{3x+5} + 6 = 20$, we get $2e^{3x+5} = 14$, then $e^{3x+5} = 7$. We can now take the logarithm of both sides: $\ln(e^{3x+5}) = \ln 7$, hence $3x + 5 = \ln 7$ and finally $x = (\ln 7 - 5)/3$.

Linear, Quadratic, and Exponential Models

<u>Example</u>

Describe what kind of function grows by equal differences over equal intervals, and prove your answer

A function that grows by equal differences over equal intervals is a *linear function*, a function of the form $f(x) = mx + b$.

To prove that a linear function meets this criterion, we can consider some arbitrary interval, Δx, and then show that $f(x + \Delta x) - f(x)$ does not depend on x—hence, that when x increases by an interval of Δx, $f(x)$ grows by a constant amount. Substituting in the linear function, we get $f(x + \Delta x) - f(x) = (m(x + \Delta x)) + b - (mx + b) = mx + m\Delta x + b - mx - b = m\Delta x$. As expected, this does not depend on x, proving that the linear function grows by equal differences over equal intervals.

<u>Example</u>

Describe what kind of function grows by equal factors over equal intervals, and prove your answer

A function that grows by equal factors over equal intervals is an *exponential function*, a function of the form $f(x) = Ae^{bx}$.

To prove that an exponential function meets this criterion, we can consider some arbitrary interval, Δx, and then show that $f(x + \Delta x)/f(x)$ does not depend on x—hence, that when x increases by an interval of Δx, $f(x)$ grows by a constant factor. Substituting in the exponential function, we get $f(x + \Delta x)/f(x) = Ae^{b(x+\Delta x)}/Ae^{bx} = Ae^{bx}e^{b\Delta x}/Ae^{bx} = e^{b\Delta x}$. As expected, this does not depend on x, proving that the exponential function grows by equal factors over equal intervals.

Phrases in a word problem indicating quantity changes

If one quantity changes at a constant rate relative to another, this means the two quantities have a linear relationship ($y = mx + b$). There are a number of common phrases in a word problem that might indicate this. Rarely are we told directly that the relationship between two quantities is linear, but there are other ways the relationship could be phrased. Consider the following statement: "For every meter you go deeper underwater, the pressure increases by ten thousand Pascals." This says that one quantity—here the pressure—increases at a constant rate—ten thousand Pascals per meter—relative to another—the depth.

Another common phrasing that indicates a linear relationship is the statement that one quantity is proportional to another. This can be expressed algebraically as $y = mx$. Note that not all linear relationships are proportional—only those in which the y intercept is zero—but all proportional relationships are linear.

Example

Describe what kind of equation you would use to model a relationship in which one quantity changes at a constant rate per unit interval relative to another

A relationship in which one quantity changes at a constant rate per unit interval relative to another is necessarily a *linear relationship*, and can be modeled by a linear equation, of the form $f(x) = mx + b$. In this equation, m is equal to the slope of the line, or to the rate at which $f(x)$ changes per unit interval. This rate may be given directly, or it may be possible to derive it from the given information: if, for example, two points in the relationship are given, we can find m by calculating $\frac{f(x_1) - f(x_2)}{x_1 - x_2}$. The constant b is the y intercept, or the value $f(0)$; again, this may be given directly, or may be derivable from given information: if you know m and you're given one data point, you can put these known values into the equation $f(x) = mx + b$ and solve for b.

Example

Suppose you're told an event ticket costs a flat fee of $20 plus $5 per person. Describe how you would write an algebraic expression to describe the total price

To write an expression based on a given situation, the first thing to observe is what quantities we will be concerned with and that will correspond to variables in the expression. In this case, we have a total price that varies by the number of people involved, so we'll be writing $y = f(x)$, where y is the total cost and x is the number of people. Secondly, we can observe exactly how one quantity varies with the other. In this case, the price increases by a fixed amount for each additional person. A situation in which one quantity changes at a constant rate per unit interval relative to the other corresponds to a linear function. In this case, with a flat fee of $20 independent of the number of people, and a fee increase of $5 per person, an appropriate equation is $y = 20 + 5x$.

- 87 -

Phrases in a word problem indicating quantity grows or decays

If one quantity grows or decays by a constant percent rate per unit interval relative to another, this means that the two quantities have an exponential relationship, $y = AB^{Cx}$—or rather, to take into account the percent rate, $y(t) = y_o(1 + P)^{Ct}$, where P is the percent rate. This relationship may be stated directly, but more often it must be partly inferred by other phrases appearing in the problem. For instance, we may be told the number of bacteria in a culture doubles every ten months—"doubles" indicates a percent rate of 100% ($1 + P = 2$, so $P = 1 = 100\%$).

Some common examples of problems involving exponential relationship involve compound interest and radioactive half-lives. In the former, the interest rate is the percent increase, while the coefficient of the exponent depends on how often the interest is compounded—for interest compounded monthly, the exponent would be $t/12$, assuming that t is measured in months. In the latter, the base of the exponent is always $\frac{1}{2}$, and the exponent is $t/t_{1/2}$, where $t_{1/2}$ is the half-life.

<u>Example</u>

> Describe what kind of equation you would use to model a relationship in which one quantity changes by a constant percent rate per unit interval relative to another.

> A relationship in which one quantity changes by a constant percent rate per unit interval relative to another is an *exponential relationship*, and can be modeled by an exponential equation, of the form $f(x) = Ae^{bx}$. If the percent rate of change is positive, then b is positive and the equation represents exponential growth; if the percent rate of change is negative, then b is negative and the equation represents exponential decay. Often in such a problem we are given the value of $f(x)$ when $x = 0$; this is simply A, as can be seen as follows: $f(0) = Ae^{b \cdot 0} = Ae^0 = A \cdot 1 = A$. Given this, if we have at least one other data point, we can use it to solve for b.

<u>Example</u>

> Suppose you're told that an item initially sold for \$200 and its price has increased by 10% per year. Show how you would write an algebraic expression to describe the price

> To write an expression based on a given situation, the first thing to observe is what quantities we will be concerned with and that will correspond to variables in the expression. In this case, we have a price that varies by year, so we'll be writing $y = f(t)$, where y is the total cost and t is the time in years from the item's initial sale. Secondly, we can observe exactly how one quantity varies with the other. In this case, the price increases by a fixed percentage per year. A situation in which one quantity changes at a constant percent rate per unit interval relative to the other corresponds to an exponential function. In this case, with an initial cost of \$200 at $t = 0$ and an increase of 10% per year, an appropriate equation is $y = 200 \cdot 1.1^t$.

Example

Given two points, such as (1,2) and (3,–1), describe how you can find a linear function that includes those points

A linear function is a function of the form $y = mx + b$, where m is the slope of the line and b is its y intercept. Suppose we are given two points, (x_1, y_1) and (x_2, y_2). We can find m by calculating the "rise over run": that is, $m = \frac{y_2 - y_1}{x_2 - x_1}$. Knowing m, we can then put the x and y values of one of the points into the equation $y = mx + b$ to solve for b, the only remaining unknown.

For example, using the sample points (1,2) and (3,–1) we have $m = \frac{-1-2}{3-1} = -\frac{3}{2}$. We can now put that into the linear equation along with the coordinates of the first point, (1,2), to yield $2 = -\frac{3}{2}(1) + b$, which we can solve for b to get $b = \frac{7}{2}$. (Had we used the second point instead of the first, we would have arrived at the same answer.) Therefore, the linear function that includes the two given points is $y = -\frac{3}{2}x + \frac{7}{2}$.

Example

Given two points, one of which has an x value of zero, such as (0,2) and (3,20), show how you can find an exponential function that includes those points

An exponential function has the form $y = Ae^{bx}$. (We could use a different base for the exponent rather than e, but in that case, by the properties of exponents, we'd simply have a different value for b; the form of the equation wouldn't change, and neither would the means of solving it.) If one of the given points has an x value of zero, then finding A is easy: we can just put the x and y values of this point into the equation, and we'll find that $y = A$. For the sample points, using (0,2) we find $2 = Ae^{b \cdot 0} = A$, so $A = 2$.

Knowing A, we can now use the x and y values of the other point to solve for b. For the sample points, putting in (3,20) we get $20 = 2e^{b \cdot 3}$. Dividing both sides by 2 yields $10 = e^{3b}$, and now we can take the natural logarithm of both sides, giving $\ln 10 = 3b$, thus $b = \frac{\ln 10}{3}$. Therefore, our final equation is $y = 2e^{\frac{\ln 10}{3}x} = 2(e^{\ln 10})^{x/3} = 2 \cdot 10^{\frac{x}{3}}$.

<u>Example</u>

Given two points with nonzero x values, such as $(2,4)$ and $(6,60)$, show how you can find an exponential function that includes both point.

An exponential function has the form $y = Ae^{bx}$. Putting the x and y values for the given points into this equation yields two equations: in the case of the sample points, $4 = Ae^{2b}$ and $60 = Ae^{6b}$. We have two equations and two unknowns (A and b), so in principle it should be possible to solve for the unknowns.

There are many ways of doing this. We could, for instance, solve for A in one equation and substitute that value into the other. Another relatively simple method is to take the ratio of the two equations, thus canceling A: $\frac{60}{4} = \frac{Ae^{6b}}{Ae^{2b}}$, thus $15 = \frac{e^{6b}}{e^{2b}} = e^{6b-2b} = e^{4b}$. Taking the natural logarithm of both sides, $\ln 15 = 4b$, so $b = \frac{\ln 15}{4}$.

Knowing b, we can now use either point to solve for A: using $(2,4)$, we get $4 = Ae^{\frac{\ln 15}{4} \cdot 2} = Ae^{\frac{\ln 15}{2}} = A\left(e^{\ln 15}\right)^{\frac{1}{2}} = A \cdot 15^{1/2} = \sqrt{15}A$, so $A = \frac{4\sqrt{15}}{15}$. Our full equation is then $y = \frac{4\sqrt{15}}{15}e^{\frac{\ln 15}{4}x} = \frac{4\sqrt{15}}{15}\left(e^{\ln 15}\right)^{x/4} = \frac{4\sqrt{15}}{15} \cdot 15^{\frac{x}{4}}$.

<u>Example</u>

Given a graph of a linear function, determine how you can construct an algebraic expression for the function

An algebraic expression for a linear function has the form $y = mx + b$. We can find both m and b from the graph of the function. b is simply equal to the y intercept, and can be read from the graph by observing at what point the graph of the linear function intersects the y-axis. To find m, the slope, we can take from the graph any two points that lie on the line, (x_1, y_1) and (x_2, y_2). The slope m is then equal to $m = \frac{y_1 - y_2}{x_1 - x_2}$.

There are two special cases that must be treated differently: horizontal and vertical lines. A horizontal line has a slope of zero; its equation is $y = b$, where b is, again, the y intercept (or the y coordinate of any other point on the line). Conversely, the slope of a vertical line is undefined; its equation is $x = a$, where a is the x intercept (or the x coordinate of any other point on the line).

Example

Given a graph of an exponential function, describe how you can construct an algebraic expression for the function

An algebraic expression for an exponential function has the form $y = Ae^{bx}$. A can be found directly from the graph; it is simply the graph's y intercept. To see this, consider what happens when we evaluate the expression at $x = 0$: $y = Ae^{b \cdot 0} = Ae^0 = A \cdot 1 = A$. Once we know A, we can choose any other point (x_1, y_1) that lies on the graph of the function *except* the y intercept. We can then use this to solve for b: $y_1 = Ae^{bx_1}$, so $\frac{y_1}{A} = e^{bx_1}$, $\ln\left(\frac{y_1}{A}\right) = \ln(e^{bx_1}) = bx_1$, and finally $b = \frac{1}{x_1}\ln\left(\frac{y_1}{A}\right)$. For instance, if the y intercept is $(0, 2)$ and the graph also passes through the point $(5,4)$, then we have $4 = 2e^{b \cdot 5}$, hence $2 = e^{5b}$, $\ln 2 = 5b$, and $b = \frac{\ln 2}{5}$. So an algebraic expression for the function is $y = 2e^{\frac{\ln 2}{5}x}$. This can be simplified: $2e^{\frac{\ln 2}{5}x} = 2\left(e^{\ln 2}\right)^{\frac{1}{5}x} = 2 \cdot 2^{\frac{1}{5}x} = 2^{\frac{1}{5}x+1}$. So $y = 2 \cdot 2^{\frac{1}{5}x}$ and $y = 2^{\frac{1}{5}x+1}$ are both acceptable ways to write the expression.

Example

Describe how you can write an algebraic expression for an arithmetic sequence given two (not necessarily consecutive) terms of the sequence

An arithmetic sequence is a sequence in which there is a constant difference d between consecutive terms. It can be expressed by the formula $f(n) = a_1 + d(n - 1)$. Suppose we are given two terms of the sequence, $f(n_1)$ and $f(n_2)$. Since the difference between consecutive terms is d, the difference between terms Δn terms apart is simply $\Delta n \cdot d$. In this case, $\Delta n = (n_2 - n_1)$, so $f(n_2) - f(n_1) = (n_2 - n_1)d$, and $d = \frac{f(n_2)-f(n_1)}{n_2-n_1}$. Knowing d, we can use one of the given terms to solve for a_1: $f(n_1) = a_1 + d(n_1 - 1)$, so $a_1 = f(n_1) - d(n_1 - 1)$.

For example, suppose we are told that the third term of an arithmetic sequence is 5 and the seventh term is 17—that is, $f(3) = 5$ and $f(7) = 17$. Then $17 - 5 = (7 - 3)d$, hence $d = \frac{17-5}{7-3} = \frac{12}{4} = 3$. We can now solve for a_1: $5 = a_1 + 3(3 - 1)$, so $a_1 = 5 - 3(3 - 1) = 5 - 3(2) = -1$. So an expression for this arithmetic sequence is $f(n) = -1 + 3(n - 1)$.

<u>Example</u>

Describe how you can write an algebraic expression for a geometric sequence given two (not necessarily consecutive) terms of the sequence

A geometric sequence is a sequence in which there is a constant ratio r between consecutive terms. It can be expressed by the formula $f(n) = a_1 r^{n-1}$. Suppose we are given two terms of the sequence, $f(n_1)$ and $f(n_2)$. Since the ratio of consecutive terms is r, the ratio of terms Δn terms apart is simply $r^{\Delta n}$. In this case, $\Delta n = (n_2 - n_1)$, so $f(n_2)/f(n_1) = r^{n_2 - n_1}$, and $r = \left(f(n_2)/f(n_1)\right)^{1/(n_2 - n_1)}$. Knowing r, we can use one of the given terms to solve for a_1: $f(n_1) = a_1 r^{n_1 - 1}$, so $a_1 = f(n_1)/r^{n_1 - 1}$.

For example, suppose we are told that the ninth term of an arithmetic sequence is 40 and the fifteenth term is 5—that is, $f(9) = 40$ and $f(15) = 5$. Then $\frac{5}{40} = r^{15-9} = r^6$, hence $r = \left(\frac{5}{40}\right)^{1/6} = \left(\frac{1}{8}\right)^{1/6} = \frac{1}{8^{\frac{1}{6}}} = \frac{1}{\sqrt[6]{8}} = \frac{1}{\sqrt{2}} = \frac{\sqrt{2}}{2}$. We can now solve for a_1: $40 = a_1 \left(\frac{\sqrt{2}}{2}\right)^{9-1} = a_1 \left(\frac{\sqrt{2}}{2}\right)^8 = a_1 \left(\frac{1}{16}\right)$, so $a_1 = 40/(1/16) = 40 \cdot 16 = 640$. So an expression for this arithmetic sequence is $f(n) = 640 \cdot \left(\frac{\sqrt{2}}{2}\right)^{n-1}$.

Exponential functions (with a positive exponent) eventually exceeds any polynomial function

An exponential function has the form $y = Ae^{bx}$. A polynomial function has the form $y = a_n x^n + a_{n-1} x^{n-1} + \cdots + a_1 x + a_0$. The exponential always exceeds the polynomial for sufficiently large x, regardless of the values of A, b, n, and $a_0 \ldots a_n$.

One way to see this is to consider the rate of change. One characteristic of an exponential function is that over a fixed interval it changes by a constant ratio: when x increases by 1, Ae^{bx} increases by e^b. This isn't true of polynomials; for large x, when only the leading term of the polynomial is significant, when x increases by 1 the polynomial increases by a ratio of $\frac{(x+1)^n}{x^n} = \left(\frac{x+1}{x}\right)^n$, which *decreases* as x increases, converging at very large x to 1. Therefore, eventually the rate of change of the polynomial will drop below the rate of change of the exponential, and thereafter at some point the exponential will surpass the polynomial.

<u>Example</u>

The graph below shows a cubic function, an exponential function, a linear function, a logarithmic function, and a quadratic function

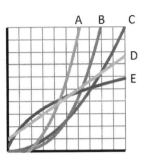

All of these functions tend toward infinity in their right end behavior, but some of them do so more rapidly than others. An exponential equation eventually increases more rapidly than any polynomial, and certainly increases more rapidly than a logarithmic function. The function that, in the end, increases most rapidly must therefore be the exponential, namely A. Conversely, the logarithmic function, the inverse of the exponential, must eventually increase more *slowly* than any polynomial. The logarithmic function must be the one that increases the most slowly in the end, namely E.

This leaves B, C, and D as the cubic, linear, and quadratic. These are all polynomial functions, and in its end behavior a polynomial of a larger order (largest exponent) increases more rapidly than one of a smaller order. This means B must be the cubic (order 3), C the quadratic (order 2), and D the linear (order 1).

Determining how to tell which is a cubic function, an exponential function, a linear function, a logarithmic function, and a quadratic function

x	1	2	3	4	5	6	7	8	9	10
$f(x)$	0.00	0.60	1.60	3.00	4.80	7.00	9.60	12.60	16.00	19.80
$g(x)$	2.00	2.12	2.43	3.05	4.07	5.58	7.70	10.52	14.13	18.65
$h(x)$	4.00	5.39	6.20	6.77	7.22	7.58	7.89	8.16	8.39	8.61
$j(x)$	0.03	0.09	0.27	0.81	2.43	7.29	21.87	65.61	196.83	590.49
$k(x)$	0.50	1.00	1.50	2.00	2.50	3.00	3.50	4.00	4.50	5.00

$k(x)$ increases by a constant rate (0.5) per unit interval, and consecutive terms of $j(x)$ differ by a constant ratio (3), so $k(x)$ must be the linear function and $j(x)$ the exponential. However, we can also determine which function is which by comparing their end behavior. The function that, in the end, increases most rapidly must be the exponential, namely $j(x)$. Conversely, the logarithmic function, the inverse of the exponential, must eventually increase more *slowly* than any polynomial. Although $k(10) < h(10)$, it's clear that $h(x)$ is increasing at a much slower rate than $k(x)$, and for sufficiently large x in the end $k(x) > h(x)$. $h(x)$ is therefore the logarithmic function.

The remaining functions are all polynomials of varying degrees. In its end behavior a polynomial of a larger order (largest exponent) increases more rapidly than one of a smaller order. Observing the end behavior of $f(x)$, $g(x)$, and $k(x)$, we therefore conclude that $k(x)$ must be the lowest degree (linear), $f(x)$ the next (quadratic), and $g(x)$ the highest degree (cubic).

Determining how to express the solution of an equation of the form $ab^{ct} = d$ in terms of a logarithm

To express the solution of an equation of the form $ab^{ct} = d$ in terms of a logarithm, we'll have to take the logarithm of both sides of the equation. Before doing that, though, we'd have to isolate the exponential on a side by itself. We can do that by dividing both sides by a: $b^{ct} = d/a$. To cancel an exponential with a base of b, we have to use a logarithm with the base of b: $\log_b b^{ct} = \log_b(d/a)$. Since the logarithm is the inverse of the exponential, the left side, $\log_b b^{ct}$, reduces to just ct. So $ct = \log_b(d/a)$, so $t = \frac{\log_b(d/a)}{c}$. (Using the rule $\log(\alpha/\beta) = \log \alpha - \log \beta$, we can also rewrite this as $t = \frac{\log_b d - \log_b a}{c}$.)

<u>Example</u>

Given an exponential equation such as $20 = 4 \cdot 2^{3x}$, show how you could solve for x

To solve an exponential equation where the variable appears in the exponent, we have to use the fact that the logarithmic function is the inverse of the exponential. First, we rearrange the expression to get the exponential expression on a side by itself. After that, we can cancel the exponential by taking the logarithm of both sides (with the same base as the exponential). From that point on, solving the equation is a matter of simple algebra.

For instance, we can divide by four both sides of our sample equation, $20 = 4 \cdot 2^{3x}$, to get $2^{3x} = \frac{20}{4} = 5$. We can now cancel the exponential with a logarithm: $\log_2 2^{3x} = \log_2 5$, or, simplifying the left hand side, $3x = \log_2 5$. So $x = \frac{1}{3}\log_2 5$.

Using a calculator to evaluate logarithms such as $\log_e 2$, $\log_{10} 7$, and $\log_2 5$

The logarithm base e is also called the natural logarithm, abbreviated ln: so $\log_e 2$ is the same thing as $\ln 2$. Scientific calculators generally have an "ln" button, so evaluating natural logarithms is straightforward: to evaluate $\ln 2$ on a TI-84 calculator, for instance, just involves hitting "LN", "2", "ENTER". Similarly, most scientific calculators have a button to calculate logarithms base 10, though it often just says "log" without the base. On a TI-84, $\log_{10} 7$ can be evaluated by hitting "LOG", "7", "ENTER".

Evaluating logarithms with bases other than 10 and e is not quite as straightforward, but still possible using the relation $\log_a b = \frac{\log_c b}{\log_c a}$ (for any base c). Therefore $\log_2 5 = \ln 5 / \ln 2$ or $\log_{10} 5 / \log_{10} 2$, either of which is readily evaluable with a calculator.

Example

In the equation of a linear function, $y = mx + b$, what is the physical significance of the parameters m and b

The parameter m is the slope of the line. Regarding the relationship between the physical quantities symbolized by x and y, m is the *rate of change* of y with respect to x: specifically, when x increases by 1, y increases by the amount m.

b is often known as the *y-intercept* of the line: it represents the y coordinate of the point where the line crosses the y-axis. Another way of saying this, and one that makes its physical significance clearer, is that b is the value of y when $x = 0$. When x represents time (as is frequently the case), then b is the *initial value* of y.

Example

Given an exponential equation such as the compound interest equation $A = P\left(1 + \frac{r}{n}\right)^{nt}$, determine how to interpret its parameters in terms of the context

While we could memorize the meaning of each parameter in the compound interest equation $A = P\left(1 + \frac{r}{n}\right)^{nt}$, it's also possible to figure out what they mean by examining the exponential equation. The amount of money in an account with compound interest rises exponentially as a function of time. The quantity that rises exponentially in this equation is A, so that must be the total amount of money in the account. The variable in the exponent is t, so that must be time. (There's also an n in the exponent, but that appears elsewhere as well.) P is the amount of money in the account when $t = 0$, so that must be the initial amount of money deposited in the account (the *principal*).

Two parameters of compound interest remain: the interest rate and the interval over which it's compounded (monthly, quarterly, etc.) The latter must be n, since it affects the exponent: interest compounded monthly would rise exponentially faster than interest compounded quarterly, for instance. That leaves r for the interest rate.

<u>Example</u>

Given a logarithmic equation such as the equation for the loudness of a sound in decibels in terms of its intensity, $\beta = 10 \log_{10}\left(\frac{I}{I_0}\right)$, determine how to interpret its parameters in terms of the context

Even if we're not familiar with this equation, we can figure out what its parameters mean by examining the equation. Since the equation is for the loudness of a sound, that must be what the β stands for. This means the intensity, the other quantity mentioned, must be either I or I_0. If the intensity were I_0, that would mean that as the sound intensity increases, the loudness decreases, which seems illogical. It stands to reason, then that I represents the sound intensity. As for I_0, since it doesn't correspond to one of the variables, it must just be a constant factor.

As it happens, I_0 is defined as 10^{-12} watts, but even without knowing that, we can still get useful information from this equation; for instance, we can tell that if a sound's intensity increases by a factor of 100, then its loudness increases by 20 decibels.

Interpreting Categorical and Quantitative Data

Dot plot, histogram, and box plot

Dot plots, histograms, and box plots are three different methods of representing data sets in graphical form. While they all have similar purposes, some are more suitable for some data sets than others. Dot plots represent each data point as a separate dot, and are most useful for relatively small data sets with a small number of possible values. When the data set contains more than a few dozen points, dot plots may become unwieldy. For larger data sets, where the data distribution is continuous rather than discrete, histograms may be more practical. Histograms are especially useful to estimate the density of the data, and to estimate probability density functions. Box plots may be used to summarize the shape of a larger number of univariate data values; they are most useful for comparing separate groups of data, such as the results of several different experiments, or the statistics of several discrete populations.

<u>Dot plot</u>
A dot plot is a representation of a data set in which each data point is represented by a dot or similar marking, with matching data points grouped in columns. For instance, the data set {2, 1, 3, 1, 1, 5, 4, 4, 3, 3, 3, 4, 1, 5} can be represented as a dot plot as follows:

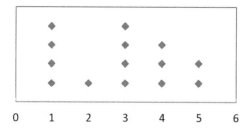

For large data sets, it is possible for each dot in a dot plot to represent more than one data point. However, for such data sets other representations may be more suitable.

Histogram

A histogram is a representation of a data set in which the data are represented by bars corresponding to discrete intervals, with the height of each bar representative of the number of data points falling in the corresponding interval. For example, the data set {101, 141, 105, 159, 122, 107, 145, 153, 183, 172, 164, 162, 144, 132, 138, 116, 155, 147, 141, 129, 168, 145, 152} can be represented by a histogram as follows:

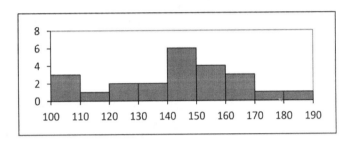

Histograms are useful for large data sets with values that may range continuously over intervals rather than being confined to discrete possibilities.

Box plot

A *box plot*, or box-and-whisker plot, is a representation of one or more data sets in which each data set is represented by a box with a bar in the middle and a "whisker" on each side. The bar represents the *median* of the data, and the edges of the box represent the first and third quartiles. The ends of the whiskers may represent the maximum and minimum data values, although often outliers are excluded and are represented instead as discrete points.

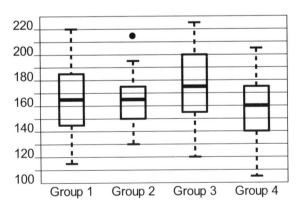

For example, given the data, 5, 5, 6, 9, 12, 14, 15, 17, 17, 21, 24, 26, 29, 31, 36, 38, 39, 46, 47, 49, the following summary statistics may be recorded: Median = 22.5, Q1 = 13, Q3 = 37, minimum = 5, and maximum = 49. Thus, a box plot of this data will show a box, with a middle bar at the value, 22.5, edges of the box at the values, 13 and 37, and whiskers at the values, 5 and 49. Box plots are useful when it is desired to compare the statistics of multiple related data sets, such as several different groups of experimental subjects.

Measures of central tendency

Mean

The mean is the average of the data points; that is, it is the sum of the data points divided by the number of data points. Mathematically, the mean of a set of data points $\{x_1, x_2, x_3, \ldots x_n\}$ can be written as $\bar{X} = \sum \frac{X}{N}$. For instance, for the data set (1, 3, 6, 8, 100, 800), the mean is $\frac{1+3+6+8+100+800}{6} = 153$.

The mean is most useful, when data is approximately normal and does not include extreme outliers. In the above example, the data shows much variation. Thus, the mean is not the best measure of central tendency to use, when interpreting the data. With this data set, the median will give a more complete picture of the distribution.

Median

The median is the value in the middle of the data set, in the sense that 50% of the data points lie above the median and 50% of the data points lie below. The median can be determined by simply putting the data points in order, and selecting the data point in the middle. If there is an even number of data points, then the median is the average of the middle two data points. For instance, for the data set {1, 3, 6, 8, 100, 800}, the median is $\frac{6+8}{2} = 7$.

For distributions with widely varying data points, especially those with large outliers, the median is a more appropriate measure of central tendency, and thus gives a better idea of a "typical" data point. Notice in the data set above, the mean is 153, while the median is 7.

Mode

The mode is the value that appears most often in the data set. For instance, for the data set {2, 6, 4, 9, 4, 5, 7, 6, 4, 1, 5, 6, 7, 5, 6}, the mode is 6: the number 6 appears four times in the data set, while the next most frequent values, 4 and 5, appear only three times each. It is possible for a data set to have more than one mode: in the data set {11, 14, 17, 16, 11, 17, 12, 14, 17, 14, 13}, 14 and 17 are both modes, appearing three times each. In the extreme case of a uniform distribution—a distribution in which all values appear with equal probability—all values in the data set are modes.

The mode is useful to get a general sense of the shape of the distribution; it shows where the peaks of the distribution are. More information is necessary to get a more detailed description of the full shape.

Relation to shape of measurement

The measurement of central tendency with the most clearly visible relationship to the shape is the mode. The mode defines the peak of the distribution, and a distribution with multiple modes has multiple peaks. The relationship of the shape to the other measurements of central tendency is more subtle. For a symmetrical distribution with a single peak, the mode, median, and mean all coincide. For a distribution skewed to the left or right, however, this is not generally the case. One rule of thumb often given is that the median is displaced from the mode in the same direction as the skew of the graph, and the mean in the same direction farther still.

First quartile

The first quartile of a data set is a value greater than or equal to one quarter of the data points (and less than the other three quarters). Various methods exist for defining the first quartile precisely; one of the simplest is to define the first quartile as the median of the first half of the ordered data (excluding the median if there are an odd number of data points).

Applying this method, for example, to the data set {3, 1, 12, 7, 17, 4, 10, 8, 9, 20, 4}, we proceed as follows: Putting the data in order, we get {1, 3, 4, 4, 7, 8, 9, 10, 12, 17, 20}. The first half (excluding the median) is {1, 3, 4, 4, 7}, which has a median of 4. Therefore the first quartile of this data set is 4.

Third quartile

The third quartile of a data set is a value greater than or equal to three quarters of the data points (and less than the remaining quarter). Various methods exist for defining the third quartiles precisely; one of the simplest is to define the third quartile as the median of the second half of the ordered data (excluding the median if there are an odd number of data points). Applying this method, for example, to the data set {3, 1, 12, 7, 17, 4, 10, 8, 9, 20, 4}, we proceed as follows: Putting the data in order, we get {1, 3, 4, 4, 7, 8, 9, 10, 12, 17, 20}. The second half (excluding the median) is {9, 10, 12, 17, 20}, which has a median of 12. Therefore the third quartile of this data set is 12.

Interquartile range of a data set

The interquartile range of a data set is the difference between the third and first quartiles. That is, one quarter of the data fall below the interquartile range and one quarter of the data above it. Exactly half of the data points fall within the interquartile range, half of those above the median and half below. (This is, of course, why the quartile points are called "quartiles", because they divide the data into quarters: one quarter of the data points are below the first quartile, one quarter between the first and second quartile (the median), and so on.) The interquartile range is useful to get a rough idea of the spread of the data. The median by itself shows where the data are centered (or rather, shows one measure of central tendency); the interquartile range gives a better idea of how much the data points vary from this center.

Standard deviation

The standard deviation of a data set is a measurement of how much the data points vary from the mean. More precisely, it is equal to the square root of the average of the squares of the differences between each point and the mean: $s_x = \sqrt{\frac{\sum(X - \bar{X})^2}{N - 1}}$.

The standard deviation is useful for determining the spread, or dispersion, of the data, or how far they vary from the mean. The smaller the standard deviation, the closer the values tend to be to the mean; the larger the standard deviation, the more they tend to be scattered far from the mean.

Outlier

An outlier is an extremely high or extremely low value in the data set. It may be the result of measurement error, in which case, the outlier is not a valid member of the data set. However, it may also be a valid member of the distribution. Unless a measurement error is identified, the experimenter cannot know for certain if an outlier is or is not a member of the distribution. There are arbitrary methods that can be employed to designate an extreme value as an outlier. One method designates an outlier (or possible outlier) to be any value less than $Q_1 - 1.5(IQR)$ or any value greater than $Q_3 + 1.5(IQR)$, where Q_1 and Q_3 are the first and third quartiles and IQR is the interquartile range. For instance, in the data set {42, 71, 22, 500, 33, 38, 62, 44, 58, 37, 61, 25}, the point 500 may be considered an outlier, since 500 is greater than 101.25 (61.5 + 1.5(26.5) = 101.25).

Effect on measurements of the center and spread of a data distribution

Regarding measurements of the center, outliers tend to have little or no effect on the mode, and in general little effect on the median, though their effects may be magnified for very small distributions. Means, however, are very sensitive to outliers; a single data point that lies far outside the range of the others may leave the mode and median almost unchanged while drastically altering the mean. For instance, the data set {2, 2, 5, 5, 5, 8, 11} has a mode and median of 5 and a mean of approximately 5.4; adding the outlying value 650 to the data set leaves the mode and median unchanged but increases the mean to 86.

Like the median, the interquartile range is little affected by outliers, though, again, the effect may be greater for small data sets. The standard deviation, like the mean, is much more sensitive to outliers, and may be significantly increased by a single outlier that lies far from the spread of the rest of the points.

Two data sets with the same center but different spreads

It's certainly possible for two data sets to have the same center but different spreads; all that's necessary is for the points in one set to be clustered closer to the center than the other. Consider, for instance, two data sets that both have the normal distribution with the same mean but different standard deviations: all usual measurements of central tendency would match—the mean, mode, and median—but their spread, as measured by either interquartile range or by standard deviation, would differ. The graph below shows the distributions of two such data sets:

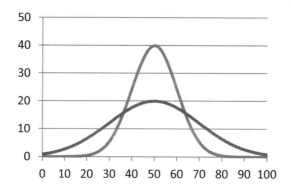

Two data sets with the same spread but different centers

It's certainly possible for two data sets to have the same spread but different centers; nothing prevents the data points of two sets from being equally near the center even if the center differs. Consider, for instance, two data sets that both have the normal distribution with the same standard deviation but different means: their spread, as measured by either interquartile range or by standard deviation, would match, but the measures of central tendency, mean, mode, and median—would differ between the data sets. The graph below shows the distributions of two such data sets:

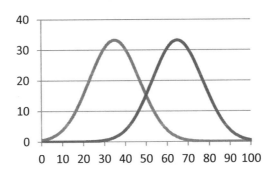

Two data distributions with the same spread and center but different shapes

It's certainly possible for two data distributions to have the same spread and center but different shapes. While the spread and the center are significant characteristics of a distribution, they are not sufficient to uniquely determine the distribution; two distributions may very well have the same spread and center but differ in the details. Consider, for instance, the data sets {5, 10, 15, 20, 25, 30, 35} and {7, 10, 11, 20, 29, 30, 33}: both these data sets have a mean and median of 20, an interquartile range of 20, and a standard deviation of approximately 10.8; yet clearly they are not identical, and have different shapes. For another example, consider an asymmetric distribution reflected about its mean; despite their different shapes, the distribution and its reflection have the same mean and necessarily the same spread.

Normal distribution

A normal distribution is a symmetrical, bell-shaped distribution that can be used to model real-world situations. In particular, the normal distribution is a good match for data that represents the sum or the mean of a large number of similar variables acting independently. If you roll a large number of dice, for instance, their mean will tend to follow close to a normal distribution. The normal distribution has a number of useful properties. Perhaps the most notable is that the distribution of the sum or difference of two variables each of which follows the normal distributions is itself another normal distribution, with the mean equal to the sum or difference of the means of the distributions of the original variables, and the standard deviation equal to the square root of the sum of the squares of the standard deviations of the original distributions.

<u>Circumstances not appropriate for normal distribution</u>
Many data sets that arise in real-world problems can be fit to or at least approximated by a normal distribution, and given the useful properties of this distribution it's often useful to

do so. However, the normal distribution is not a good fit for all data sets. In general, if a data set seems to follow a symmetrical bell curve, it is likely (though not necessarily the case) that it can be usefully fit to a normal distribution. For a data sets that is clearly skewed and asymmetrical, however, such a fit is not suitable. Nor is it appropriate to try to fit to a normal distribution data sets that have no peaks or multiple peaks (though it may be possible to fit such data to a sum of normal distributions).

<u>Generating normal distribution from the given mean and standard deviation</u>

The normal distribution is defined by the normal equation, $f(x) = \frac{1}{\sigma\sqrt{2\pi}}e^{-\frac{1}{2}\left(\frac{x-\mu}{\sigma}\right)^2}$, where μ is the mean and σ is the standard deviation. Generating a normal equation corresponding to a given mean and standard deviation, then, is as simple as putting the appropriate values for μ and σ into this equation. A standard deviation with a mean of 100 and a standard deviation of 10, for instance, would have a normal equation $f(x) = \frac{1}{10\sqrt{2\pi}}e^{-\frac{1}{2}\left(\frac{x-100}{10}\right)^2}$. The probability that the data lies within a certain range can be found by determining the area under the normal curve—the graph of the normal function—within the given range.

It's often simpler, however, to consider the standard normal distribution, with the equation $f(z) = \frac{1}{\sqrt{2\pi}}e^{-\frac{1}{2}z^2}$. This is simply a normal distribution with a mean of 0 and a standard deviation of 1. A standard z-distribution is represented by the formula, $z = \frac{X-\mu}{\sigma}$.

<u>Estimating population percentages</u>
The population percentages falling within certain ranges in a normal distribution can be estimated by finding the area under the normal curve. This can either be estimated by inspection or determined using a calculator. For certain values, however, the population percentages can be estimated more directly. About 68% of the data points in a normal distribution lie within one standard deviation of the mean, about 95% within two standard deviations, and about 99.9% within three. For a normal distribution with a mean of 100 and a standard deviation of 10, for instance, we would expect 68% of the data points to lie between 90 and 110 (100 ± 10), and 95% of the data points to lie between 80 and 120. Because of the normal distribution's symmetry, half of these would lie on each side of the mean, so, for instance, about 34% of the data points would lie between 90 and 100 and 34% between 100 and 110; about 2.5% of the data points (½(100% – 95%)) would exceed 120.

Estimating area under a normal curve

<u>Using a calculator</u>
Most scientific calculators have statistical functions that allow the easy calculation of probabilities related to common probability distributions, including the normal distribution. The details depend on the particular model of calculator. In the TI-84, one of the most commonly used calculators today, the appropriate function can be accessed from the DISTR button (press "2nd", and then "VARS"). This will bring up a menu of distribution-related functions; select "normalcdf". The parameters of this function are, in order, the lower bound, the upper bound, the mean, and the standard deviation. For a normal distribution with a mean of 100 and a standard deviation of 10, for instance, to find the probability that a data point lies between 105 and 115 you would enter "normalcdf(105, 115, 100, 10)", yielding an answer of about 0.242, or 24.2%.

If you desire to see the area visually, you can hit the right arrow from the DISTR menu to get to the DRAW menu, and choose "ShadeNorm". The parameters are the same as for the "normalcdf" function.

Using a spreadsheet

Most modern spreadsheet programs include functions that allow the user to find the area under a normal curve. In Microsoft Excel, the appropriate function is NORMDIST, which gives the total area of the graph to the left of a particular value. The first parameter of this function is the value in question, the second is the mean, and the third the standard deviation. The fourth parameter should be simply set to TRUE. (If it's set to FALSE, Excel will return the value of the normal function at that point rather than the area under the curve.) For instance, for a normal distribution with a mean of 100 and a standard deviation of 10, to find the area under the curve to the left of 115, you would enter into the cell "=NORMDIST(115,100,10,TRUE)".

To find the area within a given interval, you can simply take the difference of two results. For instance, for the previous example, the area of the curve between 105 and 115 would be generated by "=NORMDIST(115,100,10,TRUE)-NORMDIST(105,100,10,TRUE)".

Using a table

Z-tables are available and give the total area under a normal curve to the left of a given value (or the larger portion). The area within an interval can be found by taking the difference between the areas for the right and left endpoints. A mean to z table is also available and may be used to find the area between the mean and a given value. This table may also be used, in order to find the area to the left (or right) or a value, by adding half the area under the normal curve (0.5), to the mean to z area represented by the given value.

Z-tables represent standardized values. The raw values are not represented by the table. Instead, the table represents standardized z-scores. A z-score is written as: $z = \frac{X-\mu}{\sigma}$, where X represents the particular value, μ represents the population mean, and σ represents the population standard deviation. (Literally translated, a z-score represents the number of standard deviations a value is above, or below, the mean.)For instance, if we wanted to find the area under the curve between 105 and 115 for a normal distribution with a mean of 100 and a standard deviation of 10, we would first convert our values to those appropriate for a normal distribution, $\frac{105-100}{10} = 0.5$ and $\frac{115-100}{10} = 1.5$, and then look up 1.5 and 0.5 in the table and subtract the results.

# of students	SPANISH	FRENCH	GERMAN
MALE	30	20	25
FEMALE	26	28	21

Two-way frequency table

A two-way frequency table is a table that shows the number of data points falling into each combination of two categories in the form of a table, with one category on each axis. Creating a two-way frequency table is simply a matter of drawing a table with each axis labeled with the possibilities for the corresponding category, and then filling in the numbers in the appropriate cells. For instance, suppose you're told that at a given school, 30 male

- 103 -

students take Spanish, 20 take French, and 25 German, while 26 female students take Spanish, 28 French, and 21 German. These data can be represented by the following two-way frequency table:

		Category #1 (Color)			TOTALS
		yellow	grey	black	
Category #2 (Vehicle)	truck	2	5	20	27
	car	2	25	3	30
	motorcycle	15	4	3	22
TOTALS		19	34	26	79

Joint and marginal frequencies

The joint frequency, $P(X, Y)$, is the probability of belonging to two specific subcategories. It's also known as a joint probability or joint relative frequency. The marginal frequency, $P(X)$, is the probability of belonging in a specific subcategory. It's also known as a marginal probability or marginal relative frequency. For example,

The joint frequency that a vehicle is a yellow truck is equal to $\frac{2}{79}$, where 2 is the number in the table cell corresponding to both "truck" and "yellow" and 79 is the total number of all vehicles of all colors.

The marginal frequency that a vehicle is a truck is equal to the sum of the probabilities of its being a yellow truck, a grey truck, or a black truck, $P(truck) = \frac{2}{79} + \frac{5}{79} + \frac{20}{79} = \frac{27}{79}$.

Conditional frequency

The conditional frequency, $P(X|Y)$, is the probability that X is a certain value on the condition that Y is a certain value. It's also known as a conditional probability or conditional relative frequency. The conditional frequency is related to the joint frequency and the marginal frequency by the relation $P(X, Y) = P(X|Y)P(Y)$; thus knowing the joint and marginal frequencies we can find the conditional frequency.

For example, consider the two-way frequency table below.

		Category #1 (Color)			TOTALS
		yellow	grey	black	
Category #2 (Vehicle)	truck	2	5	20	27
	car	2	25	3	30
	motorcycle	15	4	3	22
TOTALS		19	34	26	79

The joint frequency that a vehicle is a yellow truck is equal to $\frac{2}{79}$, and the marginal frequency that a vehicle is a truck is $\frac{27}{79}$. Therefore, the conditional frequency that a vehicle is yellow on the condition that it is a truck (the probability that a given truck in the data set is yellow) is equal to $\frac{2}{79} \div \frac{27}{79} = \frac{2}{27}$.

Scatter plots

<u>Representing data on two quantitative variables</u>
Data sets on two quantitative variables can be represented on a scatter plot by plotting each data point as a separate point on the chart. One axis of the chart corresponds to each variable, and then the data points are plotted accordingly in the appropriate positions on each axis. For instance, if 50 widgets cost $500, 100 widgets cost $800, and 200 widgets cost $1500, this can be plotted on a scatter plot as follows:

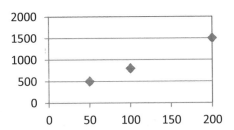

Normally, of course, a scatter plot would be used for larger data sets than this. A scatter plot is useful for seeing the relationship between the variables; one can often see at a glance if the variables have a linear or other simple relationship.

<u>Determining the function that fits the data for two variables</u>
It's often possible from examining a scatter plot to see roughly what relationship exists between the data by estimating what kind of smooth curve would best fit the data points. Linear relationships are particularly easy to spot—do the data points look like they're roughly arranged in a straight line?—but other functions may also fit the data. Actually finding the parameters of the function for the most precise fit is a more complex matter, though most calculators and spreadsheets have the capability of performing the necessary calculations. Qualitatively judging what kind of function fits the data, however, is simpler. Below are examples of scatter plots fit to quadratic and exponential functions, respectively:

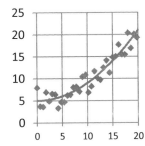 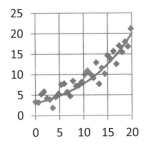

<u>Using a linear function to solve problems in the context of the data</u>
Once you have a function fitted to the scatter plot, you can use the equation of that function to solve problems regarding the data. For instance, suppose the scatter plot on the left below represents the number of bacteria that grow in a petri dish after one week, in millions, versus the amount of a certain nutrient added, in milligrams. The graph on the right shows a linear function fitted to the data.

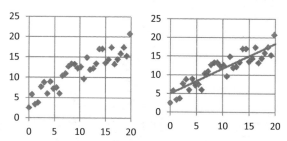

The equation of the line of best fit is $y = \frac{2}{3}x + 5$, where y is the bacteria count in millions and x is the amount of nutrient added, in milligrams. We can then use this function to solve problems; for instance, if we want to estimate how many bacteria to expect if we add 30 milligrams of nutrient, we solve $y = \frac{2}{3}(30) + 5 = 25$, or about 25 million bacteria.

Using a quadratic function to solve problems in the context of the data

Once you have a function fitted to the scatter plot, you can use the equation of that function to solve problems regarding the data. For instance, suppose the scatter plot on the left below represents the area covered by a certain patch of mold, in square centimeters, versus the time in days. The graph on the right shows a quadratic function fitted to the data.

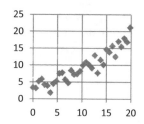

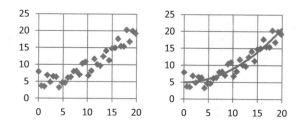

The equation of the quadratic trendline is $y = \frac{1}{25}x^2 + 5$, where x is the time in days and y is the area in square centimeters. We can then use this function to solve problems; for instance, if we want to estimate how much area to expect the mold to cover after 30 days, we solve $y = \frac{1}{25}(30^2) + 5 = 41$, or 41 square centimeters.

Using an exponential function to solve problems in the context of the data

Once you have a function fitted to the scatter plot, you can use the equation of that function to solve problems regarding the data. For instance, suppose the scatter plot on the left below represents the total assets of a certain company in millions of dollars, versus the time in years since 1990. The graph on the right shows an exponential function fitted to the data.

The equation of the trendline is $y = 3e^{0.095t}$, where t is the time in years and y is the company's assets, in millions of dollars. We can then use this function to solve problems; for instance, if we want to estimate the company's projected assets in the year 2020 (30 years after 1990), we solve $y = 3e^{0.095 \cdot 30} \approx 51.9$, or 51.9 million dollars.

Residuals of a fit to a data set

The residuals of a fit to a data set are the differences between the observed values of the data and the predicted values based on the fit. For example, consider the data set {(6,6), (8,12), (10,20), (12,30)}, shown in the scatter plot on the left below A linear fit to the graph is shown on the right:

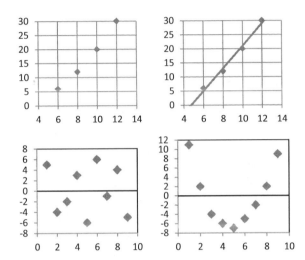

The line of best fit has the equation $y = 4x - 19$. The predicted value for x = 6 is then $4(6) - 19 = 5$, and the residual at x = 6 is $6 - 5 = 1$. At x = 8, the predicted value is $4(8) - 19 = 13$, and the residual at x = 8 is $12 - 13 = -1$. Similarly, the residuals at x = 10 and x = 12 are –1 and 1, respectively.

Note that these residuals add to 0 $(1 + (-1) + (-1) + 1 = 0)$. For the best fit curve, this is always the case; the sum and mean of the residuals will always be zero.

Residual plot

A residual plot is simply the plot of the residuals of a fit to a data set versus the independent variable (the x coordinates of the points). If the residual plot looks random—if the residuals seem to bear no relation to the independent variable—then the function fit to the model was probably a good choice. If the residual plot shows a definite pattern, then the data is probably better suited to a different kind of curve. Consider, for instance, the two residual plots shown below, both corresponding to linear fits. The plot on the left shows no obvious pattern, indicating that the linear fit in question is appropriate to the data. The plot on the left, however, shows a pronounced U shape, indicating that a nonlinear function would be a better fit to the data.

- 107 -

Calculating a fit to a linear function

Without technology
Although it's complicated to calculate an exact fit to a linear function without the aid of technology, finding an approximate fit is feasible. To produce such a fit, first draw a line that seems to follow the data points as closely as possible, probably with about as many data points above the line as below it. Then find the equation for this linear fit the same way as you would find the equation of any graphed line: choose two points on the line, (x_1, y_1) and (x_2, y_2), and then find the slope of the line as $m = \frac{y_2 - y_1}{x_2 - x_1}$. Then use this value of m and one of the known points in the equation $y = mx + b$ to solve for b (it doesn't matter which of the two points you use).

Because this method involves some eyeballing and approximation, it will generally not be completely optimal, and two people may get slightly different results. However, this approximate result will typically be good enough to find estimated solutions to problems.

Using technology
Most modern calculators and spreadsheets have the functionality to calculate linear fits to data sets. On a TI-84, you can find the fit as follows: First, press "STAT", select "EDIT", and enter your data into the table, with the independent variable in the L1 column and the dependent in the L2. Then press "STAT" again, select "CALC", and select "LinReg(ax+b)". The screen will display the coefficients a and b of the linear fit.

In recent versions of Microsoft Excel, you can put the independent and dependent variables in adjacent columns, select all the data, and insert a scatter plot. Then right-click on one of the data points of the graph and select "Add Trendline". Select "Linear", and be sure to check "Display Equation on chart" before clicking OK. The linear plot should be displayed on the graph, along with the corresponding equation of the line.

Slope

In the case of a linear fit to a data set, of the form $y = mx + b$, the slope m corresponds to the rate of change of the dependent variable y with respect to the independent variable x. This can often be expressed in a form similar to "y per x". For instance, if the data represents the distance of an object from some point as a function of time, with the distance as y and the time as x, then the slope of the linear model represents the change in distance with respect to the corresponding change in time—i.e., the velocity. If the data represents the cost to produce various quantities of products, then the slope of the linear model is the change in the cost with respect to the quantity of products produced—i.e., the production cost per unit of product.

Intercept

In the case of a linear fit to a data set, of the form $y = mx + b$, the intercept b corresponds to the value of the dependent variable y when the independent variable x is equal to zero. This often can be expressed as the "initial value" of the variable, or as its offset. For instance, if the data represents the distance of an object from some point as a function of time, with the distance as y and the time as x, then the intercept of the linear model represents the object's distance at time zero—i.e., its initial distance. If the data represents

- 108 -

the cost to produce various quantities of products, then the intercept of the linear model is the cost when no units are being produced—in other words, the overhead cost involved in the production.

Correlation coefficient of a linear fit

The correlation coefficient of a linear fit is a number that expresses how closely the linear fit approximates the function. The coefficient is negative if the line of best fit has a negative slope—the dependent variable decreases as the independent variable increases, and positive if the best fit has a positive slope—the dependent variable increases as the independent variable increases. The linear fit is most closely correlated to the data if the correlation coefficient is equal to ± 1; this means that all the data points lie exactly on the best fit line. If the correlation coefficient is equal to 0, then the data are completely uncorrelated; there is no relationship between the dependent and the independent variable. More often, the correlation coefficient is somewhere in between 0 and 1, indicating a fit that reveals some correlation between the variables.

Most modern calculators and spreadsheets have the functionality to calculate the correlation coefficients of linear fits to data sets. On a TI-84, you can find the fit as follows: First, press "STAT", select "EDIT", and enter your data into the table, with the independent variable in the L1 column and the dependent in the L2. Then press "STAT" again, select "CALC", and select "LinReg(ax+b)". In addition to the coefficients a and b of the linear fit, the screen will display the correlation coefficient, r.

In recent versions of Microsoft Excel, you can put the independent and dependent variables in adjacent columns, then in another cell type "CORREL(". Select the cells containing the independent variables, then type a comma, select the cells containing the dependent variables and type a closing parenthesis. The cell should contain something like "CORREL(A1:A10,B1:B10)", though the letters and numbers may differ. Press ENTER and the cell will show the correlation coefficient of a linear fit to the data.

Correlation

Two variables are correlated if some nonrandom relationship exists between them: if a change in one variable tends to correspond to a change in the other. While many relationships may exist between variables—they may have a quadratic relationship, or an exponential, for example—"correlation" often refers to linear correlation, the existence of a linear relationship $y = mx + b$ between the variables. The data points need not perfectly follow that line; if they do, they are perfectly correlated, but data that approximately follow close to a line may still be said to be correlated. The degree of correlation may be quantified by a value called the correlation coefficient.

Note that correlation is not the same thing as causation; just because two variables are correlated does not necessarily mean that one is the cause of the other.

Correlation and causation

Two variables are correlated if a change in one variable is accompanied by a change in the other, especially if the two variables have a linear relationship. Causation exists if one variable directly depends on the other; a change in one variable causes a change in the other. Note that correlation does not imply causation. If two variables x and y are

- 109 -

correlated, it could be because x causes y. However, it could also be that the apparent correlation is coincidental, or that y causes x, or it could be that both x and y are influenced by a third variable separate from both x and y.

Correlation not linked by causation

Many examples could be constructed of data sets with variables that are correlated but in which one variable is not the cause of the other. One way to construct such a data set is to consider two variables that might both be affected by a third. For example, suppose a survey at a given school indicates that students' shoe sizes are correlated with their spelling; the students with larger shoe sizes tend to have better spelling. Clearly it would seem strange that larger feet would lead to better spelling. In fact, there's a third variable at play here: older students would tend to have larger feet, and likewise older students will tend to have better spelling. The larger shoe sizes don't cause the better spelling, nor does the better spelling cause the larger shoe sizes; rather, both are caused by a third variable that wasn't measured.

Practice Test #1

Practice Questions

1. Choose all of the expressions that are equivalent to $2(x + 3) - 4x + (x - 3)(x + 1)$.

Ⓐ $(x - 3)(x - 1)$

Ⓑ $(x + 3)(x + 4) + 2$

Ⓒ $x(x - 4) + 3$

Ⓓ $(3x^2 + 5x - 4) - (2x^2 + 9x - 7)$

Ⓔ $3(x - 1) + x^2 - 4(x + 2)$

$2x + 3 - 4x + (x - 3)(x + 1)$
$2x + 3 - 4x + x^2 - 4x - 3 - 1)$
$x^2 + 2x - 4x - 4x + 3 - 3$
$x^2 - 6x$

2. Fill in the blanks to complete the following sentence. The graph of the equation $y = 2(x + 3) - 4x + (x - 3)(x + 1)$ is a _____ with zeros at ___ and ___ and a minimum at $y = $ ___.

For questions 3 and 4, consider the table below.

Input	Output
2	6
0	3

3. If there exists a functional relation between the input and output values, which, if any, of these input/output pairs must be excluded from the data set? Choose all that apply.

	Input	Output
Ⓐ	0	0
Ⓑ	4	6
Ⓒ	-2	0
Ⓓ	4	9
Ⓔ	-5	- 4.5

4. Part A: If there exists a linear relationship between the input and output values, which, if any, of these input/output pairs can be included in the data set? Choose all that apply.

	Input	Output
Ⓐ	0	0
Ⓑ	4	6
Ⓒ	-2	0
Ⓓ	4	9
Ⓔ	-5	-4.5

Part B: In slope-intercept form, the linear relationship between input value x and output value y can be expressed using the equation $\underline{y = \frac{1}{6}x + 54}$

Use the graph below to answer questions 5 and 6.

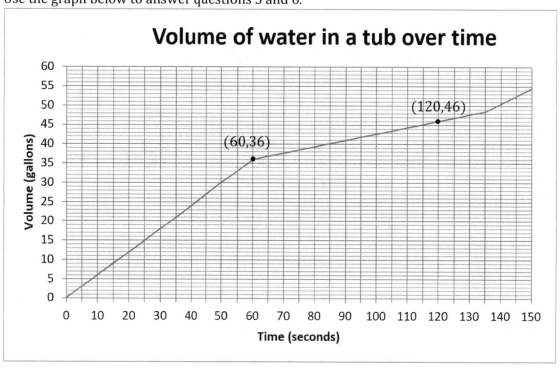

Volume of water in a tub over time

(60,36)

(120,46)

Volume (gallons)

Time (seconds)

5. Complete the piece-wise function which describes the volume as a function of time t.

$$f(t) = \begin{cases} \underline{}, & 0 \le t < 60 \\ \underline{}, & \underline{} \\ \dfrac{2}{5}t - 5.5, & 135 \le t \le 150 \end{cases}$$

6. The average rate of change is closest to which of these?

Ⓐ 3 gallons/second

Ⓑ $\frac{1}{3}$ gallons/second

Ⓒ 27 gallons/second

Ⓓ The rate of change in gallons/second on the interval [10,20]

Ⓔ The rate of change in gallons/second on the interval [70,130]

7. The graph below shows Aaron's distance from home at times throughout his morning run. Which of the following statements is (are) true?

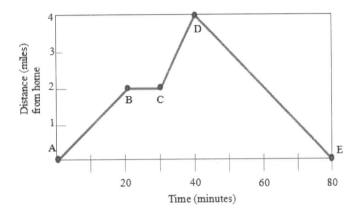

Ⓐ Aaron ran a total distance of four miles.

Ⓑ Aaron's average running speed was 6 mph.

Ⓒ Aaron's running speed from point A to point B was the same as his running speed from point D to E.

Ⓓ Aaron rested for ten minutes after running the first two miles.

Ⓔ Aaron returned home from his run 1.5 hours after starting.

8. The path of ball thrown into the air is modeled by the first quadrant graph of the equation $h = -16t^2 + 47t + 3$, where h is the height of the ball in feet and t is time in seconds after the ball is thrown. The maximum height of the ball occurs at $t =$ ____ seconds, and the ball hits the ground at $t =$ ___ seconds. If necessary, round answers to the nearest tenth.

9. Determine whether the given relation is always a function, sometimes a function, or never a function. Place check marks in the appropriate boxes.

	A relation whose graph is a line	A relation whose graph is a semicircle	A relation whose graph is a circle	$y = x^2$	$x = |y|$
Always					
Sometimes					
Never					

10. Given the functions $f(x) = 2x^2 + 4$ and $g(x) = 8x - 1$, compare the quantities using $<$, $>$, or $=$.

$$f(g(3)) \underline{\hspace{1cm}} g(f(3))$$

11. Which of these expresses the equation $y = 4x - 2$ as x in terms of y?

Ⓐ $x = 4y - 2$

Ⓑ $x = y + \frac{1}{2}$

Ⓒ $x = -4x + 2$

Ⓓ $x = \frac{1}{4}y + 2$

Ⓔ $x = \frac{1}{4}y + \frac{1}{2}$

12. The formula used to convert a temperature in degrees Celsius to degrees Fahrenheit is $F = \frac{9}{5}C + 32$. Write a formula which can be used to convert a temperature in degrees Fahrenheit to degrees Celsius by solving the given equation for C. _____ At what temperature are the readings on a Celsius and Fahrenheit thermometer the same? ___°F = ___°C

Use the combined gas law below to answer questions 13 and 14.

For a given gas, $\frac{PV}{T} = k$, where P is the pressure exerted on the gas, V is volume of the gas, T is temperature of the gas in Kelvin, and k is a constant.

13. If the pressure of a gas remains constant and the temperature of the gas rises, the volume of the gas must _____. If the temperature of a gas remains constant and the volume of the gas decreases, the pressure of the gas must _____. Fill in each blank with the "increase," "decrease," or "remain constant."

14. Graph on the number line the solution to the inequality $2|x + 3| - 9 \geq -1$.

15. To determine whether foot size is correlated with height, a student collected data from 25 fellow male tenth graders. On the given chart, create a scatter plot of the data shown in the table below.

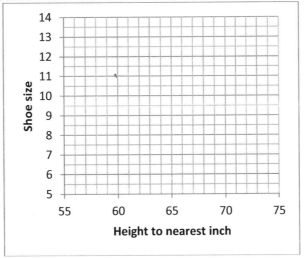

Height to nearest inch	Shoe size
55	6.5
60	8
72	11
74	13
71	10.5
69	11
58	9
72	11.5
68	11
62	9
73	12.5
70	11
69	10.5
70	11.5
56	7.5
61	9.5
72	11
64	10
57	7
59	8
63	10
72	11.5
71	11
69	11
62	9.5

Which of these most closely approximates the best fit line for the given data?

- (A) $y = \frac{1}{4}x - 7$
- (B) $y = \frac{1}{2}x - 24$
- (C) $y = x - 52$
- (D) $y = -\frac{1}{2}x + 25$
- (E) $y = \frac{3}{4}x - 38$

Use the information below to answer questions 16 and 17.

José is participating in a school fundraiser by selling packages of cookie dough and soft pretzels. His order form is shown below.

Customer name	Packages of cookie dough	Packages of pretzels	Total cost
Cedric	1	4	$42
Madhavi	3	2	$51
James	2	?	$24
Mei Ling	2	1	?

16. Determine the cost per package of cookie dough. $_____.

17. James ordered ___ packages of pretzels, and the total cost of Mei Ling's order is $_____.

18. The solution to which of the following systems of inequalities is graphed below?

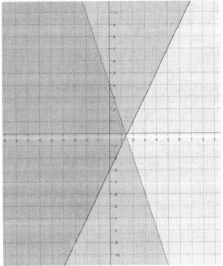

   Ⓐ $y < -3x + 4$
       $4x - 2y \leq 6$
   Ⓑ $y \geq 2x - 3$
       $y < 3x + 4$
   Ⓒ $x < -3y + 4$
       $y + 3 \leq 2x$
   Ⓓ $y > 4 - 3x$
       $y \leq 2x - 3$
   Ⓔ None of the above

19. If one side of a rectangle is described by the equation $y = 2x + 3$, which of these could describe another side of the rectangle? Choose all that apply.

   Ⓐ $y = 2x - 3$

   Ⓑ $2x + y = 6$

   Ⓒ $y = \frac{1}{2}x + 3$

   Ⓓ $2x - y = 12$

   Ⓔ $x + 2y = 6$

20. Determine whether each number is rational or irrational. Place a check in the appropriate box of the table.

	Rational	Irrational
-2		
$1.\overline{63}$		
π		
$\sqrt{2}$		
$-\dfrac{2}{3}$		
$\sqrt{\dfrac{16}{25}}$		

21. Simplify the expression.

$$\frac{5\sqrt{2}(2\sqrt{3} + 4\sqrt{3})}{3\sqrt{3}}$$

22. Fill in each blank with "sometimes," "always," or "never." The sum of two rational numbers is _____ rational, and the sum of two irrational numbers is _____ rational.

23. Fill in each blank with "sometimes," "always," or "never." The product of two rational numbers is _____ rational, and the product of two irrational numbers is _____ rational.

24. Fill in each blank with "sometimes," "always," or "never." The sum of a rational and irrational number is _____ rational, and the product of a non-zero rational number and an irrational number is _____ rational.

25. Choose the phrase or phrases which truthfully complete this statement: if $f(x) = -(x-2)^2 + 1$ and $g(x) = x^2 - 4x + 5$, then the graphs of $f(x)$ and $g(x)$ _____.

   Ⓐ Pass through the point (0,5).

   Ⓑ Are parabolas.

   Ⓒ Have a common line of symmetry at $x = 2$.

   Ⓓ Have a maximum at (2,1).

   Ⓔ Share a common vertex.

26. The graph of $y = (x + 3)(x^2 - x - 2)$ has x-intercepts _____ and y-intercept _____.

27. Graph $y = -\sqrt{x} + 2$.

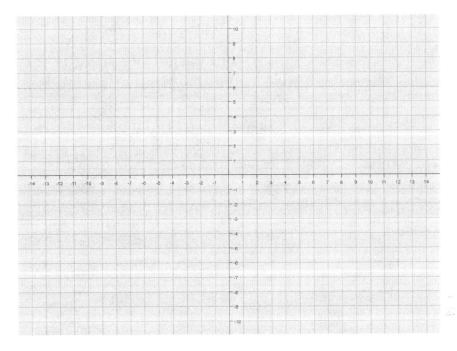

28. If function $f(x)$ is transformed by a vertical shift of 3 units upward and a horizontal shift of 2 units leftward, which one of these describes the transformed function?

    (A) $f(x + 3) - 2$

    (B) $f(x - 3) + 2$

    (C) $f(x - 2) + 3$

    (D) $f(x + 2) - 3$

    (E) $f(x + 2) + 3$

29. If $f(x) = x^3$, and the graph below represents transformation $af(x + b) + c$, then $a =$ ___, $b =$ ___, and $c =$ ___.

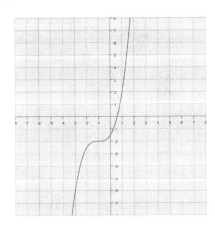

- 119 -

Use the information below to answer questions 30 and 31.

Two radioactive isotopes of Fermium, ^{252}Fm and ^{253}Fm, have half-lives of approximately one day and three days, respectively. In other words, these different forms of the material are unstable and decay to half of their original amounts with the passage of each half-life. For example, a sample of 120g of ^{252}Fm decays to 60 g of ^{252}Fm after one day, 30 g after two days, and so on.

30. A 200 mg sample of ^{252}Fm and an unknown quantity of ^{253}Fm decay for six days. If on the sixth day the mass of the two isotopes is the same, how many milligrams of ^{253}Fm were in the original sample? Include the answer in the chart below.

Day	Mass of ^{252}Fm	Mass of ^{253}Fm
0	200 mg	____?____
1	____	
2	____	
3	____	____
4	____	
5	____	
6	____	____

31. The graph below shows the decay of a sample of ^{252}Fm and a sample of ^{253}Fm over a period of eight days. Which of the following statements is (are) true? Select all that apply.

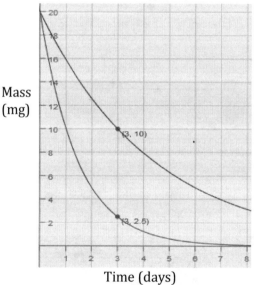

Mass (mg)

Time (days)

Ⓐ Both samples have a starting mass of 20 mg.

Ⓑ After three days, there is four times as much ^{253}Fm as ^{252}Fm.

Ⓒ After eight days, no ^{252}Fm remains.

Ⓓ Over time, the difference in the amounts of ^{252}Fm and ^{253}Fm increases and then decreases.

Ⓔ The radioactive decay of ^{252}Fm and ^{253}Fm is an example of linear regression.

32. At the end of 30 years, the account value if invested through Bank B is $_____ (more than/less than) the account value if invested through Bank C. Compare the account values rounded to the nearest cent.

33. Classify each as an example of linear or exponential growth.
The change in population of bacteria grown in a test tube containing nutrient broth
The change in the balance of an account when $50 is added weekly
The change in earnings if salary increases by 3% every year

34. A meteorologist wishes to show the forecasted change in daily high temperatures throughout the week. Which of these should she choose?

   (A) A pie chart

   (B) A frequency histogram

   (C) A line graph

   (D) A Venn diagram

   (E) A box-and-whisker plot

Use the following data to answer questions 35-36.
A company employs 66 male and 50 female non-management employees, all of whom earn less than $100,000 per year. Annual salaries (rounded to the nearest dollar) for male and female employees are shown below.

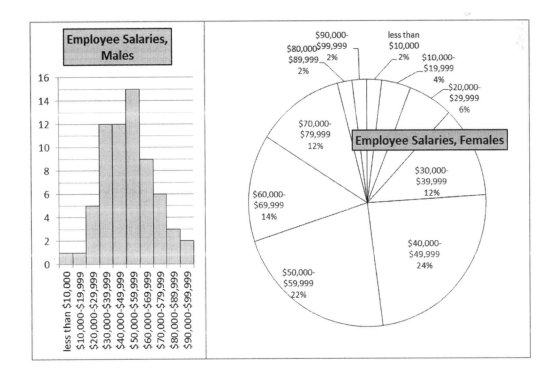

35. Which of the following statements is (are) true? Choose all that apply.

Ⓐ The number of male and female employees who earn salaries in the $40,000-$49,999 salary range is the same.

Ⓑ The percentage of male employees earning $50,000 or more is greater than the percentage of females earning $50,000 or more.

Ⓒ The percentage of female employees earning $70,000-$79,000 is greater than the percentage of male employees earning $70,000-$79,000.

Ⓓ The ratio of the number of male to female employees earning in the $30,000-$39,000 range is 2:1.

Ⓔ The number of female employees who earn salaries under $40,000 is the same as the number of male employees who earn salaries in the $30,000-$39,999 range.

36. The type of graph that displays the salaries of male employees is called a
_____.

37. The median annual salary for males lies within which interval?

Ⓐ $30,000-$39,999

Ⓑ $40,000-$49,999

Ⓒ $50,000-$59,999

Ⓓ $60,000-$69,999

Ⓔ $70,000-$79,999

38. The box-and-whisker plots to the right display student test scores by class period. Letter grades are assigned on a ten point scale: A – 90 to 100, B – 80 to 90, C – 70 to 80, D – 60 to 70, F – below 60.

Test scores by class

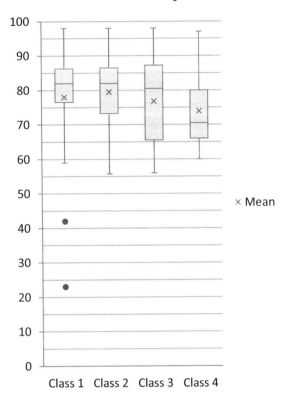

Which of the following statements is (are) true? Choose all that apply.

Ⓐ The mean better reflects student performance in class 1 than the median.

Ⓑ The mean test score for Class 1 and 2 is the same.

Ⓒ The median test score for Class 1 and 2 is the same.

Ⓓ The range of test scores for Class 3 is greater than the range of test scores for Class 1.

Ⓔ 25% of the students in Class 4 received A's or B's.

39. If a is a prime number and b is an odd integer, then the product of a and b MUST be

Ⓐ A prime number.

Ⓑ An odd number.

Ⓒ A multiple of 3.

Ⓓ A positive integer.

Ⓔ None of these

40. If a and b are positive integers, then which of these statements is (are) true about a^{-b}? Select all that apply.

(A) a^{-b} is always an integer

(B) a^{-b} is sometimes an integer and sometimes a non-integer

(C) a^{-b} is never an integer

(D) a^{-b} is always positive

(E) a^{-b} is never greater than 1

Answers and Explanations

1. A, C, and D: The expression $2(x + 3) - 4x + (x - 3)(x + 1)$ simplifies to $x^2 - 4x + 3$:

$$2(x + 3) - 4x + (x - 3)(x + 1)$$
$$2x + 6 - 4x + x^2 - 3x + x - 3$$
$$x^2 - 4x + 3$$

In factored form, $x^2 - 4x + 3 = (x - 3)(x - 1)$. Factoring an x from the first two terms of $x^2 - 4x + 3$ gives $x(x - 4) + 3$. The expression $(3x^2 + 5x - 4) - (2x^2 + 9x - 7) = (3x^2 - 2x^2) + (5x - 9x) + (-4 - (-7)) = x^2 - 4x + 3$. So, choices A, C, and D are equivalent to the each other and to the given expression.

Choice B and E are not equivalent to the given expression: $(x + 3)(x + 4) + 2 = x^2 + 3x + 4x + 12 + 2 = x^2 + 7x + 14$, and $3(x - 1) + x^2 - 4(x + 2) = 3x - 3 + x^2 - 4x - 8 = x^2 - x - 11$.

2. Parabola, 3, 1, -1: $y = 2(x + 3) - 4x + (x - 3)(x + 1)$ simplifies to $y = x^2 - 4x + 3$, and the zeros of the graph of the equation occur when $y = 0$. To solve $0 = x^2 - 4x + 3$, use the factored form $0 = (x - 3)(x - 1)$ and set each factor equal to zero. Then, solve for x:

$$(x - 3)(x - 1) = 0$$
$$(x - 3) = 0 \quad (x - 1) = 0$$
$$x = 3 \quad x = 1$$

The graph of the quadratic equation $ax^2 + bx + c$ is a parabola with an axis of symmetry $x = -\frac{b}{2a}$, and the maximum or minimum value of a parabola lies on the axis of symmetry. Find the equation which represents the axis of symmetry, and find the y-value for the determined value of x:

For $= x^2 - 4x + 3$, $a = 1, b = -4, c = 3$.

The axis of symmetry is $x = \frac{-(-4)}{2(1)} = 2$.

When $x = 2, y = (2)^2 - 4(2) + 3 = 4 - 8 + 3 = -1$.

3. A: A relationship is a function if and only if each input value is paired with exactly one output value. In the table given, the input value 0 is paired with the output value 3 and cannot, therefore, also be paired with an output value of 0. (Note: while putting a particular number into a function will always give the same output, the same output can be obtained from multiple input values.)

4. C, D, E; $y = \frac{3}{2}x + 3$: The rate of change in a linear relationship is constant. In the given table, the output, or y, value decreases by three as the input, or x, value decreases by 2. The slope m of the line between the two given points is, therefore, $\frac{-3}{-2} = \frac{3}{2}$. A linear equation can be written in slope-intercept form, $y = mx + b$. Substitute one of the given x-y pairs and the determined slope into the equation to find the y-intercept b:

$$y = mx + b$$
$$3 = \frac{3}{2}(0) + b$$
$$3 = b$$

Using the determined slope and y-intercept, the equation of the line in slope-intercept form is $y = \frac{3}{2}x + 3$. Using this equation, input values $x = 0, 4, -2, -5$ gives output values $y =$

$3, 9, 0, -4.5$, respectively. Of the answer choices, $(-2,0), (4,9)$, and $(-5,-4.5)$ lie on the same line the one which passes through given points $(2,6)$ and $(0,3)$.

$$5.\ f(t) = \begin{cases} \dfrac{3}{5}t, & 0 \le t < 60 \\[2mm] \dfrac{1}{6}t + 26, & 60 \le t < 135 \\[2mm] \dfrac{2}{5}t - 5.5, & 135 \le t \le 150 \end{cases}$$

The graph consists of three lines, each of which can be expressed in slope-intercept form $y = mx + b$, where m is the slope of the line and b is its y-intercept.

The slope is equal to the change in y-values divided by the change in x-values: in 60 seconds, the volume changes by 36 gallons; since time is graphed along the x-axis and volume along the y-axis, the slope is $\frac{36}{60} = \frac{3}{5}$. Thus, the equation for this part of the graph is $y = \frac{3}{5}x + 0$, or simply $y = \frac{3}{5}x$.

Since the first part of the graph is defined by values of t less than 60, and since the last part of the graph is defined for values of t greater than or equal to 135, the second part of the graph should be defined for values of t greater than or equal to 60 but less than 135.

The graph in this interval passes through the two labeled points. One way to find the equation for this part of the function is to use those two points to find the slope and then to substitute the slope and one point into the point-slope form of a linear equation, $y - y_1 = m(x - x_1)$, where (x_1, y_1) is a point on the line and m is the slope of the line. Afterward, rewrite the equation in slope-intercept form.

$$m = \frac{y_2 - y_1}{x_2 - x_1} = \frac{46 - 36}{120 - 60} = \frac{10}{60} = \frac{1}{6}$$
$$y - 36 = \frac{1}{6}(x - 60)$$
$$y - 36 = \frac{1}{6}x - 10$$
$$y = \frac{1}{6}x + 26$$

6. B: The average rate of change can be found by calculating $\frac{f(150) - f(0)}{150 - 0}$.

$$\frac{\left[\frac{2}{5}(150) - 5.5\right] - \frac{3}{5}(0)}{150 - 0} = \frac{54.5 - 0}{150} = \frac{54.5}{150} = \frac{545}{1500} = \frac{109}{300} \text{ or } 0.36\overline{3}$$

The rate of change in gallons/second on the interval $[10,20]$ can be found in the same manner, or it can be described using the already-determined slope of the line containing these two points, which is $\frac{3}{5}$ or 0.6. Likewise, the slope of the line on the interval $[70,130]$ is $\frac{1}{6}$ or $0.1\overline{6}$.

Of the given values, the average rate of change, $0.36\overline{3}$ gallons/second, is closest to $\frac{1}{3}$, or $0.\overline{3}$, gallons/second.

7. B, C, D: Notice that the y-axis does not show total distance traveled but rather Aaron's displacement from home.

Aaron ran four miles from home and then back home again, so he ran a total of eight miles.

Since Aaron ran eight miles in eighty minutes (one hour and twenty minutes, or $1\frac{1}{3}$ hours), he ran an average of one mile every ten minutes, or six miles per hour; he ran two miles from point A to B in 20 minutes and four miles from D to E in 40 minutes, so his running speed between both sets of points was the same – again, one mile every ten minutes, or 6 mph.

Once Aaron had run two miles, he stopped for ten minutes. Notice that his distance from home did not change between 20 and 30 minutes.

8. 1.5, 3: The ball follows a parabolic path, and the ball's maximum height occurs at the vertex of the parabola. Since the equation of the parabola is given in the form $h = at^2 + bt + c$, the t-value of the vertex can be found using $\frac{-b}{2a} = \frac{-47}{2(-16)} \approx 1.5$. The ball reaches a maximum height about 1.5 seconds after having been thrown into the air.

When the ball hits the ground, its height is zero. Substitute 0 for h into the equation and solve for t.

$$h = -16t^2 + 47t + 3$$
$$0 = -16t^2 + 47t + 3$$

Factor and use the zero-product property.

$$0 = (-16t - 1)(t - 3)$$
$$0 = -16t - 1 \quad 0 = t - 3$$
$$1 = -16t \quad 3 = t$$
$$-\frac{1}{16} = t$$

Since t cannot be negative, $t = 3$. The ball hits the ground three seconds after having been thrown into the air.

9.

	A relation whose graph is a line	A relation whose graph is a semicircle	A relation whose graph is a circle	$y = x^2$	$x = |y|, x \geq 0$
Always				✓	
Sometimes	✓	✓			
Never			✓		✓

A function is a relationship such that there is exactly one element of the range (possible y values) for every element of the domain (possible x values). One way to determine if the graph of a relation is a function is to use the vertical line test: if any vertical line passes through the graph and simultaneously touches more than one point on the graph, then the

- 127 -

graph does not represent a functional relationship. Horizontal and diagonal lines represent functions, but a vertical line does not.

A semicircle can be positioned on the coordinate plane such that it passes ⌣ or fails

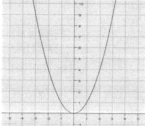the vertical line test.

A circle graphed on the coordinate plane fails the vertical line test.
Every x-value inputted into the equation $y = x^2$ yields exactly one y-value. Also, the graph

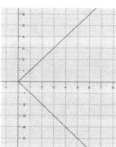

of $y = x^2$ is a parabola which opens upward and which passes the vertical line test.

For the equation $x = |y|$, is possible to obtain the same y-value for different values of the domain $\{x: x \geq 0\}$. For example, when x is 3, y can be either 3 or -3 since $3 = |3| = |-3|$. Also, the graph of this relationship fails the vertical line test.

10. >: Since $g(3) = 8(3) - 1 = 24 - 1 = 23$, $f(g(3)) = f(23) = 2(23)^2 + 4 = 2(529) + 4 = 1058 + 4 = 1062$.

Since $f(3) = 2(3)^2 + 4 = 2(9) + 4 = 18 + 4 = 22$, $g(f(3)) = g(22) = 8(22) - 1 = 176 - 1 = 175$.

$1062 > 175$, $so\ f(g(3)) > g(f(3))$.

11. E:

$$y = 4x - 2$$
$$y + 2 = 4x$$
$$\frac{y + 2}{4} = x$$
$$\frac{y}{4} + \frac{2}{4} = x$$
$$\frac{1}{4}y + \frac{1}{2} = x$$
$$x = \frac{1}{4}y + \frac{1}{2}$$

12. $= \frac{5}{9}(F - 32), -40°F = -40°C$:

Solve the equation for C.

$$F = \frac{9}{5}C + 32$$
$$F - 32 = \frac{9}{5}C + 32 - 32$$
$$\frac{5}{9}(F - 32) = \frac{5}{9} \cdot \frac{9}{5}C$$

$$\frac{5}{9}(F - 32) = C$$

To determine at what temperature both thermometers have the same reading, substitute the same variable for C and F into either the equation $F = \frac{9}{5}C + 32$ or the equation $C = \frac{5}{9}(F - 32)$ and solve.

$$F = \frac{9}{5}C + 32$$
$$x = \frac{9}{5}x + 32$$
$$\frac{5}{5}x - \frac{9}{5}x = \frac{9}{5}x + 32 - \frac{9}{5}x$$
$$-\frac{4}{5}x = 32$$
$$\left(-\frac{5}{4}\right)\left(-\frac{4}{5}x\right) = \left(-\frac{5}{4}\right)\left(\frac{32}{1}\right)$$

$$x = -40$$

Therefore, $-40°F = -40°C$.

13. Increase, increase: Since $\frac{PV}{T}$ is a constant, when one of the variables P, V, or T changes, so must at least one other variable.

If the pressure of a gas remains constant and the temperature of the gas rises, the volume of the gas must increase: if the denominator of a fraction increases, the numerator must also increase in order for the value of the fraction to stay the same; since the pressure does not change, the volume must increase in order for the numerator PV to increase along with the denominator T.

If the temperature of a gas remains constant and the volume of the gas decreases, the pressure of the gas must increase: since the denominator does not change, the numerator must also remain constant in order for the fraction to stay the same; since the volume decreases, the pressure must increase in order for the product PV in the numerator to remain constant.

14.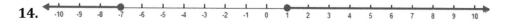

First, solve the inequality.

$$2|x+3| - 9 \geq -1$$
$$2|x+3| \geq 8$$
$$|x+3| \geq 4$$

$$x + 3 \geq 4 \qquad -(x+3) \geq 4$$
$$\boldsymbol{x \geq 1} \qquad -(x+3) \geq 4$$
$$x + 3 \leq -4$$
$$\boldsymbol{x \leq -7}$$

Then, graph the solution on the number line. When solving absolute value equations and inequalities, it is good practice to check for extraneous solutions. Choose a number in each shaded region to be sure it satisfies the given inequality.

$$2|-8+3| - 9 \geq -1? \qquad\qquad 2|2+3| - 9 \geq -1?$$
$$2|-5| - 9 \geq -1? \qquad\qquad 2|5| - 9 \geq -1?$$
$$2(5) - 9 \geq -1? \qquad\qquad 2(5) - 9 \geq -1?$$
$$10 - 9 \geq -1? \qquad\qquad 10 - 9 \geq -1?$$
$$1 \geq -1? \qquad\qquad 1 \geq -1?$$

$1 \geq -1$ is a true statement, so -8 and 2 are indeed included in the solution.

15. See scatter plot below, A:

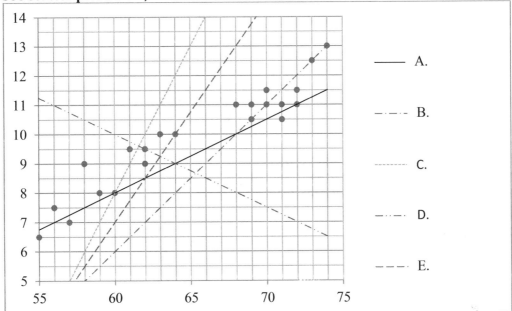

A scatter plot of the data is shown below along with the graphs of each of the linear equations given in Choices A-E. The graph of the equation given by Choice A, $y = \frac{1}{4}x + 7$, fits the data better than the others.

16. $12.00: Writing and solving a system of equations is one way to determine the cost of a package of cookie dough. Let c represent the cost of each package of cookie dough and p the cost of each package of pretzels. An individual's order cost is equal the number of packages of cookie dough ordered times the cost per package of dough plus the number of packages of pretzels ordered times the cost per package of pretzels. Using the information from the order form for Cedric's and Madhavi's order,

$$3c + 2p = 51$$
$$1c + 4p = 42$$

A system of linear equations can be solved using a variety of methods, including the elimination (or linear combination) method shown here. Since the question asks for the cost of cookie dough, eliminate the variable p by multiplying the top equation by -2

$$-2(3c + 2p = 51) \rightarrow -6c - 4p = -102$$

and combining the result with the other equation. Then, solve the resulting equation for c.

$$
\begin{aligned}
-6c - 4p &= -102 \\
+\ 1c + 4p &= \quad 42 \\
\hline
-5c \quad\ &= -60 \\
c &= 12
\end{aligned}
$$

17. 0, $31.50: James bought two packages of cookie dough for $12.00 each; since his order total was $24.00, he must not have purchased any packages of pretzels.

To determine Mei Ling's total order cost, first find the cost per package of pretzels. Madhavi bought one package of cookie dough for $12.00, and her order total was $42.00; it follows that she spent $42.00 − $12.00 = $30.00 on four packages of pretzels. Each package of pretzels therefore costs $\frac{$30}{4}$=$7.50.

Mei Ling ordered two packages of cookies at $12.00 per package and one package of pretzels at $7.50 per package, so her order total was $2(\$12.00) + (\$7.50) = \$31.50$.

18. A: The blue line has a slope of 2 and a y-intercept of -3; the line is solid, and the region above the line is shaded. Therefore, the graph illustrates the solution to the inequality $y \geq 2x - 3$.

The red line has a slope of -3 and a y-intercept of 4; the line is dashed, and the region below the line is shaded. Therefore, the graph illustrates the solution to the inequality $y < -3x + 4$.

In choice A, the second inequality when solved for y is equivalent to $y \geq 2x - 3$.
$$4x - 2y \leq 6$$
$$-2y \leq -4x + 6$$
$$y \geq 2x - 3$$
(The direction of the inequality sign changes when multiplying or diving by a negative number.)
The solution of the system of inequalities is shown by the purple region where the shading overlaps.

19. A, D, E: One of the other three sides of the rectangle must be parallel to the line described by the given equation, and the other two sides must be perpendicular to that line. Parallel lines have the same slopes, and perpendicular lines have opposite, inverse slopes. The slope of the line $y = 2x + 3$ is 2, so an equation which describes a different line with a slope of 2 can represent a parallel side of the rectangle, while an equation which describes a line with a slope of $-\frac{1}{2}$ can describe a perpendicular side of the rectangle. Both $y = 2x - 3$ (choice A) and $2x - y = 12$ (choice D) have slopes of 2 and could represent the side parallel to $y = 2x + 3$. $x + 2y = 6$ (choice E) has a slope of -1/2 and could represent one of the sides perpendicular to $y = 2x + 3$.

20.

	Rational	Irrational
-2	✔	
$1.\overline{63}$	✔	
π		✔
$\sqrt{2}$		✔
$-\dfrac{2}{3}$	✔	
$\sqrt{\dfrac{16}{25}}$	✔	

A rational number is a number which can be written as a ratio of two integers. Rational numbers include integers themselves (for example, $-2 = \frac{-2}{1} = \frac{2}{-1}$), fractions with integer numerators and denominators (for example, $-\frac{2}{3} = \frac{-2}{3} = \frac{3}{-2}$), repeating decimals (for example, $1.\overline{63} = 1\frac{63}{99} = 1\frac{7}{11} = \frac{18}{11}$), and terminating decimals. $\sqrt{\frac{16}{25}}$ simplifies to a ratio of integers, namely $\frac{4}{5}$, so it is also rational. Real numbers for which the decimal portion neither terminates nor repeats are irrational; examples of such numbers are π and $\sqrt{2}$.

21. $10\sqrt{2}$:

$$\frac{5\sqrt{2}\left(2\sqrt{3}+4\sqrt{3}\right)}{3\sqrt{3}}$$
$$\frac{5\sqrt{2}(6\sqrt{3})}{3\sqrt{3}}$$
$$\frac{30\sqrt{6}}{3\sqrt{3}}$$
$$10\sqrt{2}$$

22. Always, sometimes: The sum of two rational numbers is always rational. The sum of two irrational numbers is only rational if the sum is zero (in other words, if the two irrational numbers added together are additive inverses). For example, $\sqrt{2}+\left(-\sqrt{2}\right)=0$, a rational number.

23. Always, sometimes: The product of two rational numbers always yields a rational number, but the product of two irrational numbers may be either rational or irrational. For example, the product of irrational numbers $5\sqrt{2}$ and $3\sqrt{2}$ is $15 \cdot 2 = 30$, a rational number, while the product of irrational numbers $\sqrt{2}$ and $\sqrt{3}$ is $\sqrt{6}$, which is also irrational.

24. Never, never: The sum or product of a rational and irrational number is never rational. For example, $2\sqrt{3}+3$ is irrational and the same with $2\sqrt{3}\times 3$.

25. B, C, E: Both $f(x)$ and $g(x)$ are quadratic equations, the graph of which are parabolic. When a quadratic equation is written in vertex form $f(x)=a(x-h)^2+k$, where $a\neq 0$, the graph of the function is a parabola with a line of symmetry $x=h$ and vertex at (h,k). When written in standard form $g(x)=ax^2+bx+c$, where $a\neq 0$, the graph of the function is a parabola with line of symmetry $x=-\frac{b}{2a}$ and a vertex at $(-\frac{b}{2a},g\left(-\frac{b}{2a}\right))$. In either form, when $a>0$, the parabola opens upward, and the vertex represents the minimum value of the function; when $a<0$, the parabola opens downward, and the vertex represents the maximum value of the function.

The graph of $f(x)=-(x-2)^2+1$ has a line of symmetry $x=2$ and vertex $(2,1)$. Since it opens downward, the maximum occurs at $(2,1)$. This parabola does not pass through the point $(0,5)$ since $f(0)=-(0-2)\char`\^2+1=-(4)+1=-4=1=-3$, and $-3\neq 5$.

The graph of $g(x)=x^2-4x+5$ has a line of symmetry $x=-\frac{b}{2a}=-\frac{-4}{2(1)}=2$ and a vertex at $(2,g(2))$: since $g(2)=2^2-4(2)+5=4-8+5=-4+5=1$, the vertex is $(2,1)$, which is the minimum value of the function since the parabola opens upward. This parabola does pass through the point $(0,5)$ since $g(0)=0^2-4(0)+5=5$.

26. $x=-3,\ 2,\ -1; y=-6$: $y=(x+3)(x^2-x-2)$ is a cubic equation written as a product of a linear and quadratic factor, $x-3$ and x^2-x-2, respectively. The quadratic expression can be further factored to $(x-2)(x+1)$, so $y=(x+3)(x^2-x-2)=(x+3)(x-2)(x+1)$. The x-intercepts of the graph of y occur when $y=0$, so to find the x-intercepts, solve $0=(x+3)(x-2)(x+1)$ using the zero-product property.

$$x + 3 = 0 \qquad x - 2 = 0 \qquad x + 1 = 0$$
$$x = -3 \qquad x = 2 \qquad x = -1$$

The y-intercept of the graph of the equation occurs when $x = 0$, so solve $y = (0 + 3)(0^2 - 0 - 2) = (3)(-2) = -6$.

27.

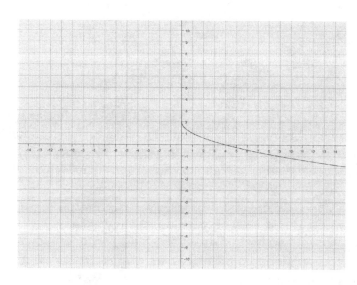

The parent function of $y = -\sqrt{x} + 2$ is the absolute value function $y = \sqrt{x}$, shown here.

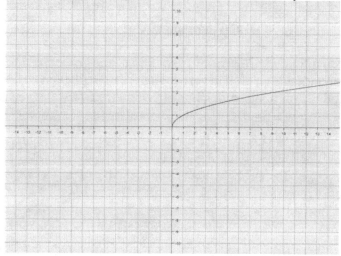

To graph $y = -\sqrt{x} + 2$, invert the graph of $y = \sqrt{x}$ and shift up two units.

28. E: $f(x) + k$ defines a function $f(x)$ shifted k units up, and $f(x + k)$ defines a function $f(x)$ shifted k units to the left. So, if a function $f(x)$ is shifted up 3 units and left 2 units, that transformed function is described by $f(x + 2) + 3$.

- 134 -

29. $a = \frac{1}{2}, b = 1, c = -2$:

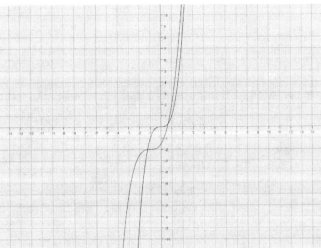

Compare the blue graph of $y = x^3$ to the red graph of its transformation. The inflection point, the point at which the graph changes from concave-upward to concave-downward or vice-versa, of $y = x^3$ is at the origin. Notice that the transformation shifts this point down two units and to the left one unit. $f(x) + k$ defines a function $f(x)$ shifted k units up, so $f(x) - 2$ shifts the inflection point on the graph 2 units; $f(x + k)$ defines a function $f(x)$ shifted k units to the left, so $f(x + 1)$ shifts the inflection point on a graph one unit to the left. Therefore, the transformation can be partially completed as $af(x + 1) - 2$, which can also be written $a(x + 1)^3 - 2$ given the original function $f(x) = x^3$.

Transformation $kf(x)$ stretches or compresses the graph vertically: when k is an integer, the graph is vertically stretched, and when k is a fraction, the graph is vertically compressed. The transformed graph is wider than the graph of $y = x^3$, so the value of a must be fractional. One way to determine the value of a is set up an equation using a point on the graph. Since the graph passes through (1,2) and since $y = a(x + 1)^3 - 2$, $2 = a(1 + 1)^3 - 2$.

$$2 = a(1 + 1)^3 - 2$$
$$2 = a(2)^3 - 2$$
$$2 = 8a - 2$$
$$4 = 8a$$
$$\frac{1}{2} = a$$

30. 12.5 mg:

Day	Mass of ^{252}Fm	Mass of ^{253}Fm
0	200 mg	12.5 mg
1	100 mg	
2	50 mg	
3	25 mg	6.25 mg
4	12.5 mg	
5	6.25 mg	
6	3.125 mg	3.125 mg

- 135 -

Since the amount of ^{252}Fm is halved each day, a 200 mg sample decays to 3.125 mg after six days. If on the sixth day there is 3.125 mg of ^{253}Fm, then there was twice as much, or 6.25 mg three days prior, and twice that amount, or 12.5 mg, at the start.

31. A, B, D: At time zero, both samples have a mass of 20 mg.

After three days, there remains 0.25 mg of ^{252}Fm and 10 mg of ^{253}Fm, which is four times the mass of ^{252}Fm (0.25 mg × 4 = 10 mg).

Even though the amount of ^{252}Fm approaches zero, a very small amount, which is half of the small amount present at seven days, remains.

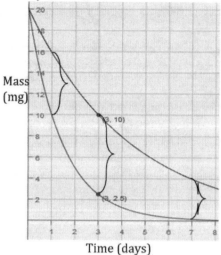

The difference in the amounts of the two isotopes remaining over times is illustrated by the space between the curves, which increases and then decreases.

Notice that the graphs representing radioactive decay are curved, not linear; radioactive decay is an example of exponential decay, not linear regression.

32. $16.43, less than: Calculate and compare the account values through Banks B and C. For Bank B,

$A = P\left(1 + \dfrac{r}{100n}\right)^{nt}$, P=$5,000, r=2.5%, n=4, t=30, so

$$A = \$5,000\left(1 + \frac{2.5}{100 \cdot 4}\right)^{4(30)}$$
$$A = \$5,000\left(1 + \frac{2.5}{400}\right)^{120}$$
$$A = \$5,000\left(\frac{400}{400} + \frac{2.5}{400}\right)^{120}$$
$$A = \$5,000\left(\frac{402.5}{400}\right)^{120}$$
$$A = \$5,000(2.112064637)$$
$$A \approx \$10,560.32$$

For Bank C, $A = P\left(1 + \dfrac{r}{100n}\right)^{nt}$, P=$5,000, r=2.5%, n=12, t=30, so

$$A = \$5,000 \left(1 + \frac{2.5}{100 \cdot 12}\right)^{12(30)}$$

$$A = \$5,000 \left(1 + \frac{2.5}{1200}\right)^{360}$$

$$A = \$5,000 \left(\frac{1200}{1200} + \frac{2.5}{1200}\right)^{360}$$

$$A = \$5,000 \left(\frac{1202.5}{1200}\right)^{360}$$

$$A = \$5,000(2.115349048)$$

$$A \approx \$10,576.75$$

Therefore, at the end of thirty years, the account value invested in Bank B is $\$10,576.75 -$ $\$10,560.32 = \$16.43$ less than the value of the account invested through Bank C.

33. B: A bar graph would best show the number of students who chose each color. Since the data is categorical rather than quantitative, a box-and whisker plot, scatter plot, and stem-and-leaf plot cannot be used. Likewise, a line graph is not the best choice since it is best used to illustrate a change in value over time.

34. C: A line graph best illustrates change over time.

35. A, B, C, D, E: Twelve male employees earn salaries in the $\$40,000$-$\$49,999$ salary range, and 24% of the fifty female employees, or $24\% \times 50 = \frac{24}{100} \times 50 = 12$ employees, earn salaries in that range.

The percentage of percentage of male employees earning $\$50,000$ or more equals $\frac{15+9+6+3+2}{66} \times 100\% = \frac{35}{66} \approx 53\%$, which is greater than the percentage of female employees earning $\$50,000$ or more, which is $22\% + 14\% + 12\% + 2\% + 2\% = 52\%$.
The percentage of female employees earning $\$70,000$-$\$79,000$ is 12%, which is greater than the percentage of male employees earning $\$70,000$-$\$79,000$: $\frac{6}{66} \times 100\% \approx 9\%$.
The number of male employees earning in the $\$30,000$-$\$39,000$ is 12, while the number of female employees earning salaries in that range is $12\% \times 50 = \frac{12}{100} \times 50 = 6$. The ratio of male to female employees earning salaries in the $\$30,000$-$\$39,000$ range is therefore 12:6, which reduces to 2:1.

36. Frequency histogram: A frequency histogram is a type of bar graph in which the heights of bars correspond to the frequency of data and the widths of bars span certain class intervals.

37. C: The median is the middle number or average of the two middle numbers of a set of data written in order from least to greatest. There are 66 male employees, so there are 66 salaries, the median of which is half-way between the 33rd and 34th salaries written from least to greatest. The data on the frequency histogram is ordered from least to greatest, and both the 33rd and 34th values are within the $\$50,000$-$\$59,000$ interval.

38. C, E: The line through the center of each box represents the median. For class 1, the median is a better representation of the data than the mean. There are two outliers (points which lie outside of two standard deviations from the mean) which bring down the average test score. In cases such as this, the mean is not the best measure of central tendency.

The mean test score for Class 1 is less than the mean test score for Class 2.

The median test score for Classes 1 and 2 is 82.

The range of test scores is the difference in the highest and lowest values. The highest test score in both classes is the same (98), but the lowest test score in Class 1 (23) is lower than the lowest test score is Class 3 (56), so the test score range is greater in Class 1. The interquartile range, however, is greater in Class 3.

The quartiles of a set of data divide the data into fourths. On the box-and-whisker plot, the upper and lower quartiles represent the boundaries of the box. So, one-fourth, or 25%, of the data lies above the upper quartile, and 25% of the data lies below the lower quartile. Since the upper quartile is 80, 25% of the students made scores of at least 80.

39. E: The product of a and b is ab. If a is a prime number, its only factors are 1 and a. If b is an odd integer, it does not have a factor of 2. Since the only factors of 2 are 1 and itself it is the only even prime number. Therefore the product of a and b can be either odd or even.

The product of a and b can be a prime number if either a or b is 1. For example, if $a = 3$ and $b = 1$, $ab = 3$, which is prime. However, in other cases, ab is not prime. When $a = 3$ and $b = 5$, $ab = 15$, which is not prime. The example and counterexample show that ab is sometimes but not always prime.

The product of a and b can be a multiple of 3. If a and/or b is a multiple of 3, then ab is also a multiple of 3. For example, when $a = 3$ and $b = 5$, $ab = 15$, a multiple of 3. However, when neither a nor b is a multiple of 3, ab will not be a multiple of 3: when $a = 5$ and $= 7$, $ab = 35$, which is not a multiple of 3. The example and counterexample show that ab is sometimes but not always a multiple of 3.

The product of a and b can be a positive integer. For example, when $a = 5$ and $= 7$, $ab = 35$, which is a positive integer. However, since b is an odd integer, it can be negative, and the product of any negative integer with a positive number is negative: when $a = 1$ and $b = -3$, $ab = -3$, an odd integer. The example and counterexample show that ab is sometimes but not always a multiple of 3.

40. B, D, E: $a^{-b} = \frac{1}{a^b}$. When $a = 1$, then $a^{-b} = \frac{1}{1^b} = \frac{1}{1} = 1$ for all values of b. So, a^{-b} can be an integer. For any value of b and any integer $a > 1$, the denominator of $\frac{1}{a^b}$ is a positive integer greater than one, so the expression $\frac{1}{a^b}$ is a fraction between 0 and 1 (a positive non-integer); for example, if a=2 and b=2, $a^{-b} = 2^{-2} = \frac{1}{2^2} = \frac{1}{4}$.

Practice Test #2

Practice Questions

1. The path of a ball thrown into the air is modeled by the first quadrant graph of the equation $h = -16t^2 + 64t + 5$, where h is the height of the ball in feet and t is time in seconds after the ball is thrown. Complete the following statement with "greater than," "less than," or "equal to":
The average rate of change on the interval [1,3] is _____ the average rate of change on the interval [0,4].

2. Complete the table by stating the type of function (linear, exponential, absolute value, quadratic, piece-wise, square root, cube root, quadratic) and the domain of each function.

Function	Type of function	Domain
$f(x) = 2x - 4$		
$f(x) = \sqrt{2x + 6}$		
$f(x) = \begin{cases} -2x^2, & -3 \le x < 4 \\ x - 1, & x \ge 4 \end{cases}$		
$f(x) = 4\lvert x - 1 \rvert$		
$f(x) = \dfrac{1}{2}\sqrt[3]{x}$		

3. Solve for x: $2(x + 3) - 8 = 4x + 2.$ _____

4. Rewrite the equation in terms of temperature, $T =$ _____; in terms of volume, $V =$ _____; and in terms of pressure, $P =$ _____.

- 139 -

For questions 5 and 6, use the information below.

A photo center's price for one-hour, in-store printing is $0.12 for every 4x6 photo. When prints are ordered online for home delivery, the same photo center charges $0.08 for every 4x6 photo and a shipping fee of $3.00.

5. Using *n* for the number of prints and *c* for the total order cost, write and graph a system of linear equations to illustrate the cost of 4x6 prints picked up in the store or shipped to home.

System of equations: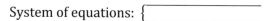

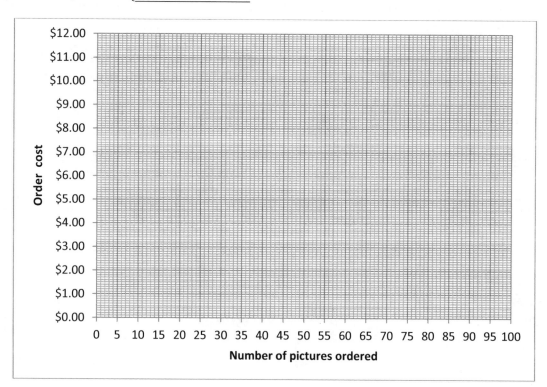

6. Which of the following statements is/are true? Select all that apply.

Ⓐ The intersection of the two lines represents the point at which the order cost is the same for the corresponding number of pictures ordered.

Ⓑ The price of pictures picked up in-store increases by $3.00 for every 25 pictures.

Ⓒ The order cost of fifty 4x6 prints is $1.00 less when picked up in-store than when shipped to home.

Ⓓ The slope of the line representing the ship-to-home order option is 3.

Ⓔ The order total for sixty prints shipped to home is $4.80.

7. Determine whether each system of equations has no solution, one solution, or infinitely many solutions. Put check marks in the appropriate boxes to complete the table.

	$y = 2x - 1$ $4x - 2y = 2$	$-3y = 12 - x$ $6y - 2x = 12$	$3x + 2y = 4$ $y = \dfrac{2}{3}x - 1$
No solution			
One solution			
Infinitely many solutions			

8. Graph each number on the number line: $2\sqrt{3}, -3.2, -2\dfrac{1}{2}, \dfrac{11}{3}, \pi.$

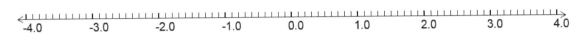

9. Write a piece-wise function to describe the graph below.

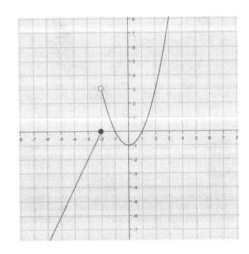

Use the information below to answer questions 10-11.

Irina intends to invest \$5,000 in an interest-earning account. Bank A makes an initial one-time deposit of \$200 into newly-opened accounts and offers an interest accrual rate of 2.25% compounded quarterly. Bank B offers an account with an interest accrual rate of 2.5%, also compounded quarterly, but does not offer a bonus deposit. Bank C offers an account with an interest accrual rate of 2.5%, compounded monthly, with no initial bonus deposit. The formula for calculating the account balance A in a compounding interest account is $A = P\left(1 + \dfrac{r}{100n}\right)^{nt}$, where P is the initial value of the account, r is the percent interest rate, n is the number of times per year interest in compounded, and t is time in years.

10. The value of each account over time illustrates _____ growth.

11. Irina creates the graph below to compare the account value trends over 30 years through Bank A and Bank B. Which of the following statements is/are true?

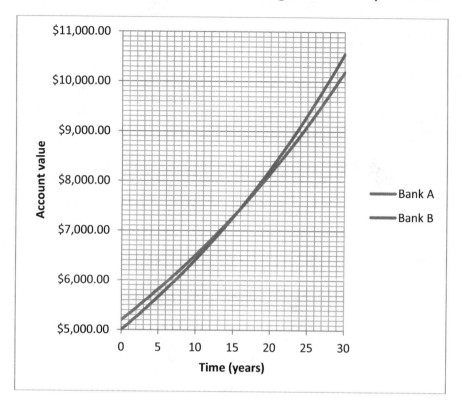

Ⓐ If Irina chooses to leave her money in the account for fewer than ten years, she should choose Bank A.

Ⓑ If Irina chooses to leave her money in either account for more than 30 years, she will not earn additional interest.

Ⓒ For every year Irina leaves her money in Bank A, the account value will increase by $100.

Ⓓ It will take approximately one year longer for Irina's initial investment to double in Bank A than Bank B.

Ⓔ After eight years, the difference in the potential account values is approximately $100 less than the initial difference in the account values.

12. Complete the statement with "never," "sometimes," or "always."
For every month after the first, the value of the account through Bank C will _____ be greater than the account value through Bank A and _____ be greater than the account value through Bank B.

- 142 -

13. A teacher asks each of his students to choose his/her favorite color among the colors of the rainbow. Which of these is the best way to illustrate the results?

(A) A line graph

(B) A bar graph

(C) A box-and-whisker plot

(D) A scatter pot

(E) A stem-and-leaf diagram

For questions 14-15, consider the set of data below.

38 49 22 36 45 27 38 47 20 21 19 38 17 28 15 18 42 17 25 33
31

14. Organize the data using a stem-and-leaf plot.

```
1 |
2 |
3 |
4 |
```

15. State the mean, median, and mode(s). If necessary, round to the nearest tenth.
Mean: _____
Median: _____
Mode: _____

16. A number is chosen at random from the set of data. As a fraction in lowest terms, what is the probability that the number is at least 22? _____

17. If all smoots are weebles and all smoots are tribits, which statement must also be true?

(A) All weebles are tribits.

(B) All weebles are smoots.

(C) If it is not a tribit, it is not a weeble.

(D) If it is not a weeble, it is not a smoot.

(E) If it is not a smoot, it is not a tribet.

18. Which of these statements is (are) true? Select all that apply.

Ⓐ All quadrilaterals have four sides.

Ⓑ Some parallelograms are rhombi.

Ⓒ All squares are rectangles.

Ⓓ All rectangles are parallelograms

Ⓔ No right triangles are equilateral triangles.

19. Complete the two-column proof to show that if $\frac{2}{3}x + 6 = 2$, then $x = -6$.

Statement	Reason
$\frac{2}{3}x + 6 = 2$	Given
$3\left(\frac{2}{3}x + 6\right) = 3(2)$	
	Distributive Property
	Subtraction Property of Equality

20. Match the word to its definition

_____Sum   a. the number resulting from the multiplication of two
numbers
_____Product   b. the number resulting from the division of two numbers
_____Square   c. the number resulting from a quantity multiplied by itself
_____Quotient   d. the number resulting from the addition of two numbers

21. A science teacher orders two boxes of test tubes, but a quarter of the test tubes from one box are broken. In a class of 28 students, there are not enough unbroken test tubes for each student to conduct their own experiment, so each student chooses one partner with whom to work. After the teacher distributes one test tube to each pair of students, seven test tubes remain unused. How many test tubes come in a box? _____

22. A seller purchases wholesale merchandise and sells it in his store with a mark-up of 25%. Store inventory that does not readily sell is marked down by 20%. What percentage profit does the seller make on clearance sales? _____

23. 210 students who graduate from a senior class will attend a university in the fall. The remaining 40% of graduates plan to attend community college, enter the workforce, or join the military at a ratio of 1:2:1. How many graduates from this class will enlist in the military? _____

24. On a map, 1.5 cm represents 60 miles. If two cities are 3.75 cm apart on the map, what is the distance between the cities in miles? _____

25. The area of a rectangular bedroom is 120 ft², and the perimeter of the room is 44 ft. On a house plan drawn to a $\frac{1}{24}$ scale, what is the length in inches of the longer side of the rectangle representing the room? _____

26. If the ratio of the volume of a small to the volume of a large cube is 1:8, what is the ratio of the length of one side of the small cube to the length of one side of the large cube?

   Ⓐ 1:2

   Ⓑ 1:4

   Ⓒ 1:8

   Ⓓ 1:64

   Ⓔ 1:512

27. Two sides of a right triangle measure 6 cm and 7 cm. Which of these can represent the length of the third side? Select all that apply.

   Ⓐ $\sqrt{13}$ cm

   Ⓑ 5 cm

   Ⓒ 8 cm

   Ⓓ $\sqrt{85}$

   Ⓔ Any of these are possible values for the third side.

*Use the table below, which shows the results of performing an operation * on values **a**, **b**, and **c**, to answer questions 28 and 29.*

*	a	b	c
a	d		a
b	c	e	b
c	a	b	c

28. If operation * is commutative, which letter goes in the empty box?

   Ⓐ a

   Ⓑ b

   Ⓒ c

   Ⓓ d

   Ⓔ e

29. For operation *, _____ is the identity element, and the inverse of a is _____.

30. A jar contains $8.05 worth of coins. In the jar, there are forty pennies, thirteen dimes, four half-dollars, and the number of nickels in the jar exceeds twice the number of quarters by three. How many nickels are in the jar? _____

Use the following information to answer questions 31-33.

Polymerase Chain Reaction, PCR, is used in a laboratory to amplify a specific portion of DNA (deoxyribonucleic acid, the genetic material found in many cells). During the reaction, double stranded DNA is separated into single strands, each of which is copied by the enzyme polymerase. The simplified diagram below illustrates this process.

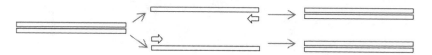

In a classroom experiment, a sample containing ten copies of double-stranded DNA targeted for amplification undergoes multiple cycles of PCR. Students A through E are asked to predict the results at different stages of the experiment.

- Student A predicts that there will be 50 copies of the DNA after four cycles because the number of DNA copies increases by ten with each PCR cycle.
- Student B predicts that there will be 10,000 copies of the DNA after three cycles because each PCR cycle produces ten times the amount of DNA as was present before the cycle.
- Student C predicts that there will be 10,240 copies after ten cycles because the amount of DNA doubles with each cycle.
- Student D predicts that there will be 160 copies of the DNA after five cycles because the number of DNA copies increases by ten during cycle 1, twenty during cycle 2, thirty during cycle 3, and so on.
- Student E predicts that there will be 18 copies of DNA after eight cycles since one additional copy of DNA is produced with every cycle.

31. Based on the students' stated predictions and explanations, complete the table to show how many double-stranded DNA molecules each student's model predicts will be present after each cycle.

Cycle	Student A	Student B	Student C	Student D	Student E
--	10	10	10	10	10
1					
2					
3		10,000			
4	50				
5				160	
6					
7					
8					18
9					
10			10,240		

32. Each student writes an expression which can be used to predict the number of strands of DNA after the nth cycle. Match each expression with each student's model of growth.

____ $5n^2 + 5n + 10$

____ $10 + 10n$

____ $10 + n$

____ $10(2^n)$

____ 10^{n+1}

33. Which student provides the best prediction and explanation?

Ⓐ Student A

Ⓑ Student B

Ⓒ Student C

Ⓓ Student D

Ⓔ Student E

Use the following information to answer questions 34 and 35.

> The midpoints of all of the sides of a square are connected to produce a second square within the first.

34. What is the probability that a point chosen at random within the larger square is also within the smaller square? Express the answer as a percent. _____

35. If the perimeter of the larger square is 120 units, what is the perimeter of the smaller square?

Ⓐ $15\sqrt{2}$ units

Ⓑ 30 units

Ⓒ $30\sqrt{2}$ units

Ⓓ 60 units

Ⓔ $60\sqrt{2}$ units

36. About half of the students in a local high school have cell phones, about three-quarters of which are smart phones. If there are 1,217 students in the school, approximately how many students do NOT have smart phones?

Ⓐ 150

Ⓑ 300

Ⓒ 450

Ⓓ 750

Ⓔ 950

37. The graph of function $f(x)$ is shown.

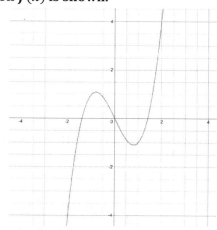

Which of the following statements is (are) true? Select all that apply.

Ⓐ $f(x) = 0$ has three solutions.

Ⓑ $f(-x) = -f(x)$

Ⓒ The graph of $f(x)$ is symmetric about the origin.

Ⓓ $f(4) = 2$

Ⓔ $f(x)$ is a cube root function.

38. If $f(x) = (x + 1)^2$ and $g(x) = x^2 + x + 4$, the graphs of $f(x)$ and g(x) intersect at point (___,___).

Use the information below to answer questions 39 and 40.

160 Algebra I students took Mr. DeMarco's final exam. The test scores were normally distributed with a mean of 72 and a standard deviation (a measure of how much data deviates from the average) of 8. In a normally distributed set of data, the graph of which forms a bell-shaped curve, about 68% of the data lies within one standard deviation of the mean, and about 95% of the data lies within two standard deviations of the mean.

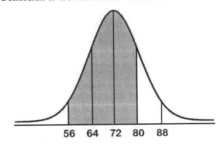

56　64　72　80　88

39. Approximately what percentage of students received scores between 56 and 80?
____%

40. Which of these statements is (are) true if Mr. DeMarco scales test scores by four points? Choose all that apply.

Ⓐ The mean increases to 76.

Ⓑ The bell curve shifts four spaces to the left.

Ⓒ The standard deviation remains the same.

Ⓓ Eight students receive failing scores (scores below 60).

Ⓔ The shape of the curve changes.

Answers and Explanations

1. Equal to: The height of the ball is a function of time, so the equation can be expressed as $f(t) = -16t^2 + 64t + 5$, and the average rate of change on the interval [1,3] can be found by calculating $\frac{f(3)-f(1)}{3-1}$.

$$\frac{-16(3)^2 + 64(3) + 5 - [-16(1)^2 + 64(1) + 5]}{3-1} = \frac{-144 + 192 + 5 - (-16 + 64 + 5)}{2} = \frac{0}{2}$$
$$= 0$$

Likewise, the average rate of change on the interval [0,4] can be found by calculating $\frac{f(4)-f(0)}{4-0}$.

$$\frac{-16(4)^2 + 64(4) + 5 - [-16(0)^2 + 64(0) + 5]}{4-0} = \frac{-256 + 256 + 5 - (0 + 0 + 5)}{4} = \frac{0}{4} = 0$$

2.

Function	Type of function	Domain
$f(x) = 2x - 4$	Linear	$\{\mathcal{R}\}$
$f(x) = \sqrt{2x + 6}$	Square root	$\{x : x \geq -3\}$
$f(x) = \begin{cases} -2x^2, & -3 \leq x < 4 \\ x - 1, & x \geq 4 \end{cases}$	Piece-wise	$\{x : x \geq -3\}$
$f(x) = 4\lvert x - 1\rvert$	Absolute value	$\{\mathcal{R}\}$
$f(x) = \frac{1}{2}\sqrt[3]{x}$	Cube root	$\{\mathcal{R}\}$

The domain of each given linear, absolute value, and cube root function is the set of all real numbers: there is no real number which, when entered into the equation for x, does not give exactly one real value for $f(x)$.

The square root function $f(x) = \sqrt{2x + 6}$ is undefined in the real number system for certain values of x, such as -4. The domain of the function must only include values which make the square-root expression positive or equal to zero: $\sqrt{2x + 6} \geq 0$. Solve for x to determine which values are included in the domain.

$$\sqrt{2x + 6} \geq 0$$
$$\left(\sqrt{2x + 6}\right)^2 \geq 0^2$$
$$2x + 6 \geq 0$$
$$2x \geq -6$$
$$x \geq -3$$

The domain only includes values of x greater than -3 since any value less than -3 produces a negative number under the square root.

The given piece-wise function is defined for all values of x such that $x \geq -3$ but is undefined for x-values less than -3.

3. $x = -2$:

$$2(x + 3) - 8 = 4x + 2$$
$$2x + 6 - 8 = 4x + 2$$
$$2x - 2 = 4x + 2$$
$$-2 = 2x + 2$$
$$-4 = 2x$$
$$-2 = x$$

4. $T = \dfrac{PV}{k}, V = \dfrac{kT}{P}, P = \dfrac{kT}{V}$:

Solve $\dfrac{PV}{T} = k$ for T:

$$\frac{PV}{T} = k$$
$$\cancel{T} \cdot \frac{PV}{\cancel{T}} = T \cdot k$$
$$PV = Tk$$
$$\frac{PV}{k} = \frac{T\cancel{k}}{\cancel{k}}$$
$$\frac{PV}{k} = T$$

Solve $\dfrac{PV}{T} = k$ for V:

$$\frac{PV}{T} = k$$
$$\frac{\cancel{T}}{\cancel{P}} \cdot \frac{\cancel{P}V}{\cancel{T}} = \frac{T}{P} \cdot k$$
$$V = \frac{Tk}{P} = \frac{kT}{P}$$

Solve $\dfrac{PV}{T} = k$ for P:

$$\frac{PV}{T} = k$$
$$\frac{\cancel{T}}{\cancel{V}} \cdot \frac{P\cancel{V}}{\cancel{T}} = \frac{T}{V} \cdot k$$
$$P = \frac{Tk}{V} = \frac{kT}{V}$$

5.

$$c = 0.12n$$
$$c = 0.08n + 3$$

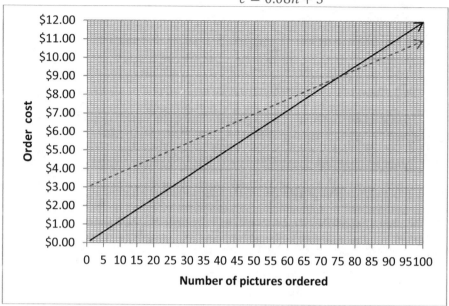

6. A, B, C: The intersection of the lines shows that 75 pictures cost $9.00 whether the pictures are picked up in the store or shipped to home.

The slope of the line representing the in-store pick-up is $0.12 = \frac{12}{100} = \frac{3}{25}$, so the price of pictures picked up in-store increases by $3.00 for every 25 pictures.

The order cost of fifty prints picked up in the store is $6.00, which is $1.00 less than $7.00 cost to have the prints shipped to home.

The slope of the line representing the ship-to-home order option is $0.08 = \frac{8}{100} = \frac{2}{25}$.

The order total for sixty prints shipped to home is $\$0.08(60) + \$3.00 = \$4.80 + \$3.00 = \$7.80$.

7. A:

	$y = 2x - 1$ $4x - 2y = 2$	$-3y = 12 - x$ $6y - 2x = 12$	$3x + 2y = 4$ $y = \frac{2}{3}x - 1$
No solution		✔	
One solution			✔
Infinitely many solutions	✔		

In a system of two linear equations with no solution, the slopes of both lines are the same while the y-intercepts differ. Since the lines are parallel, they do not intersect; therefore, there is no solution to the system of equations.

$-3y = 12 - x$: slope $= \frac{1}{3}$, y-intercept $= -4$

$6y - 2x = 12$: slope $= \frac{1}{3}$, y-intercept $= 2$

In a system of two linear equations with infinitely many solutions, the slopes and y-intercepts of the two lines are the same. Since the two equations describe the same line, the lines overlap and intersect at every point; therefore, there are infinitely many solutions.

$y = 2x - 1$: slope $= 2$, y-intercept $= -1$

$4x - 2y = 2$: slope $= 2$, y-intercept $= -1$

In a system of two linear equations with one solution, the slopes of the two lines differ, and the y-intercepts can be either the same of different. The lines intersect at exactly one point, so there is one solution.

$3x + 2y = 4$: slope $= -\frac{3}{2}$, y-intercept $= 2$

$y = \frac{2}{3}x - 1$: slope $= \frac{2}{3}$, y-intercept $= -1$

8. The numbers are graphed are -3.2, $-2\frac{1}{2}$, π, $2\sqrt{3}$, and $\frac{11}{3}$, respectively:

9. $f(x) = \begin{cases} 2x + 4, & x \leq -2 \\ x^2 - 1, & x > -2 \end{cases}$

The graph as x approaches -2 from the left is linear; the slope of the line is 2, and, if the line were extended, it would cross the y-axis at 4. Therefore, in slope-intercept form, the equation of the line is $y = 2x + 4$. The function is defined by this line for all x-values less than or equal to -2.

Once x exceeds -2, the graph is a parabola. This parabola is the graph of $y = x^2$ shifted down one unit, so its equation is $y = x^2 - 1$.

10. Exponential: Since interest is earned on top of interest, the growth of the account value is exponential. An exponential growth equation is in the general form $y = c^x$, where c is a constant. For all three banks, the initial account value, the interest rate, and the number of times interest is compounded are constants; the exponent t, time, is variable.

11. A, D, E: The value of the account invested through Bank A is greater for every year through ten years than the value of the account invested through Bank B.

Even though the graph only shows the value of the accounts over a 30 year period, both accounts will continue to accrue interest as long as the accounts remain in the bank.

For every year the money remains in the bank, the account value will increase more than it did the previous year since the account earns interest on top of interest: if the growth of the account value were linear, the increase in the account value per year would be a constant representing the slope of the line; however, the growth is exponential, so the change is not constant.

- 153 -

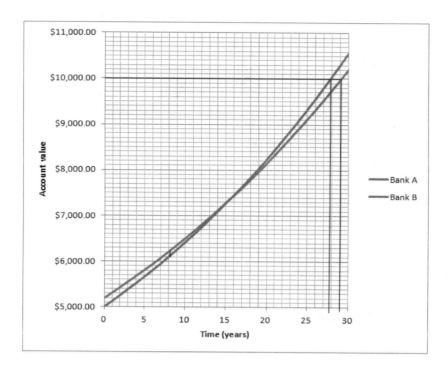

Irina initially invested $5,000, and the value of her account is $10,000, twice her original investment, at approximately 28 years in Bank B and approximately 29 years in Bank A.

At eight years, the account value through Bank A is approximately $6,200, while the account value through Bank B is approximately $6,100. This difference of $100 is $100 less than the initial difference of $200 in account values ($5,200 in Bank A and $5,000 in Bank B).

12. Sometimes, always: Bank B offers the same interest rate as Bank C, but interest is compounded monthly rather than quarterly; this means that interest payments are added to the account twelve times per year rather than four times per year, and since interest in earned on top of that interest, the account value in Bank C is higher, albeit slightly at first, than the account value in Bank B. The difference in the account values through Banks A and C follows the same trend as the difference in account values through Banks A and B: the account value through Bank A exceeds the value through Bank C for several years, after which the value through Bank C exceeds the value through Bank A.

13. Exponential, linear, exponential: Bacteria reproduce asexually by binary fission, which means to split into two parts. Once the genetic material of a single-celled bacterium replicates, the cell splits into two daughter cells, each of which reproduces by splitting into two, and so forth. So, if the population of bacteria which double every minute starts at 100 cells, there will be 200 cells after one minute, then 400 after a two minutes, 800 after three minutes, and so one. This is an example of exponential growth. The change in population is not constant but increases predictably and proportionally with every minute as long as there space and available nutrients do no limit the growth of the bacteria.

Since the change in the account value is constant every week, the balance grows linearly. If there is a starting balance of $100, after one week the balance would be $150, then $200 after the second, $300 after the third, and so on.

If salary increases by 3% every year, the yearly change in salary is not a constant dollar amount but increases predictably and proportionally with each passing year. For example, if a starting salary is $100,000, the salary will become $103,000 ($100,000 + 0.03 · $100,000) after the first year, $106,090 ($103,000 + 0.03 · $103,000) after the second, $109,272.70 after the third, and so on. This is an example of exponential growth.

14. 1 | 5 = 15:

1	5, 7, 7, 8, 9
2	0, 1, 2, 5, 7, 8
3	1, 3, 6, 8, 8, 8
4	2, 5, 7, 9

15. Mean: 29.8; Median: 28; Mode: 38: The mean, or average, is equal to the sum of the data divided by the number of values in the data set.

$$\text{Mean} = \frac{15+17+17+18+19+20+21+22+25+27+28+31+33+36+38+38+38+42+45+47+49}{21} = \frac{626}{21} = 29.8$$

The median is the middle number or the average of the two middle numbers in the set of data organized from least to greatest. Since there are 21 numbers in the data set, the median is the eleventh number, below and above which there are ten numbers. The eleventh number is 28.

The mode is the value that occurs with the greatest frequency in the set. If all values occur with equal frequency, there is no mode; if more than one value appears with the highest frequency, there is more than one mode. In this set, there is one mode, namely 38, which appears three times in the set of data.

16. $\frac{2}{3}$: There are fourteen numbers in the set of data that are greater than or equal to 22, and there are twenty-one numbers in the set. The probability of choosing a number that is at least 22, therefore, is $\frac{14}{21}$, which reduces to $\frac{2}{3}$.

17. D: Since the words are nonsensical, it may be helpful to rewrite given statements using other words. For instance, substitute the word "smoots" with "cats," "weebles" with "mammals," and "tribits" with "felines" to make the true statements "all cats are mammals" and "all cats are feline." If interchanging these words in any of the answer choices creates a false statement, then the original statement is not necessarily true. If interchanging these words in the answer choice creates a true statement, the original statement *may* be true; however, if another counterexample can be given, the original statement is not necessarily true.

"All mammals are felines" is not true. (For example, dogs are mammals, but they are not feline.)

"All mammals are cats" is not true. (For example, dogs are mammals, but they are not cats.)

"If it is not a mammal, then it is not a feline" is true. However, if "weebles" were defined as "feline" and "tribit" were defined as "mammal," then the statement would read "if it is not a feline, it is not a mammal." That is not true. (For example, dogs are not feline, but they are mammals.)

"If it is not a mammal, then it is not a cat" is true. There is no counterexample which can disprove this statement. The contrapositive (if not q, then not p) of a true statement (if p, then q) is always true.

If it is not a cat, then it is not a mammal is not true. (For example, dogs are not cats, but dogs are mammals.)

18. A, B, C, D, E: A polygon which has four sides is a quadrilateral.

A quadrilateral with two pairs of parallel sides is a parallelogram, and a parallelogram with four congruent sides is a rhombus; therefore, all rhombi are parallelograms, but only some parallelograms are rhombi.
A rectangle is a parallelogram with four right angles, and a square is a rectangle with four congruent sides; therefore, all squares are rectangles, but only some rectangles are squares, and all rectangles are parallelograms, but only some parallelograms are rectangles.

An equilateral triangle has three congruent sides and three congruent angles, each of which measures 60°. Since a right triangle contains a 90° angle, the triangle cannot be equilateral.

19.

Statement	Reason
$\frac{2}{3}x + 6 = 2$	Given
$3\left(\frac{2}{3}x + 6\right) = 3(2)$	**Multiplication Property of Equality**
$2x + 18 = 6$	Distributive Property
$2x = -12$	Subtraction Property of Equality
$x = -6$	**Division Property of Equality**

20. D, A, C, B

21. 12: In a class of 28, there are 14 groups of two students. If seven remain after distributing 14 test tubes to the pairs, then there are 14+7=21 unbroken test tubes. Let x represent the number of test tubes in a box. If a quarter, or $\frac{1}{4}$, of the test tubes in one box are broken, then the number of unbroken test tubes in that box is $x - \frac{1}{4}x = \frac{3}{4}x$. So, the total number of unbroken test tubes from both boxes is $x + \frac{3}{4}x$, which is 21. Solve for x.

$$x + \frac{3}{4}x = 21$$
$$\frac{4}{4}x + \frac{3}{4}x = 21$$
$$\frac{7}{4}x = 21$$
$$\frac{4}{7} \cdot \frac{7}{4}x = \frac{4}{7} \cdot \frac{21}{1}$$
$$x = 12$$

22. 0%. (The seller does not profit.): Suppose the seller purchases an item for $100. A mark-up of 25% is $\frac{25}{100} \times \$100 = \$25$, so the store price is set at $125. If that $125 item is marked down 20%, or $\frac{20}{100} \times \$125 = \$25$, the clearance price is $100. Since $100 is the amount of the seller's initial investment, he makes no profit on the sale of clearance merchandise.

A general expression describing the price of the clearance merchandise is $0.80(1.25x)$, where x is the seller's purchase price. The expression simplifies to x, so the clearance price is the same as the seller's investment price.

23. 35: The 210 students who will attend a university represent 60% of the graduates $(100\% - 40\% = 60\%)$. If $x=$number of graduates, then $60\% \cdot x = 210 \rightarrow 0.60 \cdot x = 210 \rightarrow x = \frac{210}{0.60} = 350$. If 40% of the 350 graduates plan to attend community college, enter the workforce, or join the military at a ratio of 1:2:1, then 10% of the graduates will attend community college, 20% will enter the workforce, and 10% will join the military $(10\%: 20\%: 10\% = 1: 2: 1$ and $10\% + 20\% + 10\% = 40\%)$. Therefore, 10% of 350, or $0.10 \cdot 350 = 35$, students will enlist in the military.

24. 150 miles: On the map, the scale factor is proportional to the ratio of the distance on the map between the cities and the actual distance between the cities. So,

$$\frac{1.5 \text{ cm}}{60 \text{ miles}} = \frac{3.75 \text{ cm}}{x}$$
$$(1.5 \text{ cm})x = (3.75 \text{ cm})(60 \text{ miles})$$
$$\frac{(1.5 \text{ cm})x}{1.5 \text{ cm}} = \frac{(3.75 \text{ cm})(60 \text{ miles})}{1.5 \text{ cm}}$$

$x = 150 \text{ miles}$

25. 6 inches: The area of a rectangle is equal to its length times its width, while the perimeter is the sum of the four sides, or the sum of twice the length and twice the width. So, to find the dimensions of the rectangle, set up and solve a system of equations. Here, the substitution method of solving is shown.

$$lw = 120 \rightarrow l = \frac{120}{w}$$
$$2l + 2w = 44$$
$$2\left(\frac{120}{w}\right) + 2w = 44$$
$$\frac{240}{w} + 2w = 44$$
$$w\left(\frac{240}{w} + 2w\right) = w(44)$$
$$240 + 2w^2 = 44w$$
$$2w^2 - 44w + 240 = 0$$
$$2(w^2 - 22w + 120) = 0$$
$$w^2 - 22w + 120 = 0$$
$$(w - 10)(w - 12) = 0$$
$$w = 10 \text{ or } w = 12$$

If the width is 10 ft, the length is 12 ft, or if the width is 12 ft, the length is 10 ft.

On the house plan, the scale is $\frac{1}{24}$, which means that a 1 ft length is represented as 1/24th of a foot on the plan. 1/24th of a foot is $\left(\frac{1}{24}\right)(12") = \frac{12"}{24} = \frac{1"}{2}$. So, the 12' side of the room is represented as a 6" side of a rectangle on the house plan.

26. A: The volume, V, of a cube is the cube of the length of one side, l^3: $V = l^3$. It follows that the length of one side of a cube is the cube root of its volume: $\sqrt[3]{V} = l$. Therefore, the ratio of the length of one side of the small cube to the length of one side of the large cube equals $\sqrt[3]{1} : \sqrt[3]{8} = 1 : 2$.

27. A, D: The sides of a right triangle must satisfy the Pythagorean Theorem, $a^2 + b^2 = c^2$, where a and b are the legs of the right triangle and c is the hypotenuse. The hypotenuse is always the longest of the three sides, so 6 cm cannot represent the length of the hypotenuse. However, the hypotenuse could measure 7 cm, or the hypotenuse could be the side whose length is not given. Thus, either $6^2 + b^2 = 7^2$ or $6^2 + 7^2 = c^2$.

$$6^2 + b^2 = 7^2$$
$$36 + b^2 = 49$$
$$b^2 = 13$$
$$b = \sqrt{13}$$

Or

$$6^2 + 7^2 = c^2$$
$$36 + 49 = c^2$$
$$85 = c^2$$
$$c = \sqrt{85}$$

28. C: If the operation * is commutative, then $a * b = b * a = c$.

29. C, B: $a * c = c * a = a$; $b * c = c * b = b$, and $c * c = c$, so performing operation $* c$ on any element does not change that element's value; therefore, c is the identity element. Two values are inverses if an operation performed on those yields the operation's identity element. Since c is the identity element for operation *, and since $a * b = b * a = c$, a and b are inverse elements.

30. 27: The jar contains $8.05 worth of coins. There are forty pennies, so $0.40 of that amount is in pennies; likewise, there are thirteen dimes and four half-dollars, so $13(\$0.10) = \$1.30$ of the amount is in dimes and $4(\$0.50) = \$2.00$ is in half-dollars. Therefore, the value of the nickels and quarters together is $8.05 − $0.40 − $1.30 − $2.00 = $4.35. Since each nickel contributes $0.05 to that amount and each quarter contributes $0.25 to the amount, $0.05n + 0.25q = 4.35$, where n is the number of nickels and q is the number of quarters.

The number of nickels exceeds twice the number of quarters by three: $n = 2q + 3$. This equation, together with the other equation relating the number of nickels and quarters, can be used to find the number of nickels in the jar. Apply substitution method of solving a system of equations to first solve for q and then for n.

$$\mathbf{0.05(2q + 3) + 0.25q = 4.35}$$
$$0.1q + 0.15 + 0.25q = 4.35$$
$$\mathbf{0.35q + 0.15 = 4.35}$$
$$0.35q = 4.20$$

- 158 -

$$q = 12$$

$$n = 2q + 3 \rightarrow n = 2(12) + 3 = 24 + 3 = 27$$

There are 27 nickels in the jar.

31.

Cycle	Student A	Student B	Student C	Student D	Student E
--	10	10	10	10	10
1	20	100	20	20	11
2	30	1,000	40	40	12
3	40	10,000	80	70	13
4	50	100,000	160	110	14
5	60	10^6	320	160	15
6	70	10^7	640	220	16
7	80	10^8	1,280	290	17
8	90	10^9	2,560	370	18
9	100	10^{10}	5,120	460	19
10	110	10^{11}	10,240	560	20

32. D, A, E, C, B: Compare the values yielded by each expression to the numbers predicted by each student.

Cycle (n)	$5n^2 + 5n + 10$	$10 + 10n$	$10 + n$	$10(2^n)$	10^{n+1}
1	$5(1)^2 + 5(1) + 10$ $= 5 + 5 + 10$ $= 20$	$10 + 10(1)$ $= 10 + 10$ $= 20$	$10 + 1$ $=11$	$10(2^1)$ $= 10(2)$ $=20$	10^{1+1} $= 10^2$ $= 100$
2	$5(2)^2 + 5(2) + 10$ $= 20 + 10 + 10$ $= 40$	$10 + 10(2)$ $= 10 + 20$ $= 30$	$10 + 2$ $=12$	$10(2^2)$ $= 10(4)$ $=40$	10^{2+1} $= 10^3$ $= 1,000$
3	$5(3)^2 + 5(3) + 10$ $= 45 + 15 + 10$ $= 70$	$10 + 10(3)$ $= 10 + 30$ $= 40$	$10 + 3$ $=13$	$10(2^3)$ $= 10(8)$ $=80$	10^{3+1} $= 10^4$ $= 10,000$
4	$5(4)^2 + 5(4) + 10$ $= 80 + 20 + 10$ $= 110$	$10 + 10(4)$ $= 10 + 40$ $= 50$	$10 + 4$ $=14$	$10(2^4)$ $= 10(16)$ $=160$	10^{4+1} $= 10^5$ $= 100,000$

33. C: During the first cycle, the ten copies of double-stranded DNA separate into twenty single strands, and each strand is copied to produce double-stranded DNA. So, at the end of the first cycle, there are twenty double-stranded DNA molecules. During the second cycle, each of these separates into forty single strands, which are copied by polymerase to make forty double-stranded DNA molecules. With each successive cycle, the number of DNA molecules doubles. This is exponential growth with a base of two and follows Student C's growth model.

34. 50%: Draw a square and connect the midpoints of all of the sides to create a smaller square. If the midpoints of opposite sides of the larger square (i.e., vertices of the smaller square) are connected, it becomes evident that the area of the smaller square is half the area of the larger square. Therefore, the probability that a point chosen at random within the larger square is also within the smaller square is 50%.

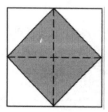

35. E: If the perimeter of the larger square is 120 units, then each side measures $\frac{120}{4} = 30$ units. The midpoints divide each side of the square into two equal parts measuring 15 units. Since a square has right angles, this produces four equivalent right, isosceles triangles, the hypotenuses of which are the side of the smaller square. Therefore, the side lengths of the smaller square can be found using the Pythagorean Theorem.

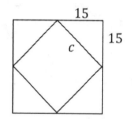

$$15^2 + 15^2 = c^2$$
$$225 + 225 = c^2$$
$$450 = c^2$$
$$\sqrt{450} = c$$
$$\sqrt{2 \cdot 3 \cdot 3 \cdot 5 \cdot 5} = c$$
$$3 \cdot 5 \cdot \sqrt{2} = c$$
$$15\sqrt{2} = c$$

The perimeter of square is four times the length of one of its side, so $P = 4\left(15\sqrt{2}\right) = 60\sqrt{2}$ units.

36. D: The number of students who do not have smart phones includes the students who have no cell phones and the students who have cell phones which are not smart phones. There are about 1200 students in the school, so approximately 600 students have no cell phones, and about 600 students do have cell phones. Since three-quarters of the cell phones are smart phones, one-quarter of the phones are not smart phones: $\frac{600}{4} = 150$. So, there are approximately $600 + 150 = 750$ students who do not have smart phones.

37. A, B, C: $f(x) = 0$ all along the x-axis. Since the graph of $f(x)$ crosses the x-axis three times, $f(x) = 0$ has three solutions.
Since $f(2) = 4$, $-f(2) = -4$. $f(-2) = -4$, so $f(-2) = -f(2)$. For every point $(x, f(x))$ on the graph, there is a point $(-x, -f(x))$, so the generalization $f(-x) = -f(x)$ is true.

A graph is symmetric about the origin when the graph can be rotated 180° with respect to the origin and look the same as the original graph. Incidentally, this happens when $f(-x) = -f(x)$ is true.

The value of $f(4)$ cannot be determined from the portion of the graph shown, but since the graph does not pass through $(4,2)$, $f(4) \neq 2$.

The graph of $y = \sqrt[3]{x}$ is shown below. No transformation results in a graph which crosses the x-axis more than once. The given function $f(x)$ is a cubic function, not a cube-root function.

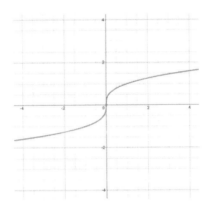

38. (3, 16): The graphs of the functions will intersect when $f(x) = g(x)$. Therefore, rather than graphing, one may determine the x-value of intersection of the graphs by solving the equation $(x + 1)^2 = x^2 + x + 4$.

$$(x + 1)^2 = x^2 + x + 4$$
$$x^2 + 2x + 1 = x^2 + x + 4$$
$$2x + 1 = x + 4$$
$$x + 1 = 4$$
$$x = 3$$

$f(3) = g(3)$, so to find the y-value of the point of intersection, find either f(3) or g(3).
$$f(3) = (3 + 1)^2 = 4^2 = 16$$

39. 81.5%: Since 68% of students scored within one standard deviation of the mean, 34% scored within one standard deviation above the mean (between 72 and 80), and 34% scored within one standard deviation below the mean (between 64 and 72). Since 95% of students scored within two standard deviations of the mean (between 56 and 88), 47.5% of students scored within two deviations either above (between 56 and 72) or below the mean (between 72 and 88); of those, 34% scored within one standard deviation, so 47.5% − 34% = 13.5% of students scored between one and two standard deviations either above or below the mean (between 56 and 64 or between 80 and 88). Only 100% − 95% = 5% of students scored outside of two standard deviations from the mean: 2.5% received scores below two standard deviations below the mean (below 56), and 2.5% received scores above two standard deviations above the mean (above 88).

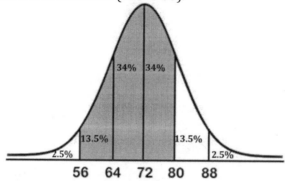

The percentage of students who received scores between 56 and 80 is 13.5% + 34% + 34% = 81.5%.

40. A, C: If Mr. DeMarco scales scores by four points, then every test score increases by four points. Therefore, the mean increases by four points from 72 to 76. Since the amount of variation in scores remains the same, the standard deviation does not change. Accordingly, the curve retains its shape but shifts four spaces to the right.

When scores are scaled, 2.5% of students receive scores below 60 since 60 is two standard deviations from the new mean (76 − 8 − 8 = 60). 2.5% of 160 students is 0.025 · 160 = 4 students.

Success Strategies

The most important thing you can do is to ignore your fears and jump into the test immediately. Do not be overwhelmed by any strange-sounding terms. You have to jump into the test like jumping into a pool—all at once is the easiest way.

Make Predictions

As you read and understand the question, try to guess what the answer will be. Remember that several of the answer choices are wrong, and once you begin reading them, your mind will immediately become cluttered with answer choices designed to throw you off. Your mind is typically the most focused immediately after you have read the question and digested its contents. If you can, try to predict what the correct answer will be. You may be surprised at what you can predict.

Quickly scan the choices and see if your prediction is in the listed answer choices. If it is, then you can be quite confident that you have the right answer. It still won't hurt to check the other answer choices, but most of the time, you've got it!

Answer the Question

It may seem obvious to only pick answer choices that answer the question, but the test writers can create some excellent answer choices that are wrong. Don't pick an answer just because it sounds right, or you believe it to be true. It MUST answer the question. Once you've made your selection, always go back and check it against the question and make sure that you didn't misread the question and that the answer choice does answer the question posed.

Benchmark

After you read the first answer choice, decide if you think it sounds correct or not. If it doesn't, move on to the next answer choice. If it does, mentally mark that answer choice. This doesn't mean that you've definitely selected it as your answer choice, it just means that it's the best you've seen thus far. Go ahead and read the next choice. If the next choice is worse than the one you've already selected, keep going to the next answer choice. If the next choice is better than the choice you've already selected, mentally mark the new answer choice as your best guess.

The first answer choice that you select becomes your standard. Every other answer choice must be benchmarked against that standard. That choice is correct until proven otherwise by another answer choice beating it out. Once you've decided that no other answer choice seems as good, do one final check to ensure that your answer choice answers the question posed.

Valid Information

Don't discount any of the information provided in the question. Every piece of information may be necessary to determine the correct answer. None of the information in the question is there to throw you off (while the answer choices will certainly have information to throw you off). If two seemingly unrelated topics are discussed, don't ignore either. You can be confident there is a relationship, or it wouldn't be included in the question, and you are probably going to have to determine what is that relationship to find the answer.

Avoid "Fact Traps"

Don't get distracted by a choice that is factually true. Your search is for the answer that answers the question. Stay focused and don't fall for an answer that is true but irrelevant. Always go back to the question and make sure you're choosing an answer that actually answers the question and is not just a true statement. An answer can be factually correct, but it MUST answer the question asked. Additionally, two answers can both be seemingly correct, so be sure to read all of the answer choices, and make sure that you get the one that BEST answers the question.

Milk the Question

Some of the questions may throw you completely off. They might deal with a subject you have not been exposed to, or one that you haven't reviewed in years. While your lack of knowledge about the subject will be a hindrance, the question itself can give you many clues that will help you find the correct answer. Read the question carefully and look for clues. Watch particularly for adjectives and nouns describing difficult terms or words that you don't recognize. Regardless of whether you completely understand a word or not, replacing it with a synonym, either provided or one you more familiar with, may help you to understand what the questions are asking. Rather than wracking your mind about specific detailed information concerning a difficult term or word, try to use mental substitutes that are easier to understand.

The Trap of Familiarity

Don't just choose a word because you recognize it. On difficult questions, you may not recognize a number of words in the answer choices. The test writers don't put "make-believe" words on the test, so don't think that just because you only recognize all the words in one answer choice that that answer choice must be correct. If you only recognize words in one answer choice, then focus on that one. Is it correct? Try your best to determine if it is correct. If it is, that's great. If not, eliminate it. Each word and answer choice you eliminate increases your chances of getting the question correct, even if you then have to guess among the unfamiliar choices.

Eliminate Answers

Eliminate choices as soon as you realize they are wrong. But be careful! Make sure you consider all of the possible answer choices. Just because one appears right, doesn't mean that the next one won't be even better! The test writers will usually put more than one good answer choice for every question, so read all of them. Don't worry if you are stuck between two that seem right. By getting down to just two remaining possible choices, your odds are now 50/50. Rather than wasting too much time, play the odds. You are guessing, but guessing wisely because you've been able to knock out some of the answer choices that you know are wrong. If you are eliminating choices and realize that the last answer choice you are left with is also obviously wrong, don't panic. Start over and consider each choice again. There may easily be something that you missed the first time and will realize on the second pass.

Tough Questions

If you are stumped on a problem or it appears too hard or too difficult, don't waste time. Move on! Remember though, if you can quickly check for obviously incorrect answer choices, your chances of guessing correctly are greatly improved. Before you completely give up, at least try to knock out a couple of possible answers. Eliminate what you can and then guess at the remaining answer choices before moving on.

Brainstorm

If you get stuck on a difficult question, spend a few seconds quickly brainstorming. Run through the complete list of possible answer choices. Look at each choice and ask yourself, "Could this answer the question satisfactorily?" Go through each answer choice and consider it independently of the others. By systematically going through all possibilities, you may find something that you would otherwise overlook. Remember though that when you get stuck, it's important to try to keep moving.

Read Carefully

Understand the problem. Read the question and answer choices carefully. Don't miss the question because you misread the terms. You have plenty of time to read each question thoroughly and make sure you understand what is being asked. Yet a happy medium must be attained, so don't waste too much time. You must read carefully, but efficiently.

Face Value

When in doubt, use common sense. Always accept the situation in the problem at face value. Don't read too much into it. These problems will not require you to make huge leaps of logic. The test writers aren't trying to throw you off with a cheap trick. If you have to go beyond creativity and make a leap of logic in order to have an answer choice answer the question, then you should look at the other answer choices. Don't overcomplicate the problem by creating theoretical relationships or explanations that will warp time or space. These are normal problems rooted in reality. It's just that the applicable relationship or explanation may not be readily apparent and you have to figure things out. Use your common sense to interpret anything that isn't clear.

Prefixes

If you're having trouble with a word in the question or answer choices, try dissecting it. Take advantage of every clue that the word might include. Prefixes and suffixes can be a huge help. Usually they allow you to determine a basic meaning. Pre- means before, post- means after, pro - is positive, de- is negative. From these prefixes and suffixes, you can get an idea of the general meaning of the word and try to put it into context. Beware though of any traps. Just because con- is the opposite of pro-, doesn't necessarily mean congress is the opposite of progress!

Hedge Phrases

Watch out for critical hedge phrases, led off with words such as "likely," "may," "can," "sometimes," "often," "almost," "mostly," "usually," "generally," "rarely," and "sometimes." Question writers insert these hedge phrases to cover every possibility. Often an answer choice will be wrong simply because it leaves no room for exception. Unless the situation calls for them, avoid answer choices that have definitive words like "exactly," and "always."

Switchback Words

Stay alert for "switchbacks." These are the words and phrases frequently used to alert you to shifts in thought. The most common switchback word is "but." Others include "although," "however," "nevertheless," "on the other hand," "even though," "while," "in spite of," "despite," and "regardless of."

New Information

Correct answer choices will rarely have completely new information included. Answer choices typically are straightforward reflections of the material asked about and will directly relate to the question. If a new piece of information is included in an answer choice that doesn't even seem to relate to the topic being asked about, then that answer choice is likely incorrect. All of the information needed to answer the question is usually provided for you in the question. You should not have to make guesses that are unsupported or choose answer choices that require unknown information that cannot be reasoned from what is given.

Time Management

On technical questions, don't get lost on the technical terms. Don't spend too much time on any one question. If you don't know what a term means, then odds are you aren't going to get much further since you don't have a dictionary. You should be able to immediately recognize whether or not you know a term. If you don't, work with the other clues that you have—the other answer choices and terms provided—but don't waste too much time trying to figure out a difficult term that you don't know.

Contextual Clues

Look for contextual clues. An answer can be right but not the correct answer. The contextual clues will help you find the answer that is most right and is correct. Understand the context in which a phrase or statement is made. This will help you make important distinctions.

Don't Panic

Panicking will not answer any questions for you; therefore, it isn't helpful. When you first see the question, if your mind goes blank, take a deep breath. Force yourself to mechanically go through the steps of solving the problem using the strategies you've learned.

Pace Yourself

Don't get clock fever. It's easy to be overwhelmed when you're looking at a page full of questions, your mind is full of random thoughts and feeling confused, and the clock is ticking down faster than you would like. Calm down and maintain the pace that you have set for yourself. As long as you are on track by monitoring your pace, you are guaranteed to have enough time for yourself. When you get to the last few minutes of the test, it may seem like you won't have enough time left, but if you only have as many questions as you should have left at that point, then you're right on track!

Answer Selection

The best way to pick an answer choice is to eliminate all of those that are wrong, until only one is left and confirm that is the correct answer. Sometimes though, an answer choice may immediately look right. Be careful! Take a second to make sure that the other choices are not equally obvious. Don't make a hasty mistake. There are only two times that you should stop before checking other answers. First is when you are positive that the answer choice you have selected is correct. Second is when time is almost out and you have to make a quick guess!

Check Your Work

Since you will probably not know every term listed and the answer to every question, it is important that you get credit for the ones that you do know. Don't miss any questions through careless mistakes. If at all possible, try to take a second to look back over your answer selection and make sure you've selected the correct answer choice and haven't made a costly careless mistake (such as marking an answer choice that you didn't mean to mark). The time it takes for this quick double check should more than pay for itself in caught mistakes.

Beware of Directly Quoted Answers

Sometimes an answer choice will repeat word for word a portion of the question or reference section. However, beware of such exact duplication. It may be a trap! More than likely, the correct choice will paraphrase or summarize a point, rather than being exactly the same wording.

Slang

Scientific sounding answers are better than slang ones. An answer choice that begins "To compare the outcomes..." is much more likely to be correct than one that begins "Because some people insisted..."

Extreme Statements

Avoid wild answers that throw out highly controversial ideas that are proclaimed as established fact. An answer choice that states the "process should used in certain situations, if..." is much more likely to be correct than one that states the "process should be discontinued completely." The first is a calm rational statement and doesn't even make a definitive, uncompromising stance, using a hedge word "if" to provide wiggle room, whereas the second choice is a radical idea and far more extreme.

Answer Choice Families

When you have two or more answer choices that are direct opposites or parallels, one of them is usually the correct answer. For instance, if one answer choice states "x increases" and another answer choice states "x decreases" or "y increases," then those two or three answer choices are very similar in construction and fall into the same family of answer choices. A family of answer choices consists of two or three answer choices, very similar in construction, but often with directly opposite meanings. Usually the correct answer choice will be in that family of answer choices. The "odd man out" or answer choice that doesn't seem to fit the parallel construction of the other answer choices is more likely to be incorrect.

How to Overcome Test Anxiety

The very nature of tests caters to some level of anxiety, nervousness, or tension, just as we feel for any important event that occurs in our lives. A little bit of anxiety or nervousness can be a good thing. It helps us with motivation, and makes achievement just that much sweeter. However, too much anxiety can be a problem, especially if it hinders our ability to function and perform.

"Test anxiety," is the term that refers to the emotional reactions that some test-takers experience when faced with a test or exam. Having a fear of testing and exams is based upon a rational fear, since the test-taker's performance can shape the course of an academic career. Nevertheless, experiencing excessive fear of examinations will only interfere with the test-taker's ability to perform and chance to be successful.

There are a large variety of causes that can contribute to the development and sensation of test anxiety. These include, but are not limited to, lack of preparation and worrying about issues surrounding the test.

Lack of Preparation

Lack of preparation can be identified by the following behaviors or situations:
- Not scheduling enough time to study, and therefore cramming the night before the test or exam
- Managing time poorly, to create the sensation that there is not enough time to do everything
- Failing to organize the text information in advance, so that the study material consists of the entire text and not simply the pertinent information
- Poor overall studying habits

Worrying, on the other hand, can be related to both the test taker, or many other factors around him/her that will be affected by the results of the test. These include worrying about:
- Previous performances on similar exams, or exams in general
- How friends and other students are achieving
- The negative consequences that will result from a poor grade or failure

There are three primary elements to test anxiety. Physical components, which involve the same typical bodily reactions as those to acute anxiety (to be discussed below). Emotional factors have to do with fear or panic. Mental or cognitive issues concerning attention spans and memory abilities.

Physical Signals

There are many different symptoms of test anxiety, and these are not limited to mental and emotional strain. Frequently there are a range of physical signals that will let a test taker know that he/she is suffering from test anxiety. These bodily changes can include the following:

- Perspiring
- Sweaty palms
- Wet, trembling hands
- Nausea
- Dry mouth
- A knot in the stomach
- Headache
- Faintness
- Muscle tension
- Aching shoulders, back and neck
- Rapid heart beat
- Feeling too hot/cold

To recognize the sensation of test anxiety, a test-taker should monitor him/herself for the following sensations:

- The physical distress symptoms as listed above
- Emotional sensitivity, expressing emotional feelings such as the need to cry or laugh too much, or a sensation of anger or helplessness
- A decreased ability to think, causing the test-taker to blank out or have racing thoughts that are hard to organize or control.

Though most students will feel some level of anxiety when faced with a test or exam, the majority can cope with that anxiety and maintain it at a manageable level. However, those who cannot are faced with a very real and very serious condition, which can and should be controlled for the immeasurable benefit of this sufferer.

Naturally, these sensations lead to negative results for the testing experience. The most common effects of test anxiety have to do with nervousness and mental blocking.

Nervousness

Nervousness can appear in several different levels:

- The test-taker's difficulty, or even inability to read and understand the questions on the test
- The difficulty or inability to organize thoughts to a coherent form
- The difficulty or inability to recall key words and concepts relating to the testing questions (especially essays)
- The receipt of poor grades on a test, though the test material was well known by the test taker

Conversely, a person may also experience mental blocking, which involves:

- Blanking out on test questions
- Only remembering the correct answers to the questions when the test has already finished.

Fortunately for test anxiety sufferers, beating these feelings, to a large degree, has to do with proper preparation. When a test taker has a feeling of preparedness, then anxiety will be dramatically lessened.

The first step to resolving anxiety issues is to distinguish which of the two types of anxiety are being suffered. If the anxiety is a direct result of a lack of preparation, this should be considered a normal reaction, and the anxiety level (as opposed to the test results) shouldn't be anything to worry about. However, if, when adequately prepared, the test-taker still panics, blanks out, or seems to overreact, this is not a fully rational reaction. While this can be considered normal too, there are many ways to combat and overcome these effects.

Remember that anxiety cannot be entirely eliminated, however, there are ways to minimize it, to make the anxiety easier to manage. Preparation is one of the best ways to minimize test anxiety. Therefore the following techniques are wise in order to best fight off any anxiety that may want to build.

To begin with, try to avoid cramming before a test, whenever it is possible. By trying to memorize an entire term's worth of information in one day, you'll be shocking your system, and not giving yourself a very good chance to absorb the information. This is an easy path to anxiety, so for those who suffer from test anxiety, cramming should not even be considered an option.

Instead of cramming, work throughout the semester to combine all of the material which is presented throughout the semester, and work on it gradually as the course goes by, making sure to master the main concepts first, leaving minor details for a week or so before the test.

To study for the upcoming exam, be sure to pose questions that may be on the examination, to gauge the ability to answer them by integrating the ideas from your texts, notes and lectures, as well as any supplementary readings.

If it is truly impossible to cover all of the information that was covered in that particular term, concentrate on the most important portions, that can be covered very well. Learn these concepts as best as possible, so that when the test comes, a goal can be made to use these concepts as presentations of your knowledge.

In addition to study habits, changes in attitude are critical to beating a struggle with test anxiety. In fact, an improvement of the perspective over the entire test-taking experience can actually help a test taker to enjoy studying and therefore improve the overall experience. Be certain not to overemphasize the significance of the grade - know that the result of the test is neither a reflection of self worth, nor is it a measure of intelligence; one grade will not predict a person's future success.

To improve an overall testing outlook, the following steps should be tried:
- Keeping in mind that the most reasonable expectation for taking a test is to expect to try to demonstrate as much of what you know as you possibly can.
- Reminding ourselves that a test is only one test; this is not the only one, and there will be others.
- The thought of thinking of oneself in an irrational, all-or-nothing term should be avoided at all costs.

- A reward should be designated for after the test, so there's something to look forward to. Whether it be going to a movie, going out to eat, or simply visiting friends, schedule it in advance, and do it no matter what result is expected on the exam.

Test-takers should also keep in mind that the basics are some of the most important things, even beyond anti-anxiety techniques and studying. Never neglect the basic social, emotional and biological needs, in order to try to absorb information. In order to best achieve, these three factors must be held as just as important as the studying itself.

Study Steps

Remember the following important steps for studying:
- Maintain healthy nutrition and exercise habits. Continue both your recreational activities and social pass times. These both contribute to your physical and emotional well being.
- Be certain to get a good amount of sleep, especially the night before the test, because when you're overtired you are not able to perform to the best of your best ability.
- Keep the studying pace to a moderate level by taking breaks when they are needed, and varying the work whenever possible, to keep the mind fresh instead of getting bored.
- When enough studying has been done that all the material that can be learned has been learned, and the test taker is prepared for the test, stop studying and do something relaxing such as listening to music, watching a movie, or taking a warm bubble bath.

There are also many other techniques to minimize the uneasiness or apprehension that is experienced along with test anxiety before, during, or even after the examination. In fact, there are a great deal of things that can be done to stop anxiety from interfering with lifestyle and performance. Again, remember that anxiety will not be eliminated entirely, and it shouldn't be. Otherwise that "up" feeling for exams would not exist, and most of us depend on that sensation to perform better than usual. However, this anxiety has to be at a level that is manageable.

Of course, as we have just discussed, being prepared for the exam is half the battle right away. Attending all classes, finding out what knowledge will be expected on the exam, and knowing the exam schedules are easy steps to lowering anxiety. Keeping up with work will remove the need to cram, and efficient study habits will eliminate wasted time. Studying should be done in an ideal location for concentration, so that it is simple to become interested in the material and give it complete attention. A method such as SQ3R (Survey, Question, Read, Recite, Review) is a wonderful key to follow to make sure that the study habits are as effective as possible, especially in the case of learning from a textbook. Flashcards are great techniques for memorization. Learning to take good notes will mean that notes will be full of useful information, so that less sifting will need to be done to seek out what is pertinent for studying. Reviewing notes after class and then again on occasion will keep the information fresh in the mind. From notes that have been taken summary sheets and outlines can be made for simpler reviewing.

A study group can also be a very motivational and helpful place to study, as there will be a sharing of ideas, all of the minds can work together, to make sure that everyone understands, and the studying will be made more interesting because it will be a social occasion.

Basically, though, as long as the test-taker remains organized and self confident, with efficient study habits, less time will need to be spent studying, and higher grades will be achieved.

To become self confident, there are many useful steps. The first of these is "self talk." It has been shown through extensive research, that self-talk for students who suffer from test anxiety, should be well monitored, in order to make sure that it contributes to self confidence as opposed to sinking the student. Frequently the self talk of test-anxious students is negative or self-defeating, thinking that everyone else is smarter and faster, that they always mess up, and that if they don't do well, they'll fail the entire course. It is important to decreasing anxiety that awareness is made of self talk. Try writing any negative self thoughts and then disputing them with a positive statement instead. Begin self-encouragement as though it was a friend speaking. Repeat positive statements to help reprogram the mind to believing in successes instead of failures.

Helpful Techniques

Other extremely helpful techniques include:
- Self-visualization of doing well and reaching goals
- While aiming for an "A" level of understanding, don't try to "overprotect" by setting your expectations lower. This will only convince the mind to stop studying in order to meet the lower expectations.
- Don't make comparisons with the results or habits of other students. These are individual factors, and different things work for different people, causing different results.
- Strive to become an expert in learning what works well, and what can be done in order to improve. Consider collecting this data in a journal.
- Create rewards for after studying instead of doing things before studying that will only turn into avoidance behaviors.
- Make a practice of relaxing - by using methods such as progressive relaxation, self-hypnosis, guided imagery, etc - in order to make relaxation an automatic sensation.
- Work on creating a state of relaxed concentration so that concentrating will take on the focus of the mind, so that none will be wasted on worrying.
- Take good care of the physical self by eating well and getting enough sleep.
- Plan in time for exercise and stick to this plan.

Beyond these techniques, there are other methods to be used before, during and after the test that will help the test-taker perform well in addition to overcoming anxiety.

Before the exam comes the academic preparation. This involves establishing a study schedule and beginning at least one week before the actual date of the test. By doing this, the anxiety of not having enough time to study for the test will be automatically eliminated.

Moreover, this will make the studying a much more effective experience, ensuring that the learning will be an easier process. This relieves much undue pressure on the test-taker.

Summary sheets, note cards, and flash cards with the main concepts and examples of these main concepts should be prepared in advance of the actual studying time. A topic should never be eliminated from this process. By omitting a topic because it isn't expected to be on the test is only setting up the test-taker for anxiety should it actually appear on the exam. Utilize the course syllabus for laying out the topics that should be studied. Carefully go over the notes that were made in class, paying special attention to any of the issues that the professor took special care to emphasize while lecturing in class. In the textbooks, use the chapter review, or if possible, the chapter tests, to begin your review.

It may even be possible to ask the instructor what information will be covered on the exam, or what the format of the exam will be (for example, multiple choice, essay, free form, true-false). Additionally, see if it is possible to find out how many questions will be on the test. If a review sheet or sample test has been offered by the professor, make good use of it, above anything else, for the preparation for the test. Another great resource for getting to know the examination is reviewing tests from previous semesters. Use these tests to review, and aim to achieve a 100% score on each of the possible topics. With a few exceptions, the goal that you set for yourself is the highest one that you will reach.

Take all of the questions that were assigned as homework, and rework them to any other possible course material. The more problems reworked, the more skill and confidence will form as a result. When forming the solution to a problem, write out each of the steps. Don't simply do head work. By doing as many steps on paper as possible, much clarification and therefore confidence will be formed. Do this with as many homework problems as possible, before checking the answers. By checking the answer after each problem, a reinforcement will exist, that will not be on the exam. Study situations should be as exam-like as possible, to prime the test-taker's system for the experience. By waiting to check the answers at the end, a psychological advantage will be formed, to decrease the stress factor.

Another fantastic reason for not cramming is the avoidance of confusion in concepts, especially when it comes to mathematics. 8-10 hours of study will become one hundred percent more effective if it is spread out over a week or at least several days, instead of doing it all in one sitting. Recognize that the human brain requires time in order to assimilate new material, so frequent breaks and a span of study time over several days will be much more beneficial.

Additionally, don't study right up until the point of the exam. Studying should stop a minimum of one hour before the exam begins. This allows the brain to rest and put things in their proper order. This will also provide the time to become as relaxed as possible when going into the examination room. The test-taker will also have time to eat well and eat sensibly. Know that the brain needs food as much as the rest of the body. With enough food and enough sleep, as well as a relaxed attitude, the body and the mind are primed for success.

Avoid any anxious classmates who are talking about the exam. These students only spread anxiety, and are not worth sharing the anxious sentimentalities.

Before the test also involves creating a positive attitude, so mental preparation should also be a point of concentration. There are many keys to creating a positive attitude. Should fears become rushing in, make a visualization of taking the exam, doing well, and seeing an A written on the paper. Write out a list of affirmations that will bring a feeling of confidence, such as "I am doing well in my English class," "I studied well and know my material," "I enjoy this class." Even if the affirmations aren't believed at first, it sends a positive message to the subconscious which will result in an alteration of the overall belief system, which is the system that creates reality.

If a sensation of panic begins, work with the fear and imagine the very worst! Work through the entire scenario of not passing the test, failing the entire course, and dropping out of school, followed by not getting a job, and pushing a shopping cart through the dark alley where you'll live. This will place things into perspective! Then, practice deep breathing and create a visualization of the opposite situation - achieving an "A" on the exam, passing the entire course, receiving the degree at a graduation ceremony.

On the day of the test, there are many things to be done to ensure the best results, as well as the most calm outlook. The following stages are suggested in order to maximize test-taking potential:

- Begin the examination day with a moderate breakfast, and avoid any coffee or beverages with caffeine if the test taker is prone to jitters. Even people who are used to managing caffeine can feel jittery or light-headed when it is taken on a test day.
- Attempt to do something that is relaxing before the examination begins. As last minute cramming clouds the mastering of overall concepts, it is better to use this time to create a calming outlook.
- Be certain to arrive at the test location well in advance, in order to provide time to select a location that is away from doors, windows and other distractions, as well as giving enough time to relax before the test begins.
- Keep away from anxiety generating classmates who will upset the sensation of stability and relaxation that is being attempted before the exam.
- Should the waiting period before the exam begins cause anxiety, create a self-distraction by reading a light magazine or something else that is relaxing and simple.

During the exam itself, read the entire exam from beginning to end, and find out how much time should be allotted to each individual problem. Once writing the exam, should more time be taken for a problem, it should be abandoned, in order to begin another problem. If there is time at the end, the unfinished problem can always be returned to and completed.

Read the instructions very carefully - twice - so that unpleasant surprises won't follow during or after the exam has ended.

When writing the exam, pretend that the situation is actually simply the completion of homework within a library, or at home. This will assist in forming a relaxed atmosphere, and will allow the brain extra focus for the complex thinking function.

Begin the exam with all of the questions with which the most confidence is felt. This will build the confidence level regarding the entire exam and will begin a quality momentum. This will also create encouragement for trying the problems where uncertainty resides.

Going with the "gut instinct" is always the way to go when solving a problem. Second guessing should be avoided at all costs. Have confidence in the ability to do well.

For essay questions, create an outline in advance that will keep the mind organized and make certain that all of the points are remembered. For multiple choice, read every answer, even if the correct one has been spotted - a better one may exist.

Continue at a pace that is reasonable and not rushed, in order to be able to work carefully. Provide enough time to go over the answers at the end, to check for small errors that can be corrected.

Should a feeling of panic begin, breathe deeply, and think of the feeling of the body releasing sand through its pores. Visualize a calm, peaceful place, and include all of the sights, sounds and sensations of this image. Continue the deep breathing, and take a few minutes to continue this with closed eyes. When all is well again, return to the test.

If a "blanking" occurs for a certain question, skip it and move on to the next question. There will be time to return to the other question later. Get everything done that can be done, first, to guarantee all the grades that can be compiled, and to build all of the confidence possible. Then return to the weaker questions to build the marks from there.

Remember, one's own reality can be created, so as long as the belief is there, success will follow. And remember: anxiety can happen later, right now, there's an exam to be written!

After the examination is complete, whether there is a feeling for a good grade or a bad grade, don't dwell on the exam, and be certain to follow through on the reward that was promised...and enjoy it! Don't dwell on any mistakes that have been made, as there is nothing that can be done at this point anyway.

Additionally, don't begin to study for the next test right away. Do something relaxing for a while, and let the mind relax and prepare itself to begin absorbing information again.

From the results of the exam - both the grade and the entire experience, be certain to learn from what has gone on. Perfect studying habits and work some more on confidence in order to make the next examination experience even better than the last one.

Learn to avoid places where openings occurred for laziness, procrastination and day dreaming.

Use the time between this exam and the next one to better learn to relax, even learning to relax on cue, so that any anxiety can be controlled during the next exam. Learn how to relax the body. Slouch in your chair if that helps. Tighten and then relax all of the different muscle groups, one group at a time, beginning with the feet and then working all the way up to the neck and face. This will ultimately relax the muscles more than they were to begin with. Learn how to breathe deeply and comfortably, and focus on this breathing going in and out as a relaxing thought. With every exhale, repeat the word "relax."

As common as test anxiety is, it is very possible to overcome it. Make yourself one of the test-takers who overcome this frustrating hindrance.

Additional Bonus Material

Due to our efforts to try to keep this book to a manageable length, we've created a link that will give you access to all of your additional bonus material.

Please visit http://www.mometrix.com/bonus948/parcchsalg1 to access the information.